Get Psyched!

Meg Mulcahy | Jodie Warner

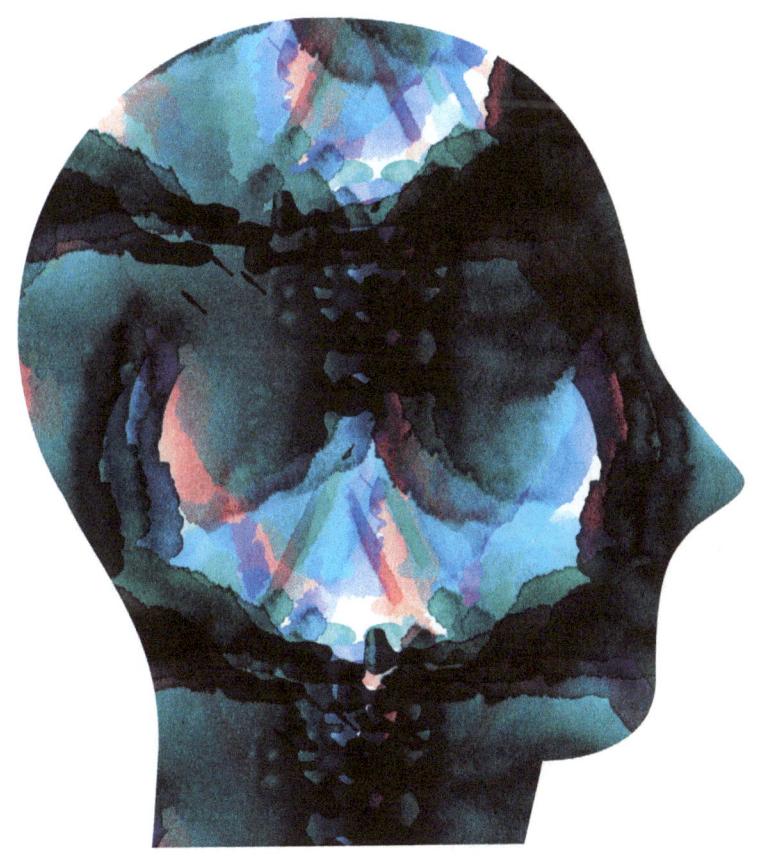

CAMBRIDGE
UNIVERSITY PRESS

477 Williamstown Road, Port Melbourne, VIC 3207, Australia

Cambridge University Press is part of the University of Cambridge.

It furthers the University's mission by disseminating knowledge in the pursuit of education, learning and research at the highest international levels of excellence.

www.cambridge.org
Information on this title: www.cambridge.org/9780521188487

© Meg Mulcahy, Jodie Warner 2011

This publication is in copyright. Subject to statutory exception and to the provisions of relevant collective licensing agreements, no reproduction of any part may take place without the written permission of Cambridge University Press.

First published 2011
Reprinted 2014

Edited by Marcia Bascombe
Designed by Marc Martin

A Cataloguing-in-Publication entry is available from the catalogue of the National Library of Australia at www.nla.gov.au

ISBN 978-0-521-18848-7 Paperback

Additional resources for this publication at www.cambridge.edu.au/GO

Reproduction and Communication for educational purposes
The Australian *Copyright Act 1968* (the Act) allows a maximum of one chapter or 10% of the pages of this publication, whichever is the greater, to be reproduced and/or communicated by any educational institution for its educational purposes provided that the educational institution (or the body that administers it) has given a remuneration notice to Copyright Agency Limited (CAL) under the Act.

For details of the CAL licence for educational institutions contact:

Copyright Agency Limited
Level 15, 233 Castlereagh Street
Sydney NSW 2000
Telephone: (02) 9394 7600
Facsimile: (02) 9394 7601
Email: info@copyright.com.au

Reproduction and Communication for other purposes
Except as permitted under the Act (for example a fair dealing for the purposes of study, research, criticism or review) no part of this publication may be reproduced, stored in a retrieval system, communicated or transmitted in any form or by any means without prior written permission. All inquiries should be made to the publisher at the address above.

Cambridge University Press has no responsibility for the persistence or accuracy of URLs for external or third-party internet websites referred to in this publication, and does not guarantee that any content on such websites is, or will remain, accurate or appropriate.

contents

About the authors	*vi*
Acknowledgements	*vii*
Introduction	*viii*

Chapter 1 Psychology IQ – debunking the myths and sorting fact from fiction

How to debunk myths – the scientific method	02
Correlations are not causes – why myths can occur	04
Some myths have been successfully debunked	04
Media portrayals support myth-making	05
One last word	11
End of chapter summary	14
End of chapter test	15

Chapter 2 Beautiful minds

The beginning	16
Birth of the brain	17
The anatomy of the brain	22
Tricks of the brain	26
Brain banks	27
End of chapter summary	29
End of chapter test	29

Chapter 3 Mind interrupted

What are the issues facing teenagers?	32
Mental health of young Australians	32
What is mental health and what is mental illness?	33
Conduct disorder	33
Anxiety	35
Depression	36
Substance dependence disorder	37
Eating disorders	38
Causes and treatments	42
Advice if you think your family and friends may be affected	44
End of chapter summary	46
End of chapter test	47

Chapter 4 Brain chemistry

What's happening in the adolescent brain?	48
Addiction – how does it work?	50
Alcohol	51
Cannabis (marijuana)	53
Nicotine (smoking)	54
Meth/amphetamines	55
Ecstasy	55
LSD, cocaine and heroin	56
Where to go for help	57
End of chapter summary	58
End of chapter test	59

Chapter 5 In your dreams

What is sleep?	60
The EEG	63
Sleep phenomena	66
What are dreams?	72
Freud's psychoanalytic theory of dreaming (1900)	72
Hobson and McCarley's activation–synthesis hypothesis (1977)	74
End of chapter summary	75
End of chapter test	76

Chapter 6 Pursuing happiness

Positive psychology	77
What determines happiness?	78
Circumstances of life	80
Voluntary activities	85
The positivity ratio	86
Happiness and humour	87
End of chapter summary	88
End of chapter test	89

Chapter 7 Human relationships

Territory and personal space	91
Gestures	95
Putting it all together: human relationships	98
Heartbreak	103
End of chapter summary	103
End of chapter test	104

Chapter 8 The darker side of human nature

Psychopathy	105
Abu Ghraib and the Lucifer Effect	109
The social-psychological concepts at play	116
End of chapter summary	118
End of chapter test	118

Chapter 9 Conduct and misconduct: the right or wrong of ethics

Ethics – what are they?	119
Dr Harry Bailey and the Chelmsford Hospital scandal	121
What are our rights as patients?	128
End of chapter summary	131
End of chapter test	131

Glossary	*132*
References	*138*
Index	*145*

about the authors

Meg Mulcahy (BSci (Hons), BTeach (Hons)) majored in psychology and completed her honours thesis in visual perception at the University of Melbourne. She also tutored at Trinity and Ormond Colleges. Passionate about teaching and psychology, Meg then completed a teaching degree whilst her peers continued on to become practicing psychologists. She is Head of Psychology at her school and is a state exam assessor. She is also a keen runner and coaches athletics and cross country. Her favourite runs are the Puffing Billy Race in Emerald, Victoria, and the Great Ocean Road Marathon.

Thank you to Dr Suresh Sundram, Dr Blaine Roberts, the Mental Health Research Institute and Julian Tatton for giving up your time. Your efforts and advice are greatly appreciated. The biggest thank you of all goes to my parents and to Leighton who is my greatest support.

Jodie Warner (B. Soc.Sci (Psych), Dip Ed.) is an experienced teacher of Psychology. She has been part of the Cambridge writing team for the *Uncovering Psychology* series and loves that her job allows her to combine two of her passions: teaching and writing. Jodie has presented at many Psychology Teachers' conferences and is a state exam assessor. In her spare time, she loves walking her dog, spending time with her family and friends, and travelling.

To Luke, my family and my friends, thanks for your love and unwavering support.

acknowledgements

The author and publisher wish to thank the following sources for permission to reproduce material:

Images: AP Photo, **p. 111**; Corbis, **p. 28**/ Bob E Daemmrich, **p. 110**/ Steve Schapiro, **p. 110**; Headspace, **p. 45**; iStockphoto/ Scott Leigh, **p. 61**/ annedde, **p. 63**/ Vikram Raghuvanshi Photography, **p. 83**; Maslow, A 1943, A Theory of Human Motivation, Psychological Review, 50, **pp. 370–396**, **p. 78**; Meg Mulcahy, **p. 12**; Natural History Museum, London, **p. 95**; Newspix/ News Ltd, **p. 123**; Shutterstock/ Timothy R Nichols, **p. 1**/ Candy Box Photo, p. 2/ CREATISTA, **p. 3**/ iDesign, **p. 5**/ Randy Drumm, **p. 11**/ James Steidl, **p. 16**/ Sebastian Kaulitzki, **p. 17, 18, 51**/ Andrea Danti, **p. 20**/ Blamb, **p. 21**/ WooDoo, **p. 23**/ Tan Wei Ming, **p. 24**/ Janaka Dharmasena, **p. 24**/ Medus Art, **p. 25, 26**/ Stephen Coburn, **p. 31**/ Mikael Damkier, **p. 32**/ Vava Vladimir Jovanovic, **p. 34**/ Hannah Gleghorn, **p. 35**/ Konstantin Sutyagin, **p. 38**/ Kentoh, **p. 39**/ RDTMOR, **p. 40**/ Waterlilly, **p. 43**/ Martan, **p. 48**/ Katherine Welles, **p. 49**/ Ingrid W, **p. 50**/ Triff, **p. 53**/ Andrew Burns, **p. 55**/ Andy Farrer, **p. 56**/ Scott Leigh, **p. 61**/ Lerche&Johnson, **p. 71**/ Losevsky Pavel, **p. 81**/ dwphotos, **p. 82**/ Ilja Mašík, **p. 83**/ tonobalaguerf, **p. 86**/ Yuri Arcurs, **p. 87, 128**/ Brocreative, **p. 90**/ Sergej Khakimullin, **p. 97**/ Maya13, **p. 97**/ svand, **p. 97**/ Deklofenak, **p. 99**/ Dash, **p. 100**/ Evgeny Murtola, **p. 108**/ Alexander Raths, **p. 108**/ Mathagraphics, **p. 109**/ Matt Trommer, **p. 109**/ Rafal Olkis, **p. 110**/ Laura Gangi Pond, **p. 111**/ Nicole Paton, **p. 113**/ Graham Prentice, **p. 114**/ Luke James Ritchie, **p. 117**/ Oliver Hoffmann, **p. 125**/ Elena Elisseeva, **p. 126**; The Australian Psychological Society Ltd, **p. 120**; The Butterfly Foundation, **p. 46**; TIME & LIFE Images/Don Cravens, **p. 69**.

Text: Adapted from the Australian Bureau of Statistics 'Life Satisfaction and Measures of Progress', 2007, **p. 80**; Babsom, RW, **p. 60**; Buddha, **p. 77**; Carroll, L, 1965, Alice's Adventures in Wonderland, Macmillan, UK, **p. 31**; Emerson, RW, **p. 119**; http://www.brainyquote.com/quotes/keywords/brain_2.html, **p. 16**; http://www.cbsnews.com/htdocs/pdf/tagubareport.pdf, **p. 112**; http://thinkexist.com/quotation/there_is_no_joy_except_in_human/192319.html, **p. 90**; http://www.yuni.com/quotes/stevenson_rl.html, **p. 105**; Miller, M, **p. 48**; News Limited, Sunday Herald Sun, Caroline Marcus, June 27, 2010, **p. 39–40**; News Limited, The Daily Telegraph, Kate Sikora, February 11, 2009, **p. 41–2**; Public Domain (17 U.S.C. 105), **p. 110, 111, 115**; Searight, HR, Rottnek, F, Abby, SL, Conduct Disorder: Diagnosis and Treatment in Primary Care, American Family Physician, 2001 Apr 15; 63(8): 1579–1589, **p. 47**; Wilde, O, The Importance of Being Earnest, 1895, Act I, p. 1.

Every effort has been made to trace and acknowledge copyright. The publisher apologises for any accidental infringement and welcomes information that would redress this situation.

introduction

To be 'psyched' means to be enthused, excited and mentally prepared for the challenges ahead. It's a useful piece of slang that we all use to describe how we or others might be feeling. Rather than be 'psyched out' (to lose confidence in one's ability), we want you to be inspired and thrilled to be studying psychology. We want you to be strong and confident about your own learning. We want you to learn something new about yourself as you learn about your psychology and that of the world around you. We want you to 'get psyched'!

This text considers both past and current research in a wide variety of areas, including relationships, happiness, and even the darker side of human nature (to name but a few). There is a wide range of activities that your teacher might ask you to complete either in class or at home, including empirical research activities (ERAs), which can be found on the Cambridge GO website. These ERAs are an excellent introduction to the type of assessment you might expect as a more senior student in future years. There are also summaries at the end of each chapter and questions to help you assess your knowledge.

Get Psyched! gives you an insight into the discipline of psychology so that you can make an informed decision about what you might like to study in your final years at school or even at university.

We have loved writing this book and we hope you enjoy reading it.

Meg Mulcahy and Jodie Warner

Psychology IQ –
debunking the myths and sorting fact from fiction

CHAPTER 1

The pure and simple truth is rarely pure and never simple.
Oscar Wilde

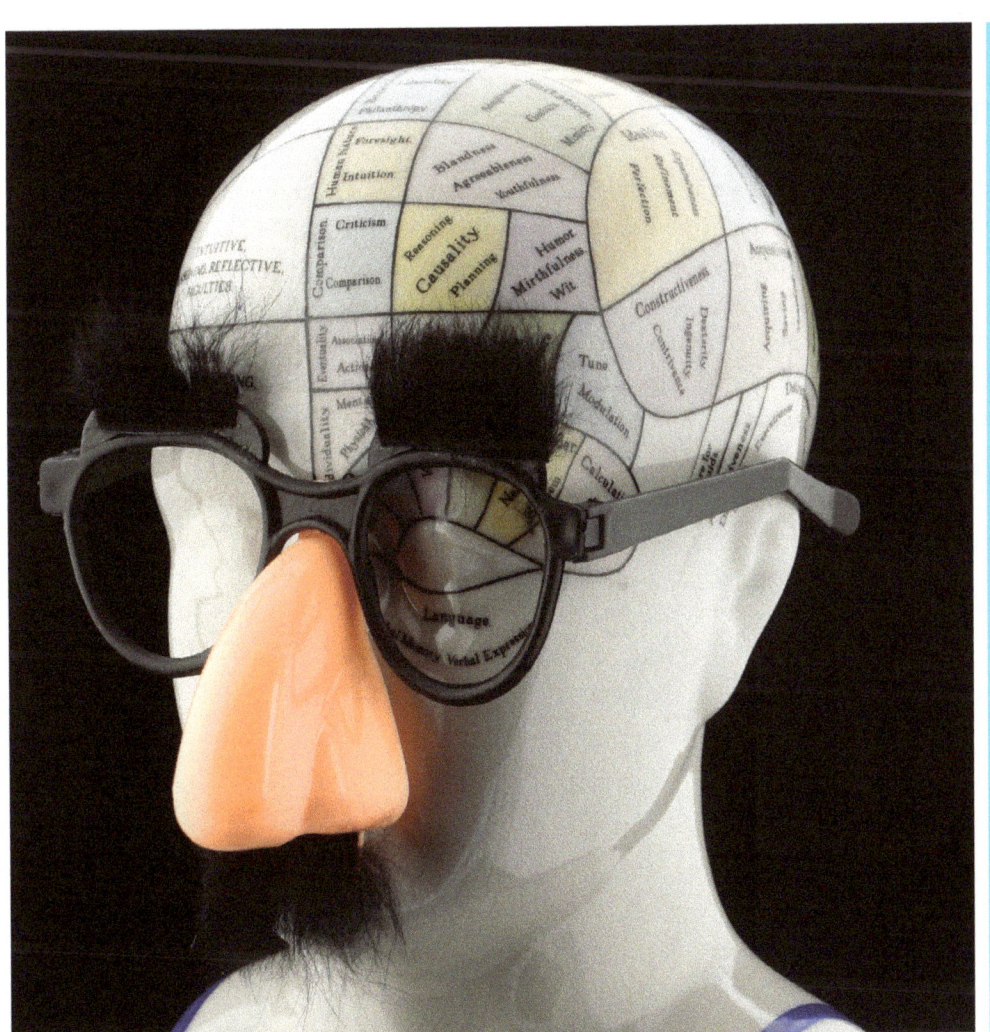

Figure 1.1 How do we sort out fact from fiction?

People often think that psychology is based upon 'common sense'. This is a misconception. Word-of-mouth, 'old wives tales', myths and urban legends are all sources of misconceptions, and create what is called 'psychomythology'. **Psychomythology** is all the misconceptions, myths and misinformation about psychology (Lilienfield et al. 2010).

Psychomythology
Misinformation or misconceptions about psychology that lay people (general population) believe

Psychology A science that studies behaviour and mental processes of human beings

The purpose of this chapter is to teach you about what psychology actually is and also set you up with the skills that you need to make up your own mind about the things you read. You need to be able to think scientifically and have an enquiring mind about what you read. For example, you should question what you read online or in the newspaper, as the article could be based upon biased or error-ridden research. **Psychology** is a science, and science is 'uncommon sense'. That is, to be scientific we have to put aside our common sense and evaluate the evidence given. We need to unlearn a tendency to believe that our gut hunches or common sense are correct. The aim of this chapter is to help you debunk or 'bust' the myths, as well as introduce you to psychology.

ACTIVITY 1.1 PSYCHOMYTHOLOGY

1. What is psychomythology? Can you think of a myth you know is not true?
2. Define psychology.
3. What is meant by psychomythology being 'common sense' whereas psychology is in fact 'uncommon sense'?

How to debunk myths – the scientific method

Empiricism The collection of information (data) through direct observation or experience, tends to also be systematic

The scientific method is a way to debunk myths. It helps us sort out fact from fiction. An important part of the scientific method is **empiricism**. All sciences collect information (data) through direct observation or experience, rather than faith or hearsay. This is called empiricism. Once information has been gathered it is then publicly shared – usually in peer-reviewed journals – so that it can either be supported or rejected. Empirical evidence that is consistent, and can be replicated by others, will be the strongest. Evidence that is *not* consistent and *cannot* be replicated by others is discarded.

Figure 1.2 Once empirical evidence has been collected, the results are published so that they can be reviewed and replicated by peers.

Another two important criteria of scientific method are the way data is collected and also how theories are constructed. The **collection of data** must be objective, controlled and be able to be replicated. Objective means unbiased, and free of personal opinion. In terms of **construction of theories**, scientists use theories to guide their research and help form hypotheses. In psychology, theories are constructed to try to understand why people behave and think they way they do. The biggest challenge for psychology compared to other sciences is that their subject matter is people – other human beings. Therefore it is very important for all psychologists and researchers to avoid bias.

Consider the following **hypothesis**, that women speak more words, on average per day, than men. Is this fact or fiction? A study in the US asked 400 college students to carry around with them electronic recorders so that their daily conversations and number of words could be counted. They found that both males and females spoke on average 16 000 words a day. There was no gender difference! Therefore the hypothesis was not supported (Mehl et al. 2007).

Collection of data Can be used to describe any method of collecting information, such as experiments, surveys, tests and observations

Construction of theories Psychological theories are constructed when observing behaviour or processes in an attempt to understand the underlying reasons

Hypothesis An estimated 'guess' or statement predicting the results of a study, or relationship between two variables. Hypotheses are tested through research.

Figure 1.3 A common myth is that women talk more than men.

Now we need to think critically. Matthias Mehl's study above is just one single study. Does this mean Mehl's results are the full truth of the matter? One of the most important things in science is for studies to be **replicated**. Therefore, hopefully, colleagues and peers of Mehl will try to measure his hypothesis again to see if they get similar results. That way we can be certain that men and women do talk an equal number of words per day.

Replicated The process of duplicating research to see if the results can be repeated, and are therefore reliable

ACTIVITY 1.2 SCIENTIFIC METHOD

1. What is the scientific method? In your answer outline the main characteristics of a scientific method.
2. When would empirical evidence be rejected and why?
3. Why should research be replicated?

Correlated Variables are described as being correlated if a change in one variable appears to occur at the same time as another (however, sometimes a third unknown variable may be causing the change)

Variable A factor in research that may be manipulated or controlled by the experimenter (the independent variable) or factor that changes as a result (dependent variable)

Correlations are not causes – why myths can occur

If two things occur together statistically they are said to be **correlated**. However, an error that many people make is that they think that if two things are correlated then they must cause each other. If **Variable** 1 (V1) correlates with Variable 2 (V2) then people think V1 causes V2. Yet there might be a Variable 3 that causes *both*. This unknown Variable 3 is why we should *not* say that V1 causes V2.

For example, studies on depression have investigated the hypothesis that there is a genetic link with children being more likely to suffer from depression if their parents suffer the illness. That is parental depression (V1) causes child depression (V2). However, could it not be that parents suffering from depression may change their parenting style and the way they interact with their children? Therefore parenting style (V3) might actually be the cause.

ACTIVITY 1.3 VARIABLES

1. Define the term 'variable'.
2. If variables are correlated, what does this mean?
3. If V1 causes V2, which one is the dependent variable and which one is the independent variable?
4. In research, correlated does not mean 'cause'. Why?
5. One of your friends notices that all the best athletes in school do not do well academically at school. They tell you that they think all athletes are poor students. How might you explain to your friend the problems with their deduction?

ACTIVITY 1.4 ERA: CONDUCT YOUR OWN RESEARCH

The details of this ERA are available on the Cambridge GO website.

Some myths have been successfully debunked

Hippocampus A brain structure that has a mirror image half in each hemisphere of the brain, and is involved in memory formation

Neurogenesis The growing of new neurons

A common myth is: 'We have a set number of brain cells and once they're lost, they're lost forever'.

This is not true. In the 1990s scientists discovered that new brain cells can be formed in the **hippocampus** of the brain. This growth is known as **neurogenesis** (see Chapter 4). Although most of our brain development happens before we are 10 years old, our brain's neurons can grow and make new connections as we learn new things. Therefore, it is very important for us to stay active!

Another common myth is that mental illness is due to brain damage, or even that it is a form of intellectual damage. There is no evidence to support such claims. For more myth debunking, see pages 7, 8 and 9.

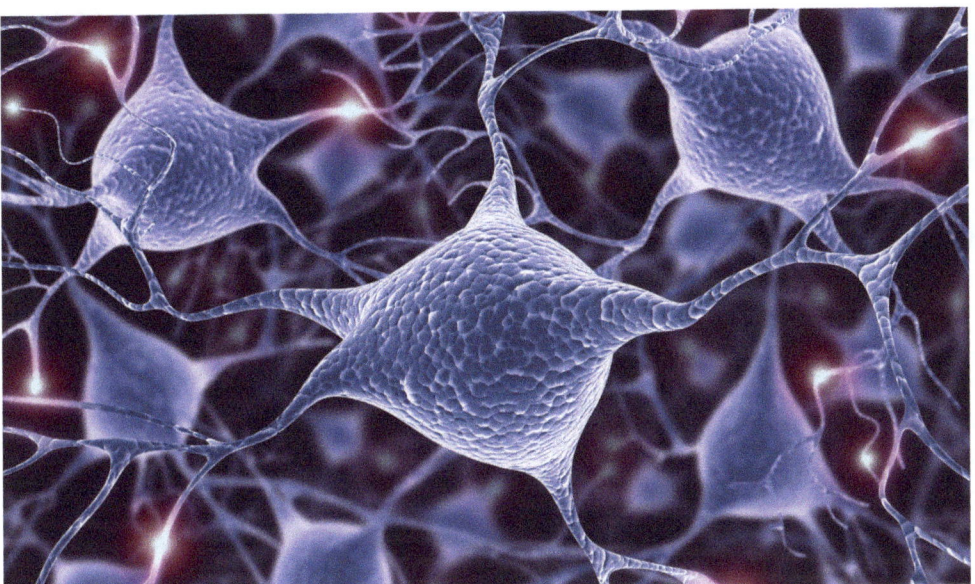

Figure 1.4 Although science has discovered that new neurons can grow, some people still believe the myth that once neurons are lost, they're lost forever.

Media portrayals support myth-making

Movies and television tend to sensationalise and exaggerate areas of psychology. For example, the roles of psychologists and psychiatrists are often portrayed on screen and not always accurately. Nor are the symptoms of mental illness portrayed accurately. These media depictions further perpetuate our misunderstandings and misconceptions.

INTERVIEW

Dr Suresh Sundram is Head of Molecular Psychopharmacology at the Mental Health Research Institute, Director of the Northern Psychiatry Research Centre, Director of Clinical Services of the Northern Area Mental Health Service, and an Associate Professor with the Department of Psychiatry at the University of Melbourne.

What made you decide to become a psychiatrist?

When I was in my fourth year at university completing my medical degree, I had a tutorial with the Professor of Psychiatry at the time. He recommended reading Shakespeare, Goethe and other famous writers. I was really attracted to the notion of madness. So I decided on psychiatry as my specialty after we had studied it in fifth year.

Figure 1.5 Dr Suresh Sundram – psychiatrist.

Schizophrenia A mental illness characterised by psychosis, a loss of contact with reality. Sufferer may have delusions or hallucinations

Psychiatry A specialised area of medicine where doctors focus on mental illnesses

Electroconvulsive therapy (ECT) A form of medical therapy where low levels of electrical impulses are applied to an anaesthetised patient's skull (and brain)

Catatonia When muscles in the body go partly rigid, and the person remains in the same position they are in. It is also associated with muteness (no speech) and withdrawal from their environment.

How long did it take you to become a psychiatrist?

I have spent more years at uni than at school! First I completed six years of medicine, and then I did one year internship and one year residency. During a research year at the Mental Health Research Institute, they talked me into doing a PhD in biochemistry of schizophrenia. I then went to the Royal Melbourne Hospital and did psychiatry training for five years and as well as a Masters degree in psychiatry. This was followed by sitting my fellowship exams for RANZP. Therefore, I had 14 years of university study but thankfully I was able to work for about half of this time as well.

Is it common for a psychiatrist to complete a PhD?

No, it is uncommon for psychiatrists to do a PhD.

Do you find that people can sometimes confuse what a psychiatrist and psychologist do?

Lay people who are not familiar with the health system have little idea of the distinction between psychologists and psychiatrists.

What do you think are the main differences?

Psychiatrists are medical specialists and they therefore understand how the body works. They spend five years of their training studying the diseases of the brain resulting in mental illnesses or mental disorders.

Psychiatrists are experts in the diagnosis and treatment of mental disorders, especially the use of physical treatments, such as medication, hospitalisation and electroconvulsive therapy (ECT). ECT is one of the most effective treatments for depression, as well as other mental illnesses.

So a major difference is that psychiatrists can use medication?

Yes. Psychologists cannot. A psychologist in comparison uses therapies. Psychologists are generally experts in therapies they've been trained in.

Psychiatrists can also be trained in therapies, but it comes down to who has more experience and has more time. We tend to assist more severe patients who need medication or hospitalisation.

How do psychologists and psychiatrists work together?

In the public health system psychologists are employed and work with psychiatrists and medical staff in a multi-disciplinary team, bringing their own expertise to treatment of patients. There is a high degree of cross-referral.

How does referral work?

Generally psychiatrists would assess, diagnose and begin medication if needed. As patient starts to recover, psychiatrists then refer them to a psychologist for therapy. Eventually, psychologists and psychiatrists discuss the cases together. There would be situations when we would handover the majority of the care of patients over to the GP and psychologist and they would only contact the psychiatrist if there were problems.

ACTIVITY 1.5 PSYCHOLOGY AND PSYCHIATRY

1. According to Dr Sundram, how does someone become a psychiatrist?
2. What are the main differences between psychiatry and psychology?
3. How might psychologists and psychiatrists help each other?
4. Sarah is suffering from depression and visits a psychologist in the hope of getting antidepressants (medication). She is surprised when the psychologist does not prescribe the medication. Explain why Sarah's psychologist does not give medication.

MYTH #1 ECT IS SHOCK TREATMENT.

No. This name gives the procedure a bad reputation. ECT is a medical procedure used to treat a range of mental illnesses including severe depression, catatonia and schizophrenia. The patient is anesthetised and electrodes are placed at strategic points on the patient's skull. A sequence of brief and low frequency electrical pulses are applied to cause mini seizures in the brain. The patient does not feel these as they are anesthetised, and their muscles are relaxed.

MYTH #2 ECT IS RARELY USED.

No. ECT remains a commonly used treatment – but only for cases where individuals have not responded to other treatments. ECT continues to be practised safely and successfully here in Australia – approximately 80 per cent of patients significantly improve (Better Health Channel 2008).

MYTH #3 ECT IS DANGEROUS AND CAN CAUSE BRAIN DAMAGE.

No. ECT does not cause brain damage as the amount of electricity used is very low. However, like any surgical procedure it does carry a certain amount of risk. For example, some patients who undergo ECT may have memory difficulties (although this is uncommon). This misconception that ECT causes brain damage is probably due to the long history of ECT where it has been misused in the past. (Such unethical use by doctors and psychiatrists is investigated in Chapter 9.)

MYTH #4 IF YOUR PSYCHIATRIST SUGGESTS ECT AS A THERAPY, YOU HAVE NO CHOICE. YOU MUST HAVE ECT.

No. Patients have many rights. Their first right is to refuse treatment. They're also entitled to get a second opinion. Their psychiatrist or doctor must also clearly explain to them the nature and purpose of the procedure, that is, they must explain everything and answer all questions.

ACTIVITY 1.6 ECT

1. What does ECT stand for?
2. What is the procedure for ECT?
3. Why does ECT have a bad reputation?
4. One of your friends is unwell, and their psychiatrist suggests ECT. Your friend is unsure of their rights. What rights does your friend have?

DID YOU KNOW?

MYTH #1 MENTAL ILLNESS IS A FORM OF INTELLECTUAL DAMAGE OR BRAIN DAMAGE.

No. There is *no* evidence to suggest this is the case. In Australia, regardless of age, one in five Australians will develop a mental illness at some stage of their life (Australian Bureau of Statistics 2007).

MYTH #2 MENTAL ILLNESS IS CONTAGIOUS. IF YOU HANG AROUND WITH MENTALLY ILL PEOPLE YOU COULD BECOME MENTALLY ILL TOO.

No. This is not the case. Mental illness is not like the measles or the flu; it cannot be caught.

MYTH #3 MENTAL ILLNESSES ARE LIFELONG.

No. Mental illnesses tend to last for a stage of life rather than be lifelong. Some people will, unfortunately, struggle with their illness for their lifetime but they are the minority.

MYTH #4 MENTAL ILLNESSES ARE INCURABLE.

No. Many mental illnesses are treatable and sufferers can fully recover. Some mental illnesses as yet still have no cure, but for the most part, mental illnesses can be successfully treated – especially if help is sought in its early stages.

MYTH #5 PEOPLE ARE BORN WITH A MENTAL ILLNESS.

No. There appear to be some genetic links that cause people to be more vulnerable to mental illness, however, there are many factors the contribute, such as stress, major physical illness, relationship breakdowns, abuse or disability.

ACTIVITY 1.7 UNDERSTANDING MENTAL ILLNESS

1. Your cousin has been diagnosed with a mental illness. Your uncle is very upset about this as he's worried about what people are going to say. What could you say to help your uncle and his colleagues understand mental illness?
2. Your mother is worried that mental illness could 'run in the family' and that you could have inherited it too. Your father, on the other hand, thinks that your cousin should just 'grow up and snap out of it'. Is your mother worrying unnecessarily? Is your father correct?

DID YOU KNOW?

MYTH #1 PEOPLE WHO SUFFER FROM SCHIZOPHRENIA HAVE MULTIPLE PERSONALITIES.

No. Someone with multiple personalities is likely to suffer from dissociative identity disorder (multiple personality disorder), which is a distinctly different mental illness from schizophrenia. This misconception probably began when schizophrenia was first given its name in 1911 by Swiss psychiatrist Eugen Bleuler. Schizophrenia means 'split mind' so it is likely that since then people have misinterpreted his definition (Lilienfield et al. 2010).

MYTH #2 BOYS ARE MORE LIKELY TO SUFFER FROM SCHIZOPHRENIA THAN GIRLS.

No. There is no gender difference in schizophrenia. However, boys tend to have an earlier onset (beginning) of the illness – which may be where this misconception has stemmed from.

MYTH #3 CATATONIA IS A SYMPTOM OF SCHIZOPHRENIA.

This is not the case – catatonia can also occur with depression, not just schizophrenia. Catatonia is when muscles in the body go partly rigid, and the person remains in the same position they are in. It is also associated with muteness (no speech).

MYTH #4 PEOPLE WITH SCHIZOPHRENIA ARE DANGEROUS AND VIOLENT.

No. The majority of people with mental illnesses, including schizophrenia, never commit violent acts. Approximately only 3 to 5 per cent of violent crime is committed by people with severe mental illnesses (Lilienfield et al. 2010).

MYTH #5 PEOPLE WITH SCHIZOPHRENIA ARE PSYCHOPATHIC.

No. People with schizophrenia are *psychotic*, as they experience *psychosis*. Psychotic is *not* the same as psychopathic. **Psychopathy** is a personality disorder, while **psychosis** is where a person loses their sense of reality and cannot function effectively in everyday life. (Psychopaths are discussed in more detail in Chapter 8.)

MYTH #6 PEOPLE WHO SMOKE MARIJUANA (CANNABIS) WILL DEVELOP SCHIZOPHRENIA.

No. There is no clear relationship between marijuana and schizophrenia. Marijuana can cause psychosis – so there is a shared feature. (Marijuana is discussed in more detail in Chapter 4.) There has also been evidence that people who are more vulnerable (such as family history) to schizophrenia may have the illness triggered by marijuana use. However, people who use marijuana would not suffer schizophrenia (although they are likely to suffer from psychosis).

Psychopathy A personality disorder characterised by impulsive and reckless behaviour, and little remorse or guilt for antisocial behaviour

Psychosis A mental state characterised by a loss of sense of reality that results in delusions, hallucinations and bizarre behaviour

ACTIVITY 1.8 UNDERSTANDING SCHIZOPHRENIA

1. Schizophrenia means 'split mind'. Does this mean a sufferer will have multiple personalities? Explain.
2. Are schizophrenics psychopathic? Explain.
3. Lizzy finds out that her neighbour, Mrs Watkins, has schizophrenia. Lizzy's confused because she thinks only men can have schizophrenia. What might you say to Lizzy?
4. Lizzy decides that Mrs Watkins must have smoked a lot of marijuana. What would your response to this be?

ACTIVITY 1.9 RESEARCH ASSIGNMENT – FACT OR FICTION?

Research one of the following topics to find out if it is fact or fiction.

- Women are worse drivers than men.
- People cannot lie (hide the truth) when hypnotised.
- Most psychotherapists use a couch and explore the patient's past.
- There is no such thing as global warming.
- Natural substances are safe.
- Playing classical music to babies in the womb increases their intelligence.
- We are more likely to die in a plane crash than a car crash.
- Happiness depends on our circumstances, such as wealth.
- People who are blind have more sensitive hearing.
- People with bigger brains are more intelligent.
- People's attitudes are highly predictive of their behaviour.
- Obese people are jollier (more cheerful) than non-obese people.
- Psychiatrists can read minds.
- Children raised by homosexual parents have a higher rate of homosexuality than other children.
- Murder is more common than suicide.
- Our handwriting gives clues to our personality.
- Teenagers are becoming more violent.
- Most colour-blind people see the world in black and white.
- High levels of anger in a marriage are predictive of divorce.
- People who confess to a crime are guilty.

One last word

Don't believe everything you read. We shouldn't, or at least we like to think we wouldn't. Yet a study in 1993 found that initially we do tend to believe what we read regardless of its truth. Gilbert and colleagues (1993) gave participants a story to read about a criminal, with the true facts written in green and the false facts written in red. One group of participants was given less time than the other group. They found that participants who did not have time to reflect or evaluate (that is pay attention to what was green or what was red) tended to think everything they read was true. So what? How does this apply to me? Well, reading is a fairly automatic process for us by the time we're in our adolescence, and we do read things quickly. How many times do you stop to question everything you read? It appears that we have a natural tendency to believe everything we read, as to understand something we want to believe it.

Don't believe everything you hear. Word of mouth can be a dangerous thing. In fact, research shows that if we hear something often enough we'll start to believe it – a principle advertisers use in their marketing. A study found that if we hear an opinion expressed 10 times by one person we are likely to believe that as much as we would if we heard 10 people say it once (Weaver et al. 2007 as cited in Lilienfield et al. 2010).

Figure 1.6 One person says something and then it spreads – this is how misconceptions can occur.

Be critical. The purpose of science is to question everything. Be critical. In particular, be very critical of what you read on the internet unless you are certain of the credibility of the source.

Motor neuron disease (MND) A disease where motor neurons fail to work properly and leading to muscles weakening and wasting; can lead to death

Neuroscience A term applied to any discipline that studies the nervous system. Any specialist can be a neuroscientist if they research the nervous system

INTERVIEW

Dr Blaine Roberts is a neuroscientist and researcher at the Mental Health Research Institute.

What made you decide to move to Australia?

I grew up on a farm in Michigan. I studied a B.S. in chemistry and then did my PhD in biochemistry and biophysics and researched amyotrophic lateral sclerosis, ALS (which is also known as **motor neuron disease**), at Oregon State University and Linus Pauling Institute. I met my wife who was an Australian National Volleyballer at the time. We married in 2002 and moved to Australia in 2008.

Figure 1.7 Dr Blaine Roberts – neuroscientist and researcher

What is neuroscience?

Neuroscience is not a discipline. Instead, a neuroscientist is someone who has a speciality that they apply to a problem about a neuron. There are many neuroscientists who are chemists, physicists, physiologists and mathematicians. The complexity of information about the brain can be mathematical or physical problems. Once you starting using your discipline for neurological problems, then you can call yourself a neuroscientist.

So when neuroscientists meet each other they'll ask "what do you do"?

Yes.

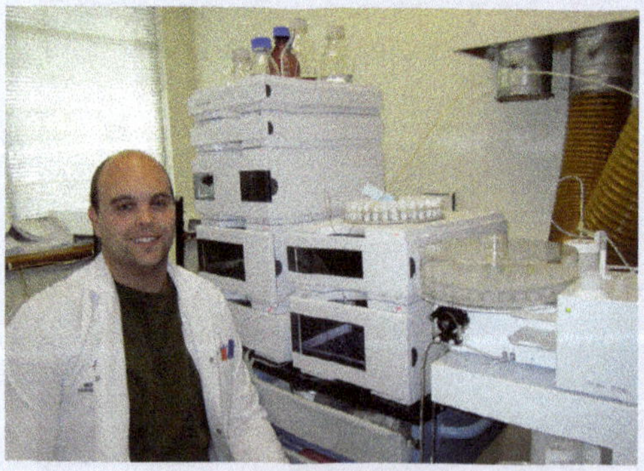

Figure 1.8 Laboratory where Dr Blaine Roberts works at the Mental Health Research Institute

What would be a normal day for you?

My day is usually half lab work and half desk job. The desk job includes processing data and writing up notebooks and consulting (helping people with other projects) as well as the usual emails and papers. I also apply for grants. The rest of the day is all lab work. Some experiments can be done in an hour and some are multi-day or multi-week.

Alzheimer's disease A progressive neurological disease of the brain that leads to the irreversible loss of neurons and dementia, and ultimately leads to death

What are you researching?

I'm a neuroscientist. I am currently conducting research on **Alzheimer's disease** and MND. In particular, I'm interested in the molecular level. For example in Alzheimer's what is causing cells to die? I look at biochemical reasons for disease and its behaviours. The questions in neuroscience can be very complex and require the input from a number of experts to answer including mathematicians, physicists, biologists and behavioural scientists.

ACTIVITY 1.10 AREAS OF PSYCHOLOGY – NEUROSCIENCE

1. What is neuroscience? Can anyone be a neuroscientist? Why or why not?
2. What is Alzheimer's disease?
3. What is motor neuron disease (MND)?

INTERVIEW

Julian Tatton is a registered psychologist who works mostly with organisations in the business world.

What are some common misconceptions or myths you come across with people?

Sometimes people imagine you sitting them on a couch and hearing about their childhood. Organisational psychologists get paid to help people and organisations perform better and find solutions, not just discuss problems. People will also say 'are you going to analyse me?' People sometimes think you have special abilities to read thoughts when they know you're a psychologist – sadly we haven't! A common misconception in the business world is that we can predict the future – whether or not they will be successful. However, there are so many reasons why people succeed or fail at work so we can never truly predict the future.

What do you do in your job then?

I spend most of my time working in professional development, such as executive coaching. I also assess people for selection for a job or for promotion within a company. I look at things like personality, their preferences and the types of things that would cause them problems when under pressure or stress. I also often help organisations in times of change – often organisations don't think of the effect of change or what is required of their staff for a change to be successful.

Figure 1.9 Julian Tatton – registered psychologist

How did you become a psychologist?

I completed a single honours degree in psychology in the UK. I ended up in Australia as my wife is from Melbourne. Then I had two years supervised practice in Victoria, approved by the Registration Board.

Are you an organisational psychologist?

Yes, I am a psychologist who works with organisations and performs all the tasks of an organisational psychologist. I have general registration as a psychologist, however, and so can perform tasks such as therapies. My business card reads 'registered psychologist'.

Is being registered important?

Psychologists need to be registered, otherwise anyone could call themselves a psychologist. Psychologists perform services and make decisions that affect peoples' lives, so professionalism is very important. The Psychology Board of Australia gives you your licence to practice, otherwise it's illegal to call yourself a psychologist.

For more information visit the Australian Health Practitioners Regulation Agency (AHPRA) at **http://www.ahpra.gov.au/**

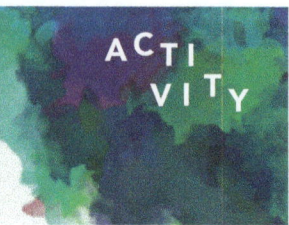

ACTIVITY 1.11 BECOMING A PSYCHOLOGIST

1. According to Julian Tatton, what is one way of becoming a psychologist?
2. In Australia who should a psychologist be registered with?
3. Why is registration important?

END OF CHAPTER SUMMARY

- Psychomythology is all the misconceptions, myths and misinformation about psychology, e.g. word of mouth, old wives tales.
- Psychology is a science and science is uncommon sense – we have to put aside our common sense and evaluate the evidence given.
- The scientific method involves empiricism, collection of data, construction of theories and replication.
- Correlations are when two things occur together statistically. Correlations, however, do not mean that two things cause each other.
- Variables are a factor in research that may be manipulated or controlled by the experimenter (the independent variable) or factor that changes as a result (dependent variable).
- Psychiatrists and psychologists can work together to help a client. Psychiatrists differ in that they have a medical degree and can prescribe medication.
- Be critical – the purpose of science is to question everything you hear and read.
- To become a psychologist in Australia you need to study a recognised four-year course followed by either two years supervised training or two years postgraduate study. You must then register with the Psychology Board of Australia.

END OF CHAPTER TEST

Multiple-choice questions

1. Science collects data by:
   A direct observation or experience
   B faith or hearsay
   C word of mouth
   D reading journals.

2. One of the most important things in science is:
   A sharing results by word of mouth
   B replication of studies
   C observations in uncontrolled environments
   D using subjective and biased data.

3. Psychomythology is:
   A old wives tales
   B misinformation
   C false stories and untruths about psychology
   D all of the above.

4. A correlation has been found between tall people and good maths results. This means that:
   A height influences maths performance
   B tall better are better at maths than small people
   C tall people and maths performance occur together statistically
   D tall people are the best at maths.

5. What variable is controlled by the experimenter?
   A independent variable
   B dependent variable
   C additional variable
   D none of the above.

Short-answer questions

Dr Finn is interested in the effect of music listening on literacy skills. He conducts a study and his results indicate a correlation between classical music listening and high literacy skills.

1. Write a possible hypothesis for Dr Finn's study.
2. What are the dependent and independent variables in his research?
3. What does the correlation between classical music listening and high literacy skills mean?
4. Why would it be important for Dr Finn to replicate his study?

Beautiful minds

CHAPTER 2

The chief function of the body is to carry the brain.

Thomas A. Edison

The brain is one of our most amazing organs. It contains over 100 billion specialised nerve cells, and is responsible for 640 muscles in our body! In addition to ruling our behaviour, the brain is also responsible for our thoughts, emotions, dreams, perceptions, personalities and motivations. Simply put, our brain makes us who we are.

Yet it remains a huge mystery. How can it be that we all have the same organ in our heads but have different abilities? Why are we not all the same? Why is it that a brain cannot be transplanted like a lung or heart? Researchers, especially psychologists, continue to make exciting new discoveries about how our brain works. This chapter will look at the features of our brain and how it makes us who we are.

The beginning

The brain begins to develop from the moment the sperm enters the egg during fertilisation. By the fourteenth day of life the **zygote** is developing its nervous system.

By the end of the eighth week, the **foetus** is 1.8 centimetres in total length and is producing 250 000 **neuroblasts** a minute, which will eventually develop into **neurons**.

Zygote An egg that has been fertilised by a sperm. It will develop into an embryo, then a foetus and finally a baby.

Foetus A developing human being in the womb

Neuroblasts Primitive cells that develop into neurons

Neurons Nerve cells in our body. They have three major parts: cell body, axon and dendrites.

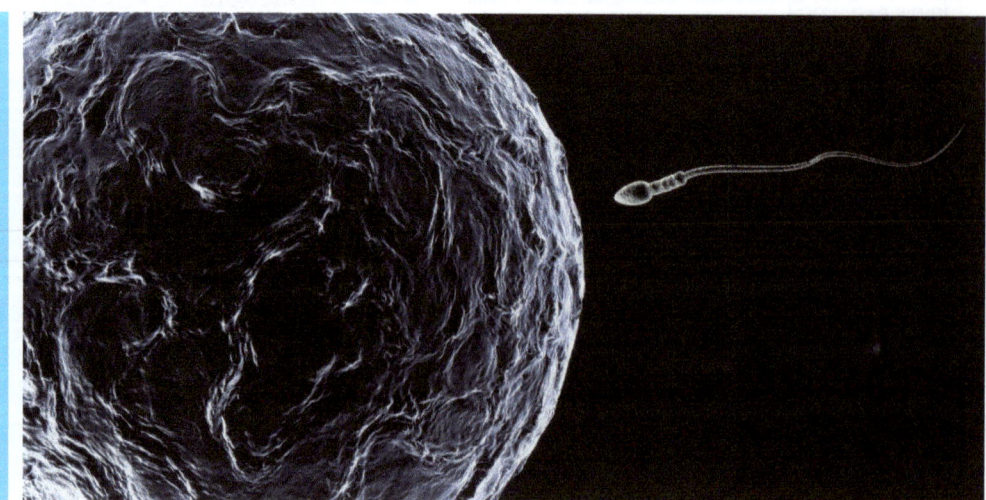

Figure 2.1 The brain begins to develop from the moment a human egg and sperm form a zygote.

DID YOU KNOW?

When we are born our brain weighs 400 grams, but by the time we celebrate our first birthday our brain weighs a kilogram – so the brain more than doubles its mass in just one year! An adult brain will be, on average, 1.4 kilograms. Surprisingly, 85 per cent of the brain's weight is water.

The largest brain in the world belongs to the sperm whale and is 9 kilograms. But a sperm whale's brain is 0.02 per cent of its overall mass, whereas our brain is 2 per cent of our mass – a significant difference.

This may be why humans have evolved so steadily and are arguably the most intelligent animal species on Earth.

By the eighth month of pregnancy, the development of the brain is almost complete. Unsurprisingly, the brain of a foetus is very vulnerable.

This is one of the reasons why pregnant women need to be careful in their habits.

Drugs, smoking and alcohol interfere with the development of the brain.

For example, the brain of a baby with **foetal alcohol syndrome (FAS)** has fewer wrinkles compared to the brain of a healthy baby. This is not good news for this baby. The more wrinkled the brain, the more powerful it is, since it has a greater surface area and therefore more neurons. The brain of a baby with FAS is significantly smaller.

Foetal alcohol syndrome (FAS) Injuries and defects inflicted on a foetus in the womb and caused by the pregnant woman's consumption of alcohol, which has a significant impact on the brain

Birth of the brain

By the time we are born our child brain has twice as many neurons as our adult brain. Why are we born with so many? As we grow, neurons that are too weak or not needed will die. By having twice as many neurons as we need, we ensure that only the strongest survive.

To understand the lifespan of neurons, we need to understand how the brain communicates with our body. Our brain 'talks' to our body through the nervous system, which is made up of neurons. The body has two major nervous systems – the central nervous system and the peripheral nervous system. The **central nervous system** is the boss of our body – like the master control centre. It consists of the brain and the spinal cord. In contrast, the **peripheral nervous system** is all the other connections in our body outside the brain and spinal cord. The peripheral nervous system carries messages (in the form of electrochemical impulses) from the central nervous system to the rest of the body and back again.

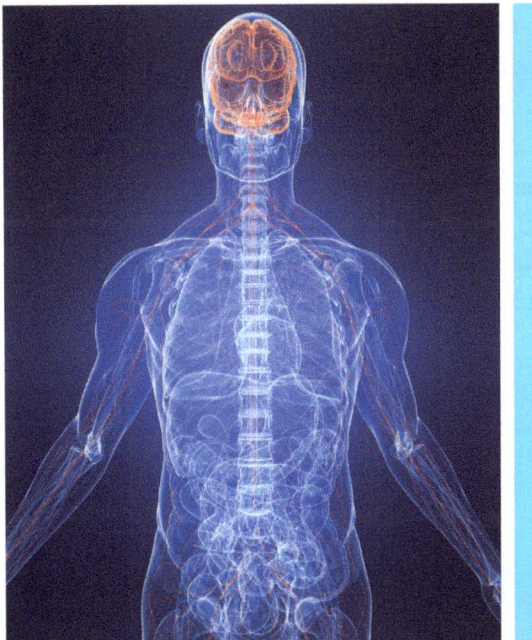

Figure 2.2 The central nervous system consists of the brain and spinal cord. The peripheral nervous system is all the connections outside the brain and spinal cord.

Central nervous system A subdivision of the human nervous system that contains the brain and spinal column

Peripheral nervous system A subdivision of the human nervous system that contains the autonomic, somatic, sympathetic and parasympathetic nervous systems

Dendrites Branch-like extensions at the front end of a neuron that receive messages from other neurons

Soma The cell body of a neuron, containing its nucleus and DNA

Axon A cable-like extension from the cell body of a neuron that sends messages to other neurons

Synapse A minute gap between neurons

Neurotransmitters Chemical messengers released by the axon that travel across the synapse (a gap) to neighbouring neurons

Acetylcholine A neurotransmitter that plays a large role in learning

Endorphins Chemical substances in our brains that act as natural painkillers in times of pain or stress. Endorphins can also cause people to feel better after strenuous exercise (a runner's 'high').

Enkephalin A powerful opiate/painkiller created by the human nervous system

Every neuron inside us has three main parts. The first part is the neuron's set of **dendrites** which receive messages from neighbouring neurons. This is how neurons 'talk'. The dendrites carry the message through to the **soma**, which is the control centre of the neuron. The message then continues from the soma along the **axon**. Axons carry neural impulses very quickly – our speed of thinking can range from 3 to 320 kilometres per hour!

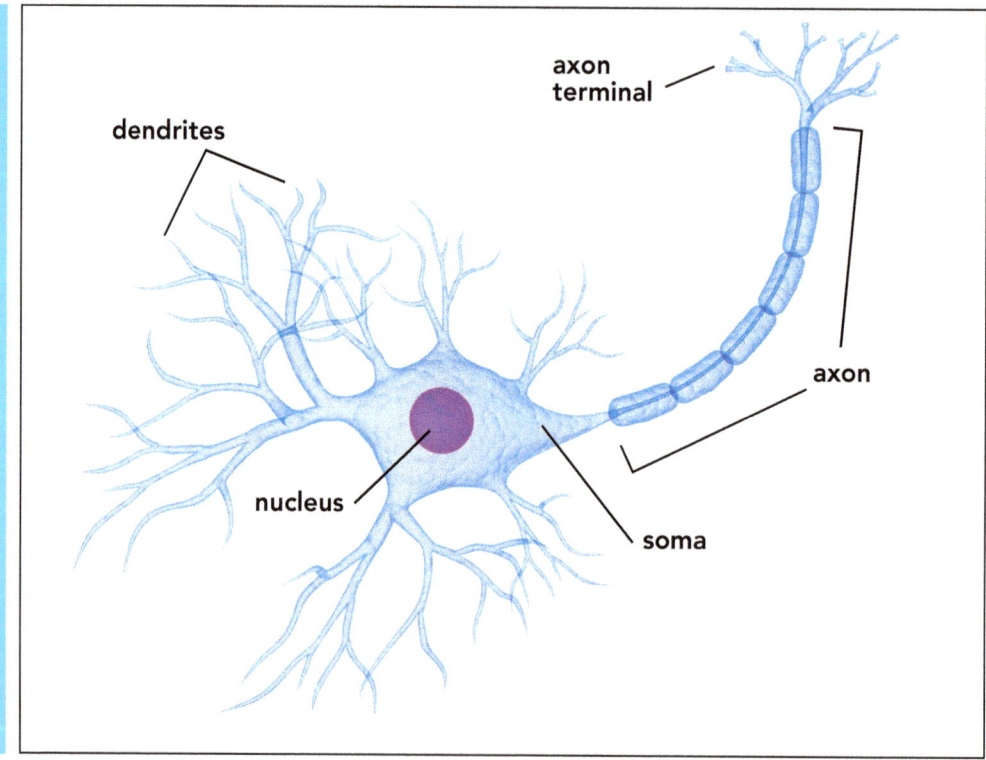

Figure 2.3 A neuron

Once the message reaches the end of the axon, it hits a dead end. There is a small gap called **synapse** between each neuron. The message needs to travel from the end of the axon across the gap to the next neuron's dendrites. How does it do this? The axon of a neuron releases **neurotransmitters**, which 'talk' to the dendrites of a neighbouring neuron. There are about 1000 neurotransmitters in the human body and each has a different role. For example, one type of neurotransmitter called **acetylcholine** plays a role in our learning. People who continue to challenge themselves, such as with complex puzzles that stretch their ability, tend to have more acetylcholine in their system.

Endorphins are another type of neurotransmitter. Endorphins are natural painkillers that are released when we experience pain.

Our brain also creates its own opiate, called **enkephalin**, thought to be more powerful than morphine – one of the strongest man-made painkillers. Scientists have also discovered that being in love can act as a painkiller. The euphoric phase of a new romance is linked to the release of dopamine, a 'feel good' chemical synthesised by neurons in the brain.

ACTIVITY 2.1 BRAIN GAMES

Search online for Dr Eric Chudler's website 'Neuroscience for Kids' and do some of the brain games and worksheets.

ACTIVITY 2.2 BRAINS

1. How much does an adult brain weigh?
2. If a sperm whale's brain is 0.02 per cent of its mass, how much does the whale weigh? Remember that its brain weighs 9 kilograms.
3. When does the brain begin to develop?
4. What is the difference between a neuroblast and a neuron?
5. What is the central nervous system made up of?
6. Draw a diagram of a neuron into your notes and label its features.
7. What is a neurotransmitter?
8. Explain what the neurotransmitters acetylcholine and endorphins are responsible for.

How our brain talks

When we learn, our brain's neurons make more connections. They do this by growing more dendrites, which can then receive messages from axons of other neurons by the chemical messengers – the neurotransmitters. For example, if a neuron only had one dendrite, it would only be able to communicate with one axon of another neuron. But if it has five dendrites, it can talk to five other neurons, and so on. Some neurons have thousands of dendrites!

As children, the number of connections between our neurons is 50 per cent greater than as adults. During adolescence, however, there is massive pruning of these connections as neurons die. It is a case of 'use it or lose it' – the neurons that die are the ones we don't end up using. Theoretically, we could keep all the neurons we had at birth if we used them all.

Our brains are like muscles, and you can actually cause your brain to grow by learning and trying new things. Any animal, humans included, can increase their brain density and number of neural connections by stimulating their brain. The brain becomes stronger if it is exercised. Stimulated neurons develop 25 per cent more dendrites and increase in size, blood supply and number of connections.

The more connections your neurons make, the faster you are able to access your knowledge. The human brain can make a million connections between its neurons each *second*. Each one of your 100 billion neurons can make up to 10 000 synaptic connections with other neurons. This means that you could have about 40 quadrillion different pattern of connections in your brain – 40 000 000 000 000 000!

The brain is a little like the Google search engine. Our brains access knowledge faster if there are more links. The more we learn about a topic, the more links we make to previous stuff we have learned. The more connections we have, the faster we think. You should never stop learning or trying new things.

DID YOU KNOW? One long-standing belief is that we only use 10 per cent of our brain. This is not true! Brain scans show that we put most of our brain to good use – not much of our brain is left idle, even when we are sleeping. So how did this myth come about? Probably because neurons only make up 10 per cent of brain matter, leading to the belief that it is only that 10 per cent that counts.

Neuronal soup

Neuroimpulses The messages that travel along a neuron

Controlled environment An environment where external factors, such as temperature and hygiene, are strictly controlled. Controlled environments are important for reliable research.

Did you know that neurons can talk to electric circuits? The **neuroimpulses** in our brain are electrochemical, meaning they are both electrical and chemical in nature. Research has found that computer microchips can communicate with the neurons. Researchers created a 'soup' of neurons taken from rats. A small pot of soup can hold about 300 000 rat neurons (Marks 2008), which can survive outside the body as long as they are in a **controlled environment**.

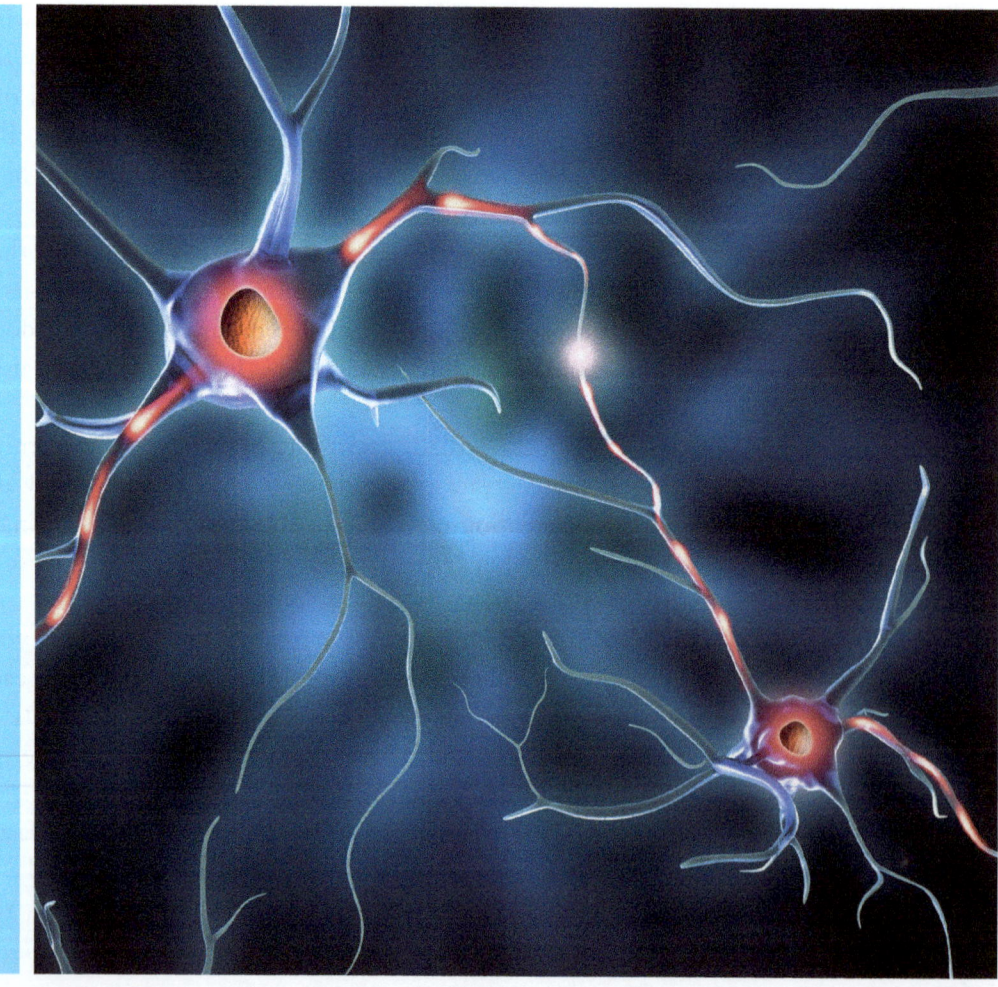

Figure 2.4 The neuroimpulses in our brain are electrochemical, meaning they are both electrical and chemical in nature.

A controller (microchip) was immersed in the neuronal soup, and researchers then programmed a robot to communicate with the neurons and respond to their messages; that is, the soup was taught what to do, like training a real animal.

ACTIVITY 2.3 RESEARCH ACTIVITY

Find a neurological disease that interests you and prepare a short presentation to your class to help teach them about it. A good place to start is the website for the National Institute of Neurological Disorders and Strokes.

Our precious brains

Fortunately, not only do we have a skull to protect our brain, but we also have other great features that work together as a security system for our brain. Aside from the layers of hair, skin, muscle and fat over the skull, there are also internal protective mechanisms of the brain.

Directly inside the skull are three layers of **membranes** known as the **meninges**. Between the two inner layers of the meninges is what is called **cerebrospinal fluid (CSF)**. Our brain literally floats in CSF, which shields it from shocks and vibrations.

Membrane A sheet of tissue that covers or connects organs

Meninges The layers of membrane under the skull surrounding the brain

Cerebrospinal fluid (CSF) The fluid that surrounds and protects the brain

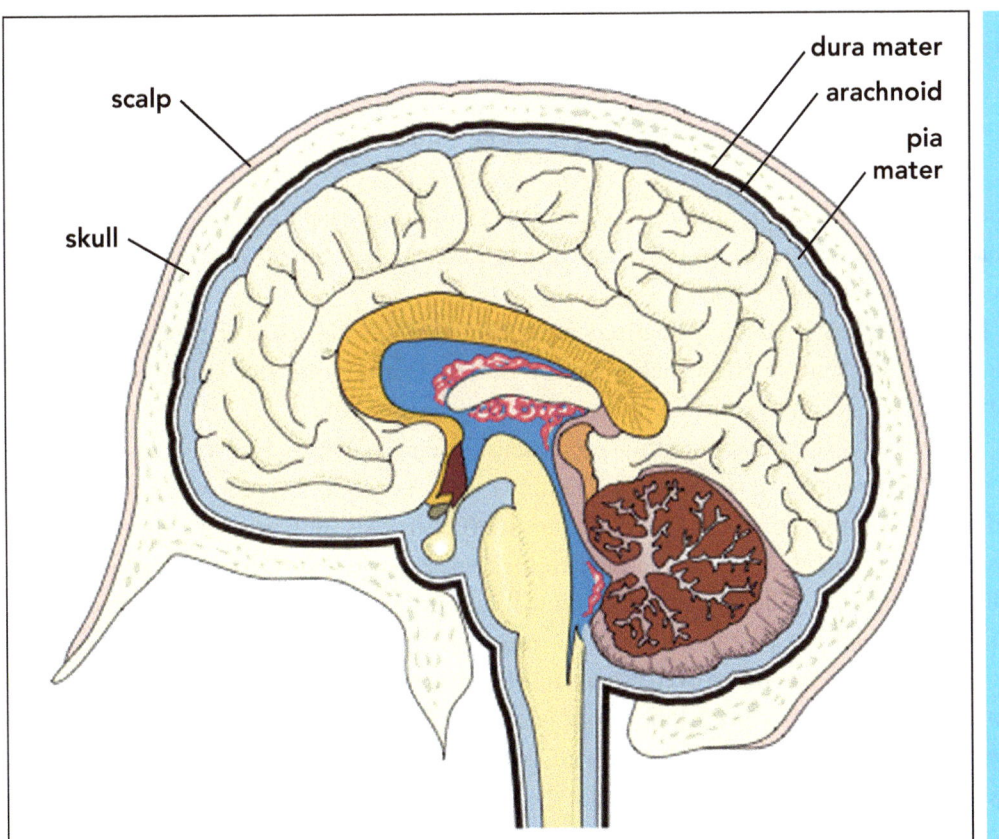

Figure 2.5 There are three meninges (layers of the brain): dura mater, arachnoid and pia mater.

There are two remaining levels of security for our brains. The first is our cells' ability to ward off any nasty or foreign chemicals that could be in our blood. The second is our behaviour; for example, we can duck when a fast-paced ball is directed at our head. Fortunately, humans have great reflexes to help us avoid damage (even if some of us have slower reflexes than others).

DID YOU KNOW?

DID YOU KNOW THAT THERE IS AN ANIMAL THAT EATS ITS OWN BRAIN?

The sea squirt is a tiny marine creature, which in its infancy swims around like a tadpole. It eventually fixes itself permanently to a rock, where it feeds by filtering plankton out of the water (an automatic process). Once a sea squirt has fixed itself permanently to its rock, it then eats its own brain as it does not need it anymore!

Figure 2.6 A sea squirt fixed to a rock.

ACTIVITY 2.4 REVIEW

1. How many neuronal connections are there thought to be in our brain?
2. In terms of connections between neurons, what is one disadvantage of ageing?
3. A neuroimpulse is electrochemical. What does this mean?
4. What are the meninges and where are they?
5. If there were no CSF in your skull, what do you think could happen to your brain?

Lobe A clearly obvious division of an organ, such as in the brain or ear

Frontal lobe The region of the brain involved in decision making, problem solving, motor control and personality

Cortex Outer layer of the brain where most processes take place, such as thinking

Parietal lobe A region of the brain involved in processing information from our sensory organs, such as the skin

Occipital lobe A region of the brain involved with vision

Temporal lobe A region of the brain involved with hearing, speech and memory

Cerebellum A primitive part of the brain responsible for balance and motor coordination

The anatomy of the brain

The brain is made up of three parts: forebrain, midbrain and hindbrain. However, it is more common for people to talk about the brain as having four **lobes**: frontal, parietal, occipital and temporal lobes.

Each lobe has its own specialised function. The **frontal lobe** is thought to house our personality and decision-making abilities. The frontal lobe also contains the motor **cortex**, which is responsible for all our voluntary movements.

The **parietal lobe** contains the somatosensory cortex, which receives messages from all the sensory organs in our body, for example, skin, eyes and tongue. More cortex space is devoted to the parts of the body that are more sensitive. For example, more cortex is given to the hands than to the feet, which makes sense when you think about how much you use your hands. The homunculus you will see later in Chapter 7 shows what we would look like if each body part grew in proportion to the amount of brain allocated to it.

The **occipital lobe** is involved in vision; while the parietal lobe receives nerve impulses from our eyes, the occipital lobe translates those impulses into images. Similarly, the **temporal lobe** translates what we hear, which makes sense as the temporal lobe is next to our ears; it also houses parts of the brain involved in memory and speech. The **cerebellum** is at the base of the brain next to the brain stem (top of spinal cord) and is responsible for balance and motor coordination.

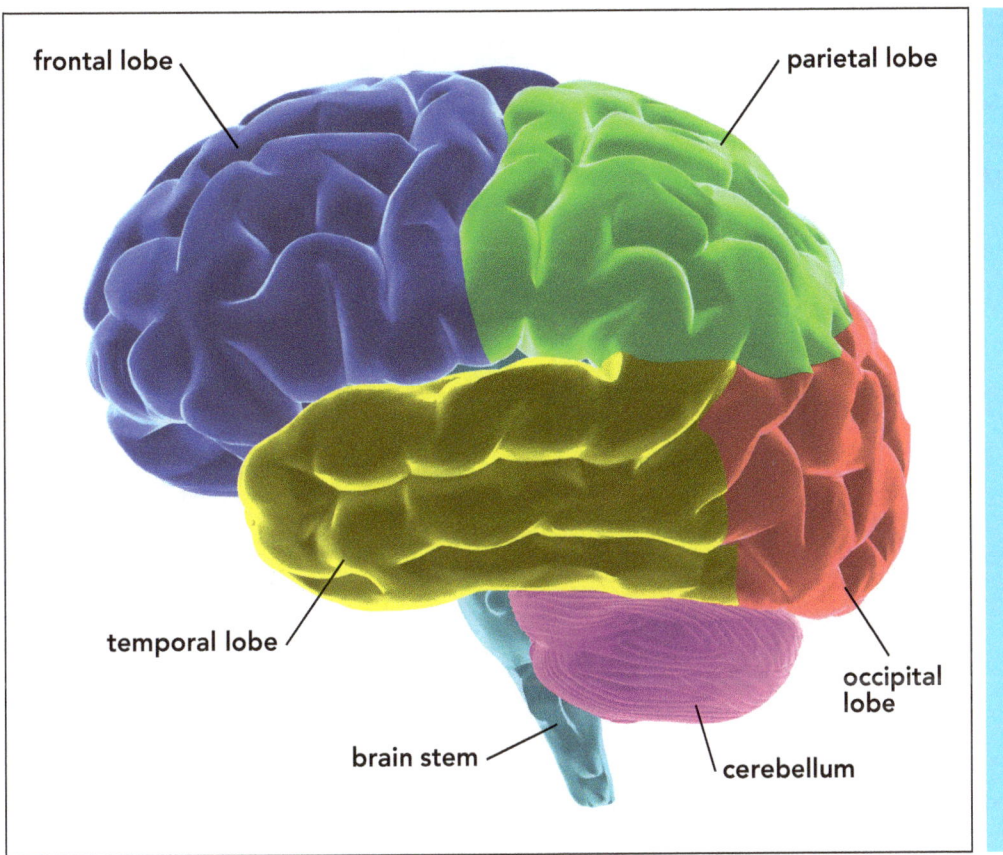

Figure 2.7 The brain has many features, including four lobes that have their own specialised functions.

> The part of the brain that helps us smell is the olfactory bulb, which is located beneath the frontal lobe – where we would expect it to be – nice and close to the nose. The olfactory bulb houses all the neurons that process smell. These neurons send information to the temporal lobes (sides of the brain) that house the olfactory cortex.
>
> Taste is processed by the limbic system. The limbic system contains the hippocampus, amygdala and hypothalamus. The hippocampus plays a large role in memory, which may explain why taste (and smell) can act as powerful cues for memory.

DID YOU KNOW?

The hemispheres of the brain

The four lobes of the brain that we have looked at so far are like state boundaries on a map of Australia, not visible to the human eye. What is visible is that the brain has two halves. Each half is called a **hemisphere**. Between the hemispheres there is a strand of tissue called the **corpus callosum**. The corpus callosum acts as a bridge of communication between the two hemispheres, connected by over 300 million nerve fibres.

Back in the 1950s, Roger Sperry, a surgeon, became very famous when he severed the corpus callosum of some of his patients in an effort to control their epilepsy. Sperry's surgical procedure is known as the 'split brain procedure'. He found that each hemisphere has its own unique functions.

Hemisphere Half of a sphere; in psychology, the left or right half of the brain

Corpus callosum Nerve tissue connecting the two hemispheres of the brain

ACTIVITY 2.5 SPLITTING THE BRAIN

Search online for the Nobel Prize Foundation's website and its suite of educational games for a game that demonstrates Sperry's split brain procedure as well as a game that explains the MRI technique.

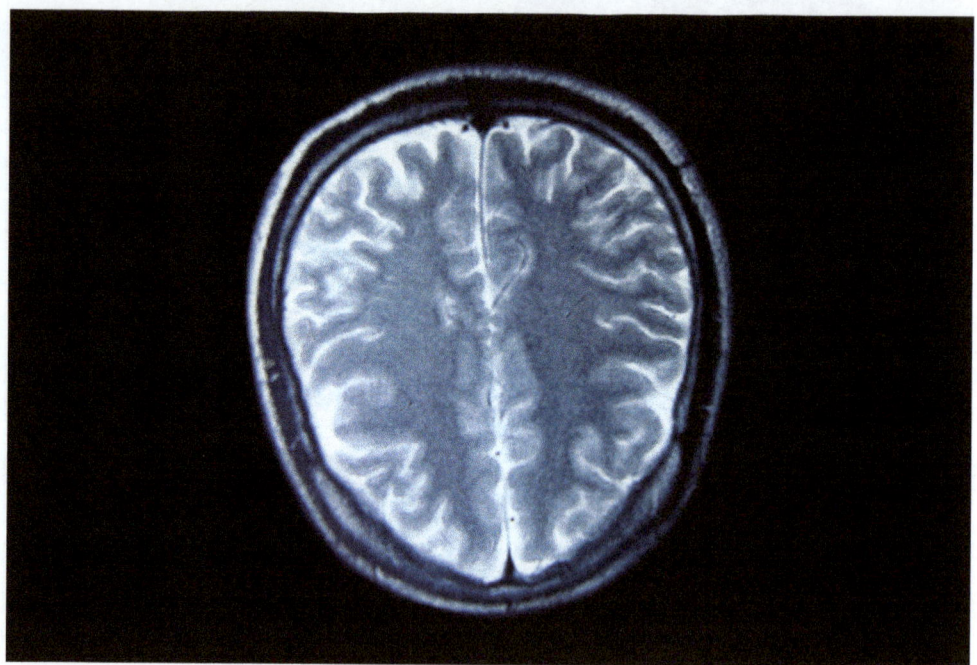

Figure 2.8 MRI scan showing the two hemispheres of the brain

What does each hemisphere control?

Contralateral On opposite sides of the body

First, our hemispheres are **contralateral**. This means that the left hemisphere controls the right side of the body, and the right hemisphere controls the left side of the body.

The left hemisphere is where language is processed – most people (around 90 per cent of right handers and 70 per cent of left handers) have their speech centre in their left hemisphere. Of the remaining people, half of them have their speech centre in the right hemisphere, and the remaining half process language bilaterally (in both hemispheres).

Leonardo da Vinci was left handed. Perhaps that is not so interesting – 10 per cent of the world's population is left handed. What *is* interesting, however, is that he wrote from the right-hand side of the page to the left-hand side, and wrote backwards. This means that the only way to read his notes is to hold them up to a mirror!

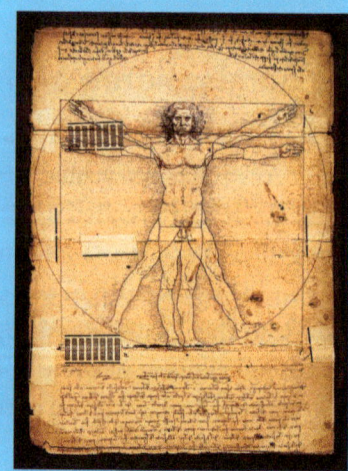

Figure 2.9 Leonardo da Vinci wrote backwards.

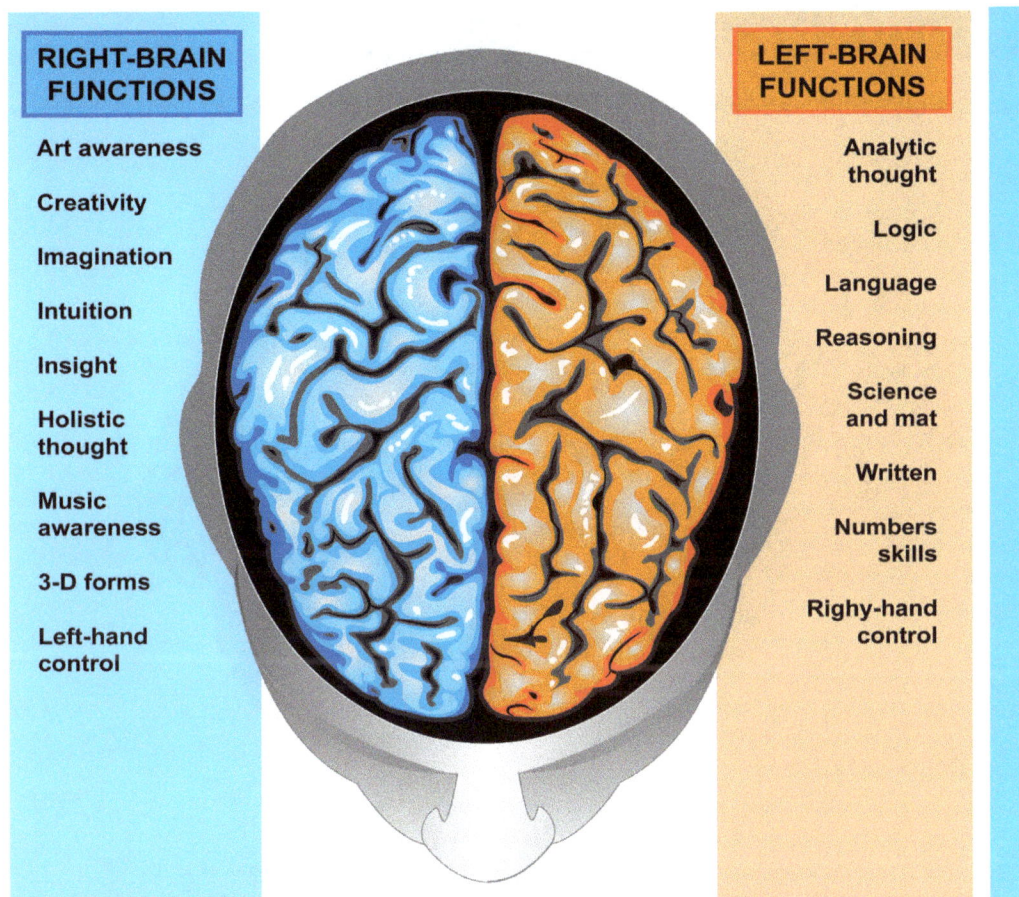

Figure 2.10 Although the hemispheres of the brain work together, it has been found that they are dominant in different functions.

In addition to language, the left hemisphere also is responsible for logical and analytical thinking, e.g. maths. In comparison, the right hemisphere is emotional and imaginative, creating ideas and insights. When we paint, play music or take part in other creative activities, we are using our right hemisphere. The right hemisphere is also important for spatial activities such as recognising shapes, patterns, faces and expressions, as well as judging the size, distance and position of objects.

Spatial neglect

Spatial neglect is where one hemisphere is damaged, resulting in a loss of awareness for the contralateral (opposite) side of the body. Spatial neglect in one of the hemispheres often occurs after a stroke. People with extreme left neglect, for instance, might only see 6 through to 12 o'clock on a clock face, only eat food from the left side of their plate, or only shave the left side of their face.

Spatial neglect not only causes problems with vision, but can also affect hearing, smell and awareness and control of one's body. For example, a sufferer may forget they have a left leg, accidentally burn their left arm while cooking and not realise, or only chew their food using the right side of their mouth. They also might bump into doorframes and people on their left side.

Spatial neglect Damage to one hemisphere of the brain that results in a loss of awareness for the contralateral (opposite side) of the body

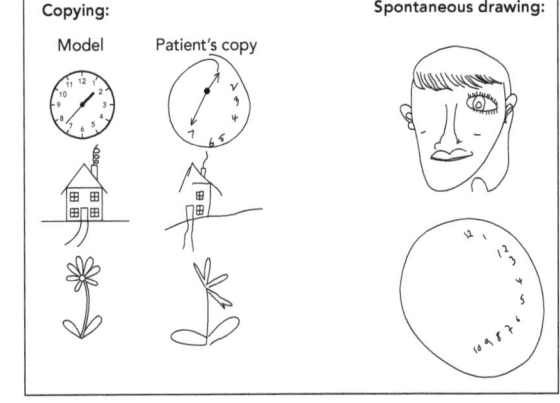

Figure 2.11 An example of a drawing by someone suffering from spatial neglect

GET PSYCHED!

ACTIVITY 2.6 HEMISPHERES OF THE BRAIN

1. Copy the following diagram. Name the four lobes of the brain and describe their functions.

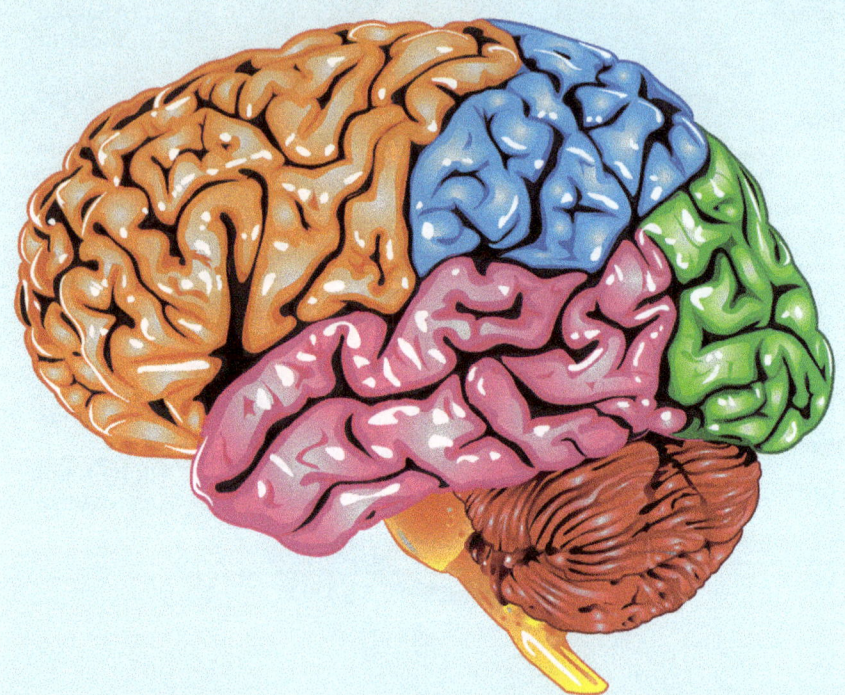

2. What does 'contralateral' mean in regards to the brain's hemispheres?
3. What is the corpus callosum and what does it do?
4. Imagine you are going to have brain surgery. Your doctor anaesthetises your left hemisphere, but you already know your speech centre is in the left hemisphere. Describe what your doctor would observe you doing following the anaesthetisation.
5. If a person was suffering from 'left neglect', what would you expect to observe them doing?

Tricks of the brain

The human brain is quite amazing. It keeps us alive and alert. However, sometimes it can also play tricks on us and make us believe things that are not quite real. Sometimes we might see or hear things that are not really there. Some examples of the tricks brains play on us are change blindness and hallucinations.

Change blindness

Do you think you would notice if the environment you were standing in changed? Most of us would definitely say 'Yes!' However, it appears that we do not pay as much attention to what is going on as we like to think.

A study at Harvard University in 2007 asked each participant to walk down a street, where they were stopped by a passerby. The passerby was a confederate (an actor working for the researcher) and asked the participant for directions. While the participant answered, two workmen carrying a door (also confederates) rudely interrupted by walking between the participant and the passerby. As they walked past, one of the workmen quickly swapped places with the passerby while hidden by the door.

Do you think the participants noticed that they were now talking to a different person? Amazingly, only seven out of fifteen participants noticed the change! Over 50 per cent did not realise a change had occurred. This is especially remarkable considering that the workmen and the passerby were different heights, had different voices, and were wearing different clothes.

So how can we be tricked like this? This phenomenon is known as change blindness. Basically, we tend to only pay attention to what we think is relevant at the time. This means we can miss things.

ACTIVITY 2.7 DO THE TEST

The Transport for London website has several short films designed to test your awareness and change blindness. Do a search for the 'Do the Test' promotion (www.dothetest.co.uk), watch the films and see whether you are as alert to changes as you think you are.

Hallucinations

Sometimes our brains make too much or too little of certain chemicals. One neurotransmitter that can have an impact on our sense of reality is **dopamine**.

Dopamine is a 'feel-good' neurotransmitter best known for its pleasurable effect in our body and the role it plays in motor control. However, too much dopamine in the body can cause **hallucinations**. For instance, sufferers of **schizophrenia** tend to have too much dopamine in their body and this may explain why they suffer from hallucinations. A common hallucination is for patients to report seeing a shadowy figure that is following them.

Further evidence of the effect of dopamine comes from people suffering from **Parkinson's disease**, who need dopamine-enhancing drugs to help their motor control. They tend to report experiencing hallucinations when they begin their medication.

ACTIVITY 2.8 ERA: THE PHANTOM HAND

The details of this ERA are available on the Cambridge GO website.

Brain banks

Researching the brain is a real challenge. The easiest and best way to research the brain is by testing the brain tissue of people who have died and donated their organs to research. centres that collect and handle brain tissue are called **brain banks**. There are about five major brain banks in Australia; Victoria's is currently at the Alfred Hospital in Melbourne. Brain banks handle a variety of brain tissues, ranging from normal and healthy to neurologically diseased.

Brain banks were created after Albert Einstein's death in 1955. Harvey Thompson, a doctor and colleague of Einstein's, carried out an autopsy on Einstein's body and preserved his brain. Thompson carefully sliced the brain into 240 parts and preserved the slices in formalin to wait for science to become more sophisticated, as in the 1950s assessment of DNA was primitive. By the 1980s, science had progressed enough to begin analysing Einstein's brain. During this time, Thompson kept Einstein's brain in the boot of his car!

Dopamine A hormone that plays an important role in cognitive functions such as memory, problem solving and attention. It is also known as the 'pleasure' hormone, as it provides feelings of enjoyment and happiness.

Hallucinations Mistaken perceptions, illusions; experiencing something that is not real. Hallucinations can be visual, auditory or tactile.

Schizophrenia A psychotic disorder characterised by distorted thought and language, and social withdrawal

Parkinson's disease A disorder of the central nervous system caused by the breakdown of motor neurons in the body. Symptoms include tremors and lack of motor control.

Brain bank An organisation that collects, organises, handles and distributes brain tissue

Figure 2.12 Albert Einstein's brain was preserved after his death so that it could be dissected and studied.

Glial cells Cells that support neurons and are involved with neural transmission

Once doctors were finally able to analyse Einstein's brain, they noted he had more **glial cells** than normal in the parietal lobe, and that these lobes were wider. They also found that his brain was a little wider and more symmetrical than the average human brain. For more information on the brain, see Chapter 4.

ACTIVITY 2.9 CHANGE BLINDNESS, HALLUCINATIONS AND BRAIN BANKS

1. What is change blindness?
2. Search YouTube for examples of change blindness.
3. What are hallucinations?
4. What role does dopamine play? Refer to schizophrenia and Parkinson's in your answer.
5. What are brain banks?
6. What do glial cells do?

END OF CHAPTER SUMMARY

- The brain contains over 100 billion neurons that can make over 10 000 synaptic connections.
- There are two major divisions of the nervous system: the central nervous system and the peripheral nervous system.
- The brain 'talks' through neurons, the building blocks of the nervous system.
- A neuron is made up of three major parts: dendrites, soma and axon.
- Neurotransmitters are chemical messengers released by an axon that travel across the synapse (a gap) to the neighbouring neurons.
- Neuroimpulses are the messages that travel through neurons; they are electrochemical in nature.
- The skull protects our brain but is still vulnerable to pressure and blast waves that can cause the skull to flex. The meninges and CSF are also important for the protection of the brain. Our immune system and our reflexes play a part in protecting the brain as well.
- The brain has two hemispheres and four lobes: frontal, parietal, occipital and temporal.
- Each hemisphere is contralateral and has its own functions. Spatial neglect can occur when a hemisphere is damaged.
- Phantom limb is a phenomenon where people continue to feel the presence of a lost limb.
- Change blindness is where people only pay attention to what is relevant and miss other changes in their environment.
- Hallucinations may be caused by the presence of too much dopamine, a neurotransmitter.
- Brain banks are an excellent resource for researchers as they collect, organise and distribute brain tissue.

END OF CHAPTER TEST

Multiple-choice questions

1. What is the role of dendrites on a neuron?
   A to send messages to neighbouring neurons
   B to protect the neuron from disease
   C to receive messages from neighbouring neurons
   D to feed the neuron.

2. When we learn, our:
   A brain becomes less dense
   B neurons make more connections
   C neurons shrink
   D brain plays tricks on us.

3. The four lobes of the brain are in the following order from front to back:
   A frontal, parietal, occipital and temporal
   B temporal, frontal, parietal and occipital
   C parietal, occipital, temporal and frontal
   D temporal, occipital, parietal and frontal.

4. The left hemisphere is responsible for:
   A speaking
   B completing maths problems
   C playing the piano
   D both A and B.

5. The lobe responsible for vision is _____ and the lobe responsible for hearing is _____.
   A parietal; occipital
   B occipital; parietal
   C occipital; temporal
   D temporal; occipital.

END OF CHAPTER TEST

Short-answer questions

1. Patrick's grandfather has had the split-brain procedure. Patrick does not understand what this means. Explain the procedure to him.
2. Callum suffers from schizophrenia. He began new medication to help control his hallucinations, but noticed that he has trouble moving his arms and legs, and his tongue felt heavy, making it difficult to speak. Why might Callum have experienced this?
3. a. Sarah has suffered a physical blow to the side of her head and is having problems with her hearing and sense of touch. Explain why this may be so.
   b. After a few days, Sarah notices that she is having difficulties with her maths homework and gets pins and needles in her right arm. Explain why this might be happening.

For more information on the brain, see Chapter 4.

Mind interrupted

CHAPTER 3

'But I don't want to go among mad people', Alice remarked.
'Oh, you can't help that', said the Cat. 'We're all mad here.
I'm mad. You're mad.'
'How do you know I'm mad?' said Alice.
'You must be', said the Cat, 'or you wouldn't have come here'.

Lewis Carroll, *Alice in Wonderland*

Life is not without its stresses. At points in our lives we will experience times of great distress. For many of us, these stresses and the emotions we feel are a natural and appropriate reaction. If we lose a loved one, we experience grief and great sadness. If we misunderstand the actions of another, we can feel great anger. Fortunately for most of us, these periods of negative emotions last for a short time. But what if these feelings are a continual part of your life? What if you feel like you are not able to control the stresses in your life?

The time of greatest stress is our teenage years – adolescence. It is a time of massive changes and pressures, and the pressures on young people are increasing. That is, it's harder to be a teenager today than it used to be. The breakdown of families (and relationships) as well as increased drug use can contribute to poorer mental health. Furthermore, the technological changes and advances in our world have caused our society to become more fast paced and consumer oriented – leading to greater pressure as everyone wants things 'now' (NACMH 2009).

Figure 3.1 Adolescence can be a time of great stress.

What are the issues facing teenagers?

In 2010, over 50 000 young Australians from age 11 to 24 years were surveyed by Mission Australia. The results showed that the major issues for young Australians included the environment, drugs and alcohol, stress and violence. Further, young Australians greatly value family and friends, independence, and good physical and mental health.

Mental health of young Australians

More than 75 per cent of all severe mental illnesses occur before 25 years of age. One in seven young Australians (12 to 17 years of age) experience a mental health problem every year. Moreover, one in four people aged 16 to 24 years in Australia has a mental illness (ABS 2010).

Figure 3.2 Mental health problems not taken care of in adolescence can develop into a mental illness.

Sadly, however, young Australians are likely to wait years before seeking help for their problems. Less than a quarter of all young Australians with a mental disorder will seek help (ABS 2010). Of those who seek help, boys are less likely to. This may be due to reluctance to discuss their emotions, or feeling that they should be able to cope on their own, or fear and anxiety about what will happen if they get help, as well as concerns about privacy, and the costs of services. To help beat mental illness, early detection and early help is the key. In Australia, some of the most common mental illnesses facing adolescents include conduct disorder, anxiety, depression, substance dependence (drug dependence) and eating disorders. Before we consider each of these disorders we first need to discuss 'what is mental health'.

What is mental health and what is mental illness?

Mental health and mental illness do not mean the same thing. **Mental illness** is a problem that significantly affects how the person behaves, feels, thinks, and is diagnosed according to criteria. Mental illness is sometimes also described by the term 'mental disorder'.

A **mental health problem** also affects how a person behaves, feels, thinks, but on a lesser scale and tends to be a temporary reaction to the stresses of life. Mental health problems are therefore less severe, but they can develop into mental illness if they are not effectively taken care of.

For the purpose of this chapter the criteria for mental illnesses as proposed by the **DSM-IV-TR** (Fourth edition, Text Revision) will be used. The DSM or *Diagnostic and Statistical Manual of Mental Disorders* is one of the most commonly used measurement tools and is translated into more than 22 languages around the world. The *DSM* is not a cookbook – that is, you simply can't just diagnose someone by having this book and carefully reading it. To use the DSM you need to be clinically trained.

Mental illness (or mental disorder) is a problem that significantly affects how the person behaves, feels, thinks, and is clinically diagnosed according to criteria.

Mental health problem Affects how a person behaves, feels, thinks, but is less severe than a mental illness and tends to be a temporary reaction to the stresses of life

DSM-IV-TR is the version of the *Diagnostic and Statistical Manual of Mental Disorders* that gives guidelines and criteria for classifying and diagnosing mental illnesses. In 2012 the fifth edition will be published.

ACTIVITY 3.1 MENTAL ILLNESS

1. What are the most common mental illnesses facing adolescents today?
2. Define the term 'mental illness'.
3. What is the difference between a mental illness and a mental health problem?
4. Name one measurement tool that professionals could use to clinically diagnose mental illness.
5. Do you agree that adolescence is a time of stress? Privately list down some of the pressures and stresses you face at the moment. You may like to share this with the class. You may find some of you face similar pressures.

ACTIVITY 3.2 ERA: THE PERCEPTION OF MENTAL HEALTH IN TEENAGERS

The details of this ERA are available on the Cambridge GO website.

Conduct disorder

Conduct disorder is the most common childhood and adolescent mental disorder in the world. The World Health Organisation (2009) estimated that 40 per cent of children with conduct disorder continue into adulthood with a range of mental health problems. Boys are twice as likely to suffer from conduct disorder than girls (Sawyer et al. 2000). Children who have conduct disorder are also four times more likely to commit crime, and twice as likely to use drugs (Fergusson et al. 2005).

Conduct disorder is a persistent and repetitive pattern of behaviour where the societal rules and basic rights of others are infringed upon, that is, antisocial behaviour. There are four main types of behaviour that sufferers demonstrate: aggressive conduct, non-aggressive conduct, deceitfulness or theft, and serious violations of rules.

Conduct disorder A mental illness characterised by antisocial behaviour, including aggressive conduct, non-aggressive conduct, deceitfulness or theft, and serious violations of rules

Features and diagnostic criteria of conduct disorder

To be diagnosed with conduct disorder, three or more of the behaviours listed below must be shown over 12 months across a variety of settings such as home, school, work and community settings.

1. Aggressive conduct includes bullying, threatening, initiating physical fights, using a weapon that can cause physical harm (e.g. brick, bat, broken bottle, knife or gun), being physically cruel to others.
2. Non-aggressive conduct is behaviour that causes property loss or damage, such as breaking windows, vandalism, setting fire to a car or house. The intention of the behaviour is to cause serious damage.
3. Deceitfulness or theft includes shoplifting, forgery, or breaking into someone's house or car, and frequently lying or breaking promises to others in order to obtain goods or avoid obligations.
4. Serious violation of rules includes breaking school and parental rules, and also societal rules that are age appropriate (that is, the child would understand the rule as they are considered old enough to understand). Examples include running away from home (must occur more than once), wagging/truancy from school, or not turning up to work for no acceptable reason.

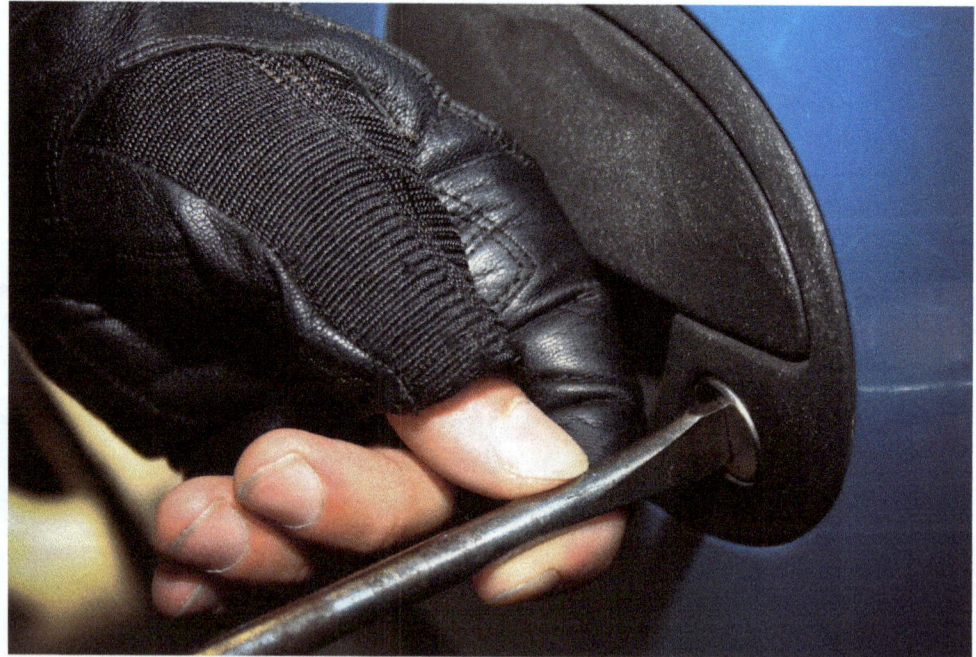

Figure 3.3 Breaking into someone's car is one of the many symptomatic behaviours of conduct disorder.

ACTIVITY 3.3 CONDUCT DISORDER

1. Define conduct disorder.
2. According to WHO, what is the risk that children with conduct disorder will face implications later in life?
3. What are the four types of behaviour of conduct disorder? Name and give two examples for each of the four types.
4. Is there a relationship between crime and conduct disorder? Why do you think so? Refer to evidence shown in the text.

Link to antisocial personality disorder and other mental illnesses

Once 18 years of age, if conduct disorder has persisted most sufferers are then diagnosed as having **antisocial personality disorder (APD)**. However, a diagnosis of APD is not possible for individuals under the age of 18 years.

Children and adolescents who suffer from conduct disorder are also at greater risk of depression, anxiety and substance-related disorders.

Antisocial personality disorder (APD) A personality disorder characterised by antisocial behaviour, and cannot be diagnosed until after the age of 18 years

ACTIVITY 3.4 PERSONALITY DISORDERS

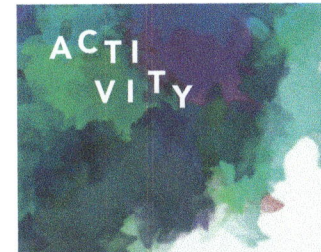

1. What other mental illnesses may adolescents be at risk of if they suffer from conduct disorder?
2. Define the term 'antisocial personality disorder'.
3. Why are adolescents with conduct disorder not diagnosed with antisocial personality disorder?

Anxiety

Feelings of **anxiety** are common to all of us. It is what we feel when we're nervous about something. If you feel anxious when it is appropriate to the situation, this is considered normal. So nerves leading up to an exam, a party, or a sports game are all natural feelings.

When you feel anxious at such an extreme level that it interferes with your daily routines and stops you from doing what you want to do, there may be a problem. Anxiety is one of the most common mental illnesses and, similar to other mental illnesses, often begins in adolescence. Currently in Australia, about 15 per cent of teenagers suffer from anxiety (ABS 2010).

In children and adolescents one of the most common types of anxiety disorder is **generalised anxiety disorder (GAD)**.

Children and adolescents with GAD are often concerned about their competence or quality of performance at school or in their sport. They also tend to have extreme concerns about punctuality as well as worrying about major catastrophic events such as earthquakes or war. Sufferers tend to be perfectionists and redo tasks due to worrying about a less-than-perfect performance. They also tend to seek continual approval and continual reassurance about their performance. They are unsure of themselves.

Anxiety Feeling of fear, nervousness, and a lack of control, or a sense of impending doom

Generalised Anxiety Disorder (GAD) An anxiety disorder that is more common amongst teenagers than adults, but can also begin in childhood. GAD is more common in girls than boys.

Figure 3.4 A common symptom of GAD is performance anxiety.

Features and diagnostic criteria of generalised anxiety disorder

There are four main features of GAD:
1 Extreme worry or anxiety for at least six months about a number of events or activities
2 Difficulty in controlling anxiety
3 At least three other symptoms of:
- tiredness
- irritability
- muscle tension
- difficulty concentrating
- restlessness (feeling on edge)
- sleep problems.
4 The anxiety is not due to substance use or another medical condition.

ACTIVITY 3.5 ANXIETY DISORDERS

1 How is an anxiety disorder different from normal feelings of anxiety? Explain.
2 Define the term 'generalised anxiety disorder (GAD)'?
3 Describe three features of GAD.

Depression

Depression A mental disorder characterised by sadness, loss of interest and pleasure in life, and other negative emotions

One in five Australians will suffer from **depression** at some point in their lifetime. Adolescents are more at risk if they have major stresses in their life, or if someone in their family has suffered from depression. The stresses for a teenager may seem insignificant to adults so it is important for parents to understand the enormity of a stress for a teenager. Stresses for teenagers include school failure, the break-up of an important friendship, bullying, parental conflict, loss of a parent, an accident, and prejudice due to sexual preferences. Adolescents who suffer from depression often don't know how to ask for help, or refuse help.

Onset Beginning point, when something begins

Approximately 3 per cent of Australian teenagers suffer from depression currently (ABS 2010). Once in adulthood, depression affects one in four women and one in six men. Like many mental illnesses, the **onset** of depression is often in adolescence.

Depression in boys and men is often not recognised. Boys and men are less likely to talk about their emotions and are less likely to seek help (as they mistakenly think they need to be 'strong' or 'in control', or they're ashamed). Men are also likely to use alcohol or drugs in an effort to cope – but this often makes the symptoms of depression worse.

Depression is treatable and people can recover from it.

Features and diagnostic criteria of depression

The symptoms described below must have persisted for at least two months or at an extreme level and the individual must exhibit at least five of the following:
- fatigue
- irritability
- tearfulness, sadness, or ' feeling blue'
- lost interest or pleasure in activities previously enjoyed
- weight change
- sleep problems
- feelings of worthlessness, guilt
- thoughts about death
- indecisiveness.

ACTIVITY 3.6 DEPRESSION

1. Define depression.
2. The onset of depression is usually in adolescence. What does this mean?
3. One in four women suffers from depression, and one in six men suffers from depression. Express these statistics as a percentage.
4. Describe four features of depression.

Substance dependence disorder

Adolescence is a time of risk taking and experimentation with drugs, as we'll see in the next chapter. Teenagers with mental illness and mental health problems have a higher rate of risk behaviour, including drug use, smoking and drinking.

Substance dependence disorder (drug dependence) is most likely to occur in adolescence and young adulthood, and boys are more likely to suffer from it than girls. In Australia, 13 per cent of adolescents suffer from a substance use disorder with 9 per cent suffering from alcohol use disorders (ABS 2010). A **substance** can include a drug of abuse (e.g. alcohol), a toxin or a medication. Drugs and their effects on us will be looked at in detail in the next chapter.

Among adolescents, conduct disorder and eating disorders often co-occur with substance dependence, and there is a particularly strong link between conduct disorder and alcohol use disorders.

> **Substance dependence disorder** A mental disorder characterised by addiction to a drug, such as alcohol, and showing tolerance and withdrawal symptoms to the drug
>
> **Substance** A drug of abuse, a toxin or a medication

Features and diagnostic criteria of substance dependence

There are two major symptoms:
1. **Tolerance** to the drug, for example, a need to increase the amount used to achieve the same desired effect (or in other words, they continue to need more than last time)
2. **Withdrawal** from the drug, for example, reduction of use of the drug leads to significant distress or impairment of their everyday functioning (social, academic and so on), or they may start using another substance with similar effects

> **Tolerance** A need to increase the amount of drugs for desired effect
>
> **Withdrawal** Reduction of use of drug leads to significant distress or impairment

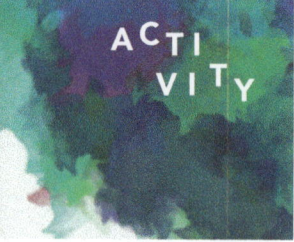

ACTIVITY 3.7 MENTAL ILLNESS AND DRUG USE

1. Define the term 'substance dependence disorder'.
2. Define the term 'substance'.
3. What other mental illnesses has substance dependence disorder been linked to?
4. Explain the symptoms of tolerance and withdrawal.

Alcohol dependence

Alcohol dependence is the most common substance dependence disorder for adolescents/teenagers.

For adolescents **alcohol dependence** is the most common substance dependence disorder. Alcohol is a drug that can have significant consequences.

Figure 3.5 Substance dependence disorder is more common amongst boys and the most widespread disorder is alcohol dependence.

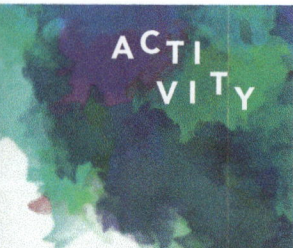

ACTIVITY 3.8 ALCOHOL AND ADOLESCENCE

Reflect on your personal observations of alcohol use. Have you or your peers had any experience with alcohol? Have you observed others? You may like to share your experiences and discuss alcohol use with the class.

Alcohol is studied further in the next chapter.

Eating disorders

Body image How you perceive, feel and think about your body

Teenagers become very aware of their bodies particularly during and after puberty. The perception adolescents have of their growing, changing bodies creates a great deal of unwanted stress. There is also a lot of external pressure – such as the media portraying the 'ideal' body shape. **Body image** is a major concern for Australian teenagers. Generally for girls, there is a tendency to link attractiveness with thinness. For boys, there is a pressure to look muscular, strong and sculpted. A poor body image can lead to low self-esteem, and in some cases mental illnesses such as eating disorders.

A big tick to women's morale

Caroline Marcus, Sunday Herald Sun, 27 June 2010

A fashion, advertising and media code of conduct will be introduced by the Federal Government in which organisations can apply for a 'body-image-friendly' symbol similar to the Heart Foundation's tick for approved foods.

The *Sunday Herald Sun* can reveal exclusively the details of the voluntary code, which will be launched by Youth Minister Kate Ellis this morning.

The announcement follows an almost two-year consultation process that began in October 2008, when Ms Ellis announced she wanted to curb the glamorisation of unhealthily thin women, which has contributed to children as young as six counting calories and developing eating disorders.

The key principles of the code include:
- not running advertisements for rapid weight loss, cosmetic surgery, excessive exercise or other commercials that may promote a negative body image.
- only using models aged 16 or older to model adult clothes, both on catwalks and in print.
- refraining from using models who are very thin or male models who are excessively muscular.
- disclosing when images have been retouched and refraining from enhancing photographs in a way that changes a person's body shape, for example, lengthening their legs or trimming their waist, or removing freckles, lines and other distinguishing marks.
- stocking clothing in a wide variety of sizes in shops to reflect the demand from customers.
- using a broad range of body shapes, sizes and ethnicities in editorial and advertising.

The government has also committed $500 000 in funding to develop education programs, together with the eating disorder group, *The Butterfly Foundation*, to promote the code.

The school program will see 2500 educators trained to teach 100 000 students aged between 8 and 18 about positive body image, covering topics such as media literacy and self-esteem.

A panel chaired by author and former *Cosmopolitan* editor Mia Freedman and comprising health and academic experts will spend the next six months defining the criteria organisations have to meet in order to be awarded the body-image-friendly symbol.

Ms Ellis urged the industry to embrace the voluntary code.

'Body image is an issue that we must take seriously because it is affecting the health and happiness of substantial sections of our community', she said.

'The symbol is a win for consumers. It will empower consumers to tell the fashion, beauty, media and modelling industries what they want and provide greater choice.'

The code has received the endorsement of leading women's and girls' magazines *The Australian Women's Weekly* and *Girlfriend*, along with plus-size agency BGM Models.

The *Australian Women's Weekly* editor Helen McCabe said the magazine would commit to identifying photographs of women that had been altered digitally.

'As Australia's biggest-selling magazine, I am proud to be taking a leading role in what is going to be a gradual process for the industry', McCabe said.

'Our readers are highly sophisticated and increasingly demand the images they see of women be more realistic.'

Anorexia nervosa An eating disorder characterised by a refusal to maintain minimum body weight

Bulimia nervosa An eating disorder characterised by binge-eating followed by compensatory behaviours; sufferers are usually a normal weight

Binge-eating disorder An eating disorder characterised by binge-eating with no compensatory behaviours; sufferers are usually overweight

The two major eating disorders are **anorexia nervosa** and **bulimia nervosa**. There is also a third but less acknowledged eating disorder called **binge-eating disorder**. Each of these disorders results in severe disruptions to normal eating patterns.

Eating disorders are more common amongst girls, and most common in adolescence. However, 10 per cent of those suffering from eating disorders are boys. It is a very real problem. Eating disorders also tend to co-occur with anxiety, depression and substance use disorders.

Features and diagnostic criteria of eating disorders

Figure 3.6 A common characteristic shared by anorexia and bulimia sufferers is their preoccupation with weight and shape.

CHAPTER 3 MIND INTERRUPTED

Table 3.1 Features and diagnostic criteria of eating disorders

Eating disorder	General symptoms	
Anorexia nervosa	• refusal to maintain minimum body weight • intense anxiety about becoming fat • irritability, **insomnia** and social withdrawal • concerns about eating in public • a strong desire for control	• obsessive thoughts about food, e.g. hoarding recipes • denial of seriousness of their problem • perfectionism • **amenorrhea** • dehydration • inflexible thinking
Bulimia nervosa	• weight at a normal level • **binges** occur – a large amount of food (typically high kilojoule) is eaten until the individual is uncomfortably full • **compensatory behaviours** include purging, fasting or excessive exercising	• binges tend to be hidden or happen in secret • most bulimics purge: a common technique is vomiting, or use **laxatives**, **diuretics** or **enemas** (less common) • enamel erosion and teeth look irregular and uneven
Binge-eating disorder	• individuals tend to be overweight • binges occur regularly • no use of compensatory behaviours (e.g. they do not purge)	• The binges are associated with: • eating very quickly (rapidly) • eating when not hungry • feeling guilty, disgusted or depressed after binge

Insomnia A sleeping disorder where a person cannot fall asleep or has trouble staying asleep

Amenorrhea The absence of three consecutive menstrual cycles

Binge A larger than normal amount of food is eaten in a short time period until the individual is uncomfortably or painfully full

Compensatory behaviour Behaviour that follows a binge to try to reverse its effects, such as purging, fasting or excessive exercise

Laxative A substance that induces bowel movements

Diuretic A drug that elevates the rate of urination

Enema Where liquid is forced into the colon to encourage elimination

ACTIVITY 3.9 BODY IMAGE

1. Define the term 'body image'.
2. Define each of the three eating disorders.
3. Describe one similarity and one difference between anorexia nervosa and bulimia nervosa.
4. Describe three features of each of the three eating disorders.
5. Describe one similarity and one difference between binge-eating disorder and bulimia nervosa.

Catena Di Mauro – the tragic face of anorexia

Kate Sikora, *The Daily Telegraph*, 11 February 2009

As Catena Di Mauro left her grandmother's home last week, she whispered the words 'You remember I love you'.

They were the last words she said to her family before she lost a seven-year battle with anorexia nervosa.

The 20-year-old Sydney woman died on Saturday, her frail body weighing just 32 kg.

Her ordeal of starving and purging was witnessed by her twin brother Paolo and father Frank, who yesterday paid tribute to his brave daughter.

Catena's obsession with food was triggered by the death of her mother when she was 11. Becoming depressed, the young girl quickly began to lose weight.

By the time she began high school, she was hiding food and her healthy 63 kg body began wasting away.

But despite pleas to doctors that his daughter was sick, Mr Di Mauro was told she 'was not sick enough'.

It was not until she was 15 that she was admitted to an adult psychiatric ward at Royal Prince Alfred. Her ravaged body withered away to 26 kg, the equivalent of an eight year old.

While Catena, whose funeral is on Friday, fought her own demons, her invalid father took on the health system and government.

Unable to watch his daughter waste away in a hospital, Mr Di Mauro waged a public fight for adequate treatment centres to be built.

Even through his grief yesterday, he pledged to keep campaigning.

In NSW there are 500 cases of anorexia each year and 20 per cent die.

Causes and treatments

In this chapter we have looked at conduct disorder, anxiety, depression, substance dependence and eating disorders. We'll now consider their causes and treatments. Interestingly, some of the causes and treatments are shared across all the disorders, so it is useful to group them together in this section.

Causes

1 **Genetic**—All five mental disorders show a genetic link. Adolescents who suffer from the disorder tend to have a parent or sibling who has also suffered from either the same mental disorder, or a similar one. Teenagers with eating disorders, for example, may have someone in the family with a history of anxiety or obesity leading to their fear of gaining weight. Parents who suffer from antisocial personality disorder are also more at risk of their teenagers suffering from conduct disorder or substance dependence.

2 **Environmental**—There is also evidence of the environment playing a role in the development of mental disorders. Teenagers with conduct disorder, for example, suffer from the disease regardless of whether they live with their biological or adoptive parents – suggesting that nurture (not just nature) is playing a role. In addition, eating disorders can also be triggered by pressures from the environment in people's pursuit to achieve the ideal body shape.

3 **Biochemical**—Some mental disorders, in particular anxiety and depression, appear to also be due to a chemical imbalance. Medication such as antidepressants try to rebalance.

4 **Drug use**—Drugs, such as alcohol and marijuana, can be a trigger. People who have a harmful level of drug use are more susceptible to depression, anxiety and substance dependence, for example.

5 **Stress**—When there is major change and major stress (such as adolescence) people can become more vulnerable. So onset of anxiety and depression, for example, can be common.

Treatments

1. **Cognitive Behaviour Therapy (CBT)** is a therapy which attempts to change how a person thinks about what they do, and change their behaviour. A sufferer of anxiety, for example, would be encouraged to address their emotions and try to decrease these. Someone with substance dependence disorder would be educated about how addiction works in an effort to decrease their behaviours and change how they think about their problem. Similarly, someone with an eating disorder would be educated about healthy eating habits in an effort to change how they think about food and how they feel about themselves.

2. **Lifestyle changes** can be very effective, and can include physical exercise, diet, and reducing drug use. Something as simple as going for a daily walk or run can really help improve how someone feels and thinks about their problem. This can be due to the endorphins released (which make us feel good) and this is discussed further in Chapter 6.

3. **Medication** can be effective, although where possible it would be preferable to avoid relying on medication. Nonetheless, for many people it can be a terrific solution and starting point for easing symptoms – particularly if the disorder is

Figure 3.7 Cognitive Behaviour Therapy (CBT) is often used to try to help sufferers of anorexia by changing how they think about themselves.

due to a chemical imbalance. People with depression, anxiety, substance dependence and eating disorders may find antidepressants really useful as they ease the emotions associated with these illnesses. Note that those suffering from any of these disorders might have depressive symptoms. Furthermore, benzodiazipines decrease feelings of anxiety and act very quickly when taken. The disadvantage, however, is that they can be highly addictive. Stimulants can assist sufferers of conduct disorder. Stimulants are thought to help decrease aggressive behaviour.

4. **Hospitalisation** for disorders would be the least preferable treatment choice. In extreme cases though, sufferers may find it helpful to have treatment in hospital. For example, those with depression may be recommended for electroconvulsive therapy (ECT), which can be effective in cases of severe depression. (For more information about ECT, see Chapter 1.) In severe cases of malnutrition, sufferers of eating disorders may be hospitalised – this is rare, however.

ACTIVITY 3.10 MENTAL ILLNESS – NATURE VERSUS NURTURE

1. Consider the genetic and environmental causes of mental disorders. What do you think is meant by the 'nature versus nurture' debate with mental health? Explain with use of examples.
2. What link might there be between drug use and stress, and the onset of mental disorders?
3. Which cause does the treatment of medication try to address?
4. What are two types of medication that can be used to treat anxiety? Why might both be useful? Define and explain the medications.
5. Why do you think hospitalisation might be the least preferable treatment?
6. Why would CBT and lifestyle changes be the most preferable treatments?
7. If someone was suffering from conduct disorder, how might CBT help them?

Advice if you think your family or friends may be affected

- Don't ignore the problem hoping it will go away.
- Encourage your family or friend to seek help – the earlier they receive help, the better.
- Be positive – try not to focus on any of the negative emotions you may be feeling but at the same time be honest about how you feel.
- It is normal and OK to feel resentful or embarrassed or scared. Talk about how you feel and encourage your family and friends to do the same.
- Talk to someone you trust (don't keep problems to yourself).
- If you don't want to talk to someone you know, then call one of the confidential helplines such as Lifeline and Kids Help Line (see below).
- Maintain your own focus on the things you like doing (so don't stop your normal routine).
- Other ways to deal with your feelings: play sport, draw, paint or play music, write about how you feel, etc.

Remember that you can't be totally responsible for their actions and feelings, but you can be supportive and helpful.

Where to get help

Lifeline's 24-hour telephone counselling service
ph. 13 11 14
www.lifeline.org.au

Kids Helpline (for ages 5–18 years) 24-hour counselling service
ph. 1800 551 800
www.kidshelp.com.au

CounsellingOnline
Free alcohol and drug counselling online 24-hours a day. Provides support for alcohol and other drug users, and others affected by alcohol and drug use in the community, including family members, relatives and friends.
www.counsellingonline.org.au

Headspace
Australia's National Youth Mental Health Foundation provides health advice, support and information for young people aged 12–25 on a variety of issues. A fantastic starting point for any questions.
www.headspace.org.au

SANE Australia
Helpline available 9 a.m.–5 p.m. Monday to Friday
ph. 1800 18 SANE (7263)
www.sane.org

Mental Illness Fellowship of Australia
www.mifa.org.au

Auseinet
For information about mental health
www.auseinet.com

Australian Government's Health*Insite*
www.healthinsite.gov.au

Beyondblue
Information line for information about depression and anxiety
ph. 1300 22 4636
www.beyondblue.org.au

The Butterfly Foundation
Information about eating disorders
www.thebutterflyfoundation.org.au

END OF CHAPTER SUMMARY

- Mental illness is a problem that significantly affects how the person behaves, feels, thinks, and is clinically diagnosed according to criteria, e.g. DSM-IV-TR.
- Mental disorders facing teenagers include conduct disorder, anxiety, depression, substance dependence and eating disorders.
- Causes of mental illnesses include factors such as genetic, environmental, drug use and biochemical imbalance.
- Treatments of mental illnesses include cognitive behaviour therapy (CBT), medications, lifestyle change and hospitalisation (less common).

END OF CHAPTER TEST

Multiple-choice questions

1 The most common mental illness affecting young Australians is:
   A depression
   B anxiety
   C eating disorders
   D substance use disorders.

2 Tolerance and withdrawal are features of:
   A substance dependence disorder
   B eating disorders
   C conduct disorder
   D anxiety.

3 Binges are features of:
   A anorexia nervosa
   B bulimia nervosa
   C binge-eating disorder
   D both B and C.

4 A unique feature of anorexia nervosa is:
   A preoccupation with being thin
   B refusal to maintain minimum body weight
   C binging
   D purging.

5 CBT stands for:
   A common behavioural treatment
   B concentrated behavioural therapy
   C cognitive behaviour therapy
   D none of the above.

Short-answer questions

Case study 1

Keith is 17 years old. His teachers are concerned about the drop in his performance at school when once he was a good student. Keith has started skipping class, as he's finding it hard to concentrate and worries about getting the correct answers. He's very anxious about what others think about him. He worries about whether he's wearing the right clothes, and whether he'll ever have a girlfriend or get a job. Keith avoids his friends and family, and spends a great deal of his time in his room at home. He has stopped going out when he's invited. Keith won't watch the news as he's worried about rising crime, and is frightened something will happen to his friends or family. Keith is often restless and gets muscle cramps. He also can't sleep and lies in beds for hours worrying each night.

1 Read the case study of 17-year-old Keith who suffers from GAD. Identify and list all the symptoms of the disorder that Keith exhibits.
2 What treatment might Keith find helpful?

Case study 2

Tim is six years old. He is not allowed to begin Grade One until his immunisations are updated. His mother explains that Tim has visited several doctors for immunisation but was so disruptive that the doctors and nurses have given up. His mum describes a long history of aggressive and destructive behaviour, as well as four school suspensions during kindergarten. Tim is often 'uncontrollable' at home and has broken furniture, started fires, and frequently pulls the family dog around by its tail. Tim's older sisters have babysat in the past but have refused to do so since he threw a can of soup at one of them.

Source: Searight, Rottnek & Abby (2001)

1 Read the case study of 6-year-old Tim who suffers from conduct disorder. Identify and list all the symptoms of the disorder that Tim exhibits.
2 What treatment might Tim find helpful?

Brain chemistry

CHAPTER 4

*I learned why they're called wonderful drugs
– you wonder what they'll do to you.*

Harlan Miller

The brain is an amazing organ. Stimulating the brain causes it to grow. This chapter will explore the adolescent brain and why it is vulnerable to drugs.

What's happening in the adolescent brain?

Grey matter Cell bodies (soma) of neurons

Cortex Outer layer of the brain where most processes take place, such as thinking

White matter Axons of neurons insulated by fatty white myelin sheath

Myelin sheath Fatty, white insulating tissue that surrounds the axons of neurons

By the age of six years, a child's brain is 95 per cent of the adult brain weight. The brain continues to grow and break neural connections, with a peak in **grey matter** just before puberty. A girl's cortex is at its thickest when she is 11 years old and a boy's at 13 years. This might explain why girls are perceived as maturing faster than boys do.

Grey matter is all the cell bodies of neurons. The major processes, such as thinking, occur in the grey matter. The outer layer, or **cortex**, of the brain is grey matter. **White matter**, in comparison, is the axons of neurons. Axons are surrounded by a fatty white **myelin sheath** – hence the name 'white matter'. White matter and grey matter are as important as each other. White matter is needed to insulate and speed up the transmission of the electrochemical impulses in your brain. Therefore grey matter would be powerless without white matter to transmit messages. Recent research also suggests that there is a link between the amount of white matter and intelligence (Young et al. 2010).

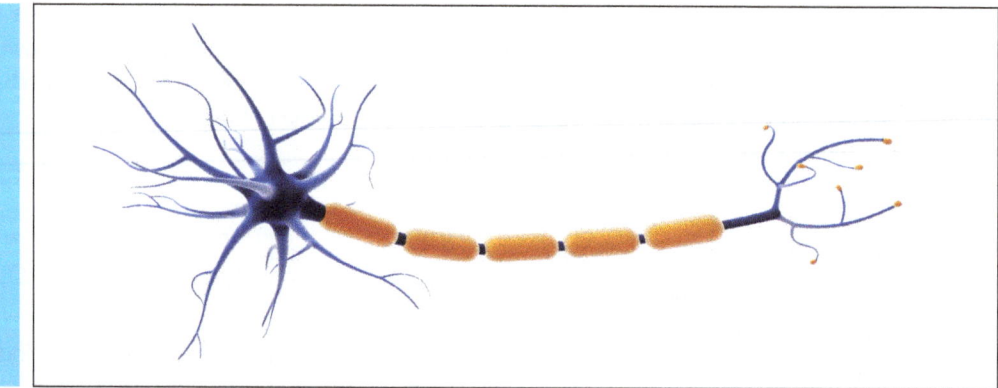

Figure 4.1 The axon of the neuron (shown here in orange) is surrounded by a fatty white myelin sheath – hence the name 'white matter'.

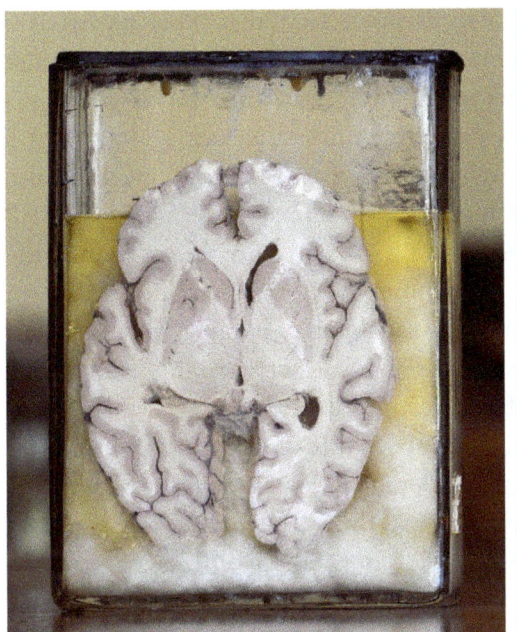

Figure 4.2 This is a cross-section of an old preserved brain. You can see the white matter and the grey matter, especially around the edges where the cortex (outer layer) lies.

The peak of development of our brain is thought to be at about 22 years of age and lasts for about five years. The decline after this is very slow. However, staying physically and mentally active, eating a good diet and avoiding drugs can slow down the decline markedly.

ACTIVITY 4.1 GREY AND WHITE MATTER

1. Define grey matter and white matter.
2. Explain the importance of both grey and white matter, and how the amount changes in an adolescent brain as it develops.
3. When does our brain supposedly peak?

Frontal lobe The region of the brain involved in decision making, problem solving, motor control and personality

Amygdala An almond-shaped piece of tissue sitting above the brainstem in the temporal lobe responsible for triggering the fight-or-flight response. There is an amygdala in each hemisphere of the brain.

Temporal lobe A region of the brain involved with hearing, speech and memory

Fight-or-flight response Physiological response to threat or intense excitement; causes the release of adrenalin in the body

Adrenalin A hormone that is released when the fight-or-flight response is triggered

Swearing Taboo words in society, or 'bad language'

Corpus callosum Nerve tissue connecting the two hemispheres of the brain

Hippocampus A brain structure that has a mirror-image half in each hemisphere of the brain, and is involved in memory formation

Neurogenesis The growing of new neurons

Amnesia A form of memory loss

The adolescent brain compared to the adult brain

Teenagers appear to use different areas of their brain from adults. Adults tend to use their **frontal lobe** more and teenagers seem to use their **amygdala** more (Yurgolen-Todd 2002). As we learnt in Chapter 2, the frontal lobe is responsible for decision making, planning the future, social judgments and controlling our behaviour.

The amygdala sits above the brainstem within the **temporal lobe**. It is responsible for triggering our **fight-or-flight response** when we are threatened causing the release of **adrenalin** in our bodies. The amygdala is therefore involved in aggressive behaviour as well as discriminating fear and other emotions. Interestingly, the amygdala is also linked to **swearing**. When people use or hear swear words (taboo words in society) their amygdala is activated. This may suggest why adolescents may use swear words more often as they mature (Spinney 2007).

Late maturation of the teenage brain

Areas that also continue to develop in adolescence are the **corpus callosum** and the **hippocampus**. Using drugs, and in high volume, can cause significant brain damage to adolescents whose brains are still growing.

The corpus callosum is the nerve tissue that connects the two hemispheres of the brain together (see Chapter 2) and is essential for effective communication between the two halves of the brain. The hippocampus lies next to the amygdala in our brain, and is involved with memory. The hippocampus plays a large role in long-term memories and begins maturing from the age of three to four years old which may explain why we find it difficult to remember anything before this age. The hippocampus continues to develop, as **neurogenesis** is occurring there. Damage to the hippocampus tends to lead to **amnesia**.

The *last* part of the adolescent brain to mature is the frontal lobe. This may explain why teenagers do not understand the arguments of adults. Therefore, even though arguments appear logical to adults, teenagers might disagree. Moreover, as teenagers may not read the emotions of adult accurately further conflict can occur.

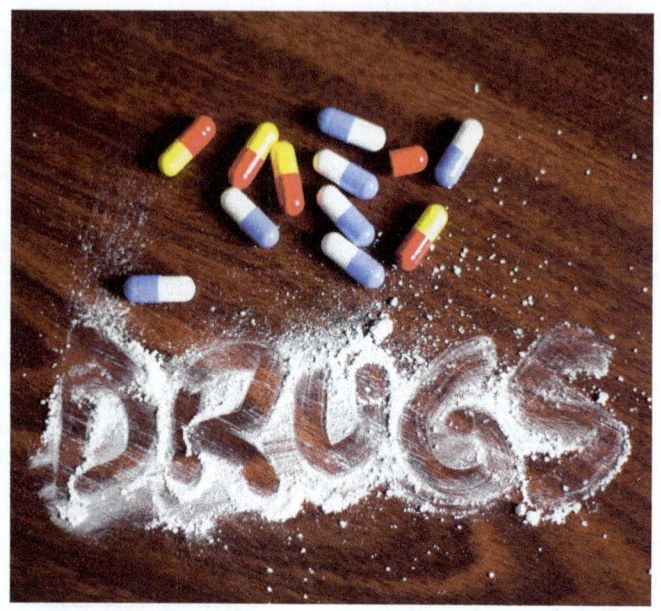

The late maturation of the frontal lobe may also explain why teenagers undertake risky behaviour. All other parts of their brain have matured other than the frontal lobe, so although they may feel in part like an adult, they have less capability of holding their emotions and behaviour in check. So despite warnings adolescents hear about drugs, many still choose to experiment.

However, the impact this drug taking can have on teenage brain development can be significant, as areas are still developing and thus vulnerable.

This chapter will look at the effects of some of the drugs on our brain. The most popular drugs for teenagers include alcohol, nicotine and cannabis, with a very small proportion of teenagers experimenting with amphetamines, cocaine, LSD and heroin. Interestingly, boys are more likely to experiment with drugs than girls.

ACTIVITY 4.2 ADOLESCENT BRAIN VERSUS ADULT BRAIN

1. Explain the major differences between an adult and an adolescent brain. You should refer to the frontal lobe and amygdala in your answer.
2. What is the link between the parts of the brain and adolescent risky behaviour?
3. What is the hippocampus? Explain its function.
4. Explain what neurogenesis is and where it has been found to occur.

Addiction Also known as dependence, is when someone compulsively takes drugs. Addiction has been linked to high levels of dopamine in the blood.

Neurotransmitters Chemical messengers released by an axon that travel across the synapse (a gap) to the neighbouring neurons.

Dopamine A hormone that plays an important role in cognitive functions such as memory, problem solving and attention. It is also known as the 'pleasure' hormone, as it provides feelings of enjoyment and happiness.

Addiction – how does it work?

The amygdala plays a role in **addiction**. As the frontal cortex is still developing in adolescents, they can be more at risk of addiction. Drugs tend to mimic **neurotransmitters** – the chemicals that our body naturally makes in our brain. Neurotransmitters are very important as they carry messages from neuron to neuron across the synapse. Some neurotransmitters, such as **dopamine**, make us feel good.

Our body has its own natural dopamine. However, drugs may increase the amount of dopamine in our bodies. Therefore our reward system goes into overdrive and we feel really good. In some cases, drugs, such as nicotine and amphetamines, can cause dopamine receptors in the brain to multiply! This is how addiction (or dependence) occurs. The increase in the number of dopamine receptors rewires the brain makes it easier for dopamine to be absorbed and can lead to compulsive drug taking.

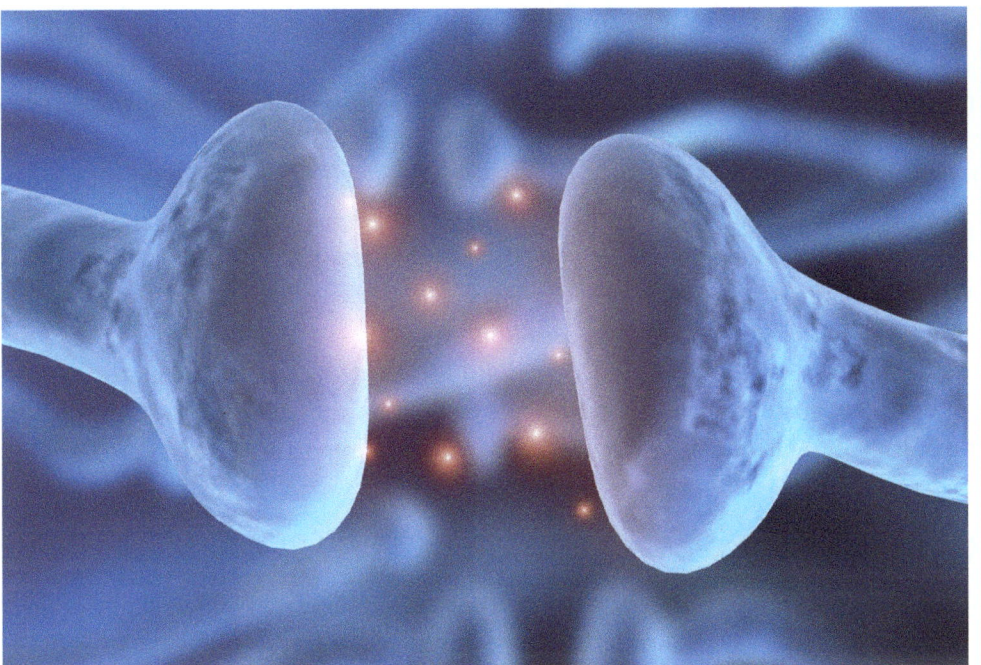

Figure 4.3 Neurotransmitters, such as dopamine, carry messages across the synapse (gap) between neurons.

Fighting addiction is incredibly tough. Addicts often suffer from the lower levels of dopamine causing **dysphoria** and a higher level of **cortisol** – a stress hormone. Researchers are looking at different types of medication and therapy that might work to fight addiction. This would clearly assist adolescents who might suffer from substance dependence disorder (see Chapter 3).

Dysphoria A depressed mood such as sadness, the opposite of euphoria

Cortisol A hormone that is released when a person is stressed. It can be very helpful in fighting stress but too much cortisol (from long periods of stress) can weaken the immune system making people vulnerable to illness.

ACTIVITY 4.3 DRUGS AND THE BRAIN

1. How do drugs affect the brain?
2. What is the relationship between drugs and dopamine? Explain.
3. Define the term 'addiction'.
4. Why can beating addiction be challenging? Explain.

Rather than tell you what to do, this chapter aims to provide you with some information about drugs and the effects they have. The information provided is not exhaustive – so if you still have some questions, a great resource is Headspace at **www.headspace.org.au**.

The important thing is this: if you decide to experiment with drugs it should not be due to peer pressure or a misconception about having more fun. Believe it or not people have a great time without drugs. You don't have to take them.

Alcohol

Alcohol is the most common drug used in Australia, and the most common drug for adolescents. Alcohol is the second largest cause of drug-related deaths and hospitalisations in Australia, with smoking as the largest cause. Alcohol is also the main cause of deaths on our roads. Of Australians who die from an alcohol-related death, 75 per cent are men (ABS 2006).

Alcohol A depressant drug that is legal and the most commonly used drug in Australia

Depressant drug A drug that slows down the body and brain, and inhibits metabolism

Alcohol is a **depressant drug**. It slows down the activity and messages from your brain to your body. Initially, alcohol relaxes the body as the body's metabolism slows down, causing your physical and mental energy to fade. However, if drinking continues (and therefore becomes heavy or risky) then alcohol will make you feel bad. It has been suggested that low to moderate alcohol consumption can have beneficial health effect (but cardiac doctors disagree). However, in higher doses it can cause unconsciousness and even death. About one in eight adults drink at a risky level in Australia. This is known as **binge drinking**.

Binge drinking Ingesting several drinks at the one time, for men five to seven drinks is considered a binge and for women three to five

Binge drinking is short-term risky drinking, e.g. on a single occasion. In Australia binge drinking for males is six or more standard drinks at the one time, and for women it is four or more standard drinks. Twenty-five per cent of those aged between 14 and 19 years drink alcohol on a daily or weekly basis, with some reporting to binge.

Adolescence and alcohol

Alcohol affects the teenage brain differently from the adult brain, as the teenage brain is still developing. Research has shown that binge drinking *decreases* the rate of neurogenesis in the hippocampus (Morris et al. 2010). Alcohol has also been found to *decrease* activity in the amygdala in response to fear and anger. This may explain why people are less able to detect threats when they are drunk, and also why they are less fearful of social situations (*New Scientist* 2008).

Adolescents also appear to be less sensitive to the sedative and motor impairment of alcohol, meaning they can stay awake for longer and not fall over (for example). So by appearances, the adolescents look like they're fine. But in fact as they continue drinking they are drinking a larger volume and therefore placing themselves at greater risk due to the continuing development of their brain.

Blackout A small period of amnesia experienced (when using alcohol) that occurs when you're awake

A worrying side effect of drinking alcohol at a risky level is suffering **blackouts**. Blackouts are a small period of amnesia where a person cannot recall an event even though they were awake and present at the time. Younger people experience more blackouts than adults do (White et al. 2002).

In addition to memory problems, adolescents also make poorer decisions when they are using alcohol. They can be more impulsive, take risks and make mistakes. Australian teenagers who drink are more likely to engage in risk-taking behaviour, such as driving whilst drunk, swimming whilst drunk, engaging in unsafe or unwanted sex, and verbal and physical abuse (ABS 2006). Additionally, teenagers who drink heavily often are not as involved in school activities and fight with their parents more frequently than non-drinkers. Teenagers often don't do well academically as alcohol may interfere with their ability to remember things.

Sadly, teenagers who drink heavily are more likely to become alcoholics as adults. Teenagers who start using alcohol before 14 years of age are much more likely to develop alcohol dependence than are those who begin drinking after 18 years. Research also shows that teenagers who drink heavily may try other drugs.

CHAPTER 4 BRAIN CHEMISTRY   53

SOME SIGNS THAT YOU MAY HAVE A DRINKING PROBLEM INCLUDE:
- you only attend social functions if there is alcohol
- you avoid your parents and your friends when you're drunk
- you drive when you've been drinking
- you have been in a car when the driver has been drinking
- you socialise only with people who drink
- you lie to your parents and your friends about your drinking
- you ignore your parents and friends who tell you that you drink too much
- you drink alcohol when you're alone.

ACTIVITY 4.4 ALCOHOL AND THE BRAIN

1. Define the term 'alcohol'. In your answer explain what a depressant drug is.
2. What is binge drinking? Is it the same for males and females? Explain.
3. What effect does alcohol have on the hippocampus and amygdala?
4. List some other effects alcohol can have on the brain and body.
5. What are blackouts and why are they a concern?
6. How does alcohol affect the risk-taking behaviour of adolescents? List three effects.

Cannabis (marijuana)

Figure 4.4 Cannabis (marijuana) is a naturally growing plant. Its use for recreational purposes is illegal in Australia.

Cannabis (marijuana), also known as 'dope', 'hash' or 'reefer', is the most widely used **illicit** drug in Australia. About one-third of the Australian population has experimented with marijuana. It is the cheapest drug available in Australia, and the easiest to obtain. This may explain why so many young Australians try it. The most common way to use

Illicit Illegal, or against the law

marijuana is to smoke the head or the leaf of the plant. Marijuana is also used in cooking with people making 'space cakes' or hash cookies. Another common method is to mix it with tobacco to form a 'joint'.

Although older Australians use it more regularly, adolescents use cannabis the most heavily. According to the Drug & Alcohol Research Centre (2007), adolescents aged between 14 and 19 years are more likely to have tried marijuana (26 per cent) than cigarettes (16 per cent).

Marijuana tends to slow down thinking, and slow coordination. People who use the drug lack motivation and often have problems concentrating. **Cannabis** may cause the brain to shrink. Research at the University of Melbourne found that the hippocampus of heavy users was 12 per cent smaller than non-users, while the amygdala was 7 per cent smaller (*New Scientist* 2008b). In Holland (where cannabis use is legal) research has found that adolescents who use marijuana have poorer academic performance and are more likely to show aggressive behaviour (Davies 2006).

There are hundreds of compounds in marijuana, but it is **THC** (delta-9-tetrahydrocannabinol) that is the most psychoactive ingredient. THC combines with CB1 receptors in our brain; these specialised receptors are found mostly in the frontal cortex and the hippocampus. Not surprising then, marijuana users have problems with their memory (Smith et al. 2010).

Other risks of cannabis use include:
- psychotic symptoms such as **hallucinations** and **delusions**
- high risk of addiction, with about a third of people who try the drug becoming dependent
- greater risk of panic attacks, cancer and driving impairment
- if there is a family history of schizophrenia, marijuana may act as a catalyst for the illness to present itself.

> **Cannabis** or marijuana is the second most used drug in Australia for adolescents. Also known by many other names such as reefer or hash.
>
> **THC** A psychoactive ingredient in cannabis
>
> **Hallucinations** Mistaken perceptions, illusions; experiencing something that is not real. Hallucinations can be visual, auditory or tactile.
>
> **Delusions** Mistaken beliefs, thoughts, thinking processes, such as paranoia and conspiracies

ACTIVITY 4.5 CANNABIS

1. Define cannabis and explain its compound THC.
2. What effects does cannabis have on the body and the brain?

Nicotine (smoking)

Nicotine Substance found in tobacco that is addictive

According to the ABS, smoking is the largest killer in Australia. **Nicotine** is also the third most common drug of choice for adolescents. Many teenagers who become heavy drinkers, also tend to smoke. In Australia, 45 per cent of males and 35 per cent of females who are heavy drinkers smoke.

Many adolescents who suffer from mental health issues also smoke, as shown in Chapter 3. A study found that those who are substance abusers and smokers are 64 per cent likely to have a mental illness (Lima et al. 2009). Nicotine and tobacco greatly increase users' risk of falling ill, e.g. cancer.

In adolescents, the speed at which addiction occurs can differ. There is research to suggest that for some teenagers it only takes one or two cigarettes before they are 'hooked'. For other teenagers they need to smoke more. Even if you are the least vulnerable of all adolescents, if you smoke 100 cigarettes then you have a 95 per cent chance of becoming addicted (Gardner et al. 2009).

How do you know you're addicted? If you show constant and repetitive use of nicotine products, such as cigarettes, and when you try to quit or stop smoking you show withdrawal symptoms. Withdrawal symptoms include irritability, restlessness and depressed mood.

ACTIVITY 4.6 REFLECT

1. Reflect back on what you have read so far in this chapter – what are the two biggest causes of death in Australia?
2. What are the risks associated with smoking?
3. Explain why addiction to smoking in adolescents can vary.
4. Are adolescents more likely to use cannabis or nicotine? Why?
5. How do you know if you are addicted? Explain by listing the symptoms.

ACTIVITY 4.7 ERA: WHAT IS IN A CIGARETTE?

The details of this ERA are available on the Cambridge GO website.

Meth/amphetamines

Meth/amphetamine is the next most widely used drug in Australia, with about 10 per cent of Australians having tried the drug. The drug is also known as 'speed', 'base', 'ice' and 'crystal meth'. Meth/amphetamine is a **stimulant drug**. Stimulant drugs speed up messages going to and from the brain, keeping a person awake and alert. People either snort, swallow, smoke through a pipe or inject it. More than one-third of regular meth-users smoke cannabis daily, and the majority of meth users are smokers (nicotine).

Risks of meth/amphetamine taking include:
- risk of **psychosis** which can include delusions, hallucinations and bizarre behaviour
- higher likelihood of mental illnesses, including anxiety and depression
- high risk of dependency (becoming addicted)
- if using needles, there is a large risk of contracting a transmissible disease such as HIV.

Meth/amphetamine A stimulant drug that tends to energise users but can cause psychosis. Also known as 'speed', 'base', 'ice' and 'crystal meth'

Stimulant drug A substance that speeds up messages going to and from the brain, keeping a person awake and alert

Psychosis A mental state characterised by a loss of sense of reality that results in delusions, hallucinations and bizarre behaviour

Ecstasy

Ecstasy or MDMA (3,4-Methylenedioxymethamphetamine) is also known as 'E', 'X' or 'love drug'. It is an amphetamine-type substance. Approximately 7.5 per cent of Australians have tried ecstasy. This drug is usually taken in tablet form or snorted. A small number of users may inject the drug. Interestingly, MDMA was used medically in the 1970s and 1980s before it was introduced as a recreational drug. This drug has been criminalised across the world (it is illegal globally). Ecstasy is meant to produce a sense of **euphoria**.

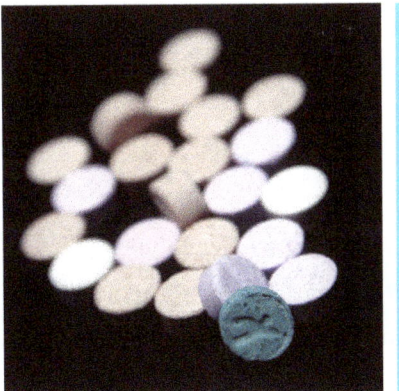

Figure 4.5 Ecstasy or 'E' is used by approximately 7.5 per cent of Australians.

Ecstasy is also known as 'E', 'X' or 'love drug'. It is an amphetamine-type substance and produces a sense of euphoria.

Euphoria A heightened mood such as joy, the opposite of dysphoria

Risks of ecstasy taking include:
- it is a major killer – of all drug related deaths, ecstasy accounts for about 46 per cent of these in Australia
- other effects are damage to brain function and memory impairment, and psychological illnesses such as depression and anxiety.

ACTIVITY 4.8 STIMULANT DRUGS

1. What is a stimulant drug?
2. List some of the effects of meth/amphetamine on the brain and body.

LSD, cocaine and heroin

LSD A hallucinogen that is usually taken with other drugs to heighten effects

Hallucinogen A drug that causes hallucinations

Cocaine A stimulant drug that is less commonly used and has a high risk of addiction

Heroin A depressant drug that is the least popular drug of choice in Australia. Users have a high risk of fatal overdose.

Depressant Any substance that slows down the central nervous system and reduces brain activity

LSD (lysergic acid diethylamine) is an **hallucinogen**. Like ecstasy about 7.5 per cent of Australians have tried it. In comparison, **cocaine** is one of the least commonly used drugs in Australia. According to the Drug & Alcohol Research Centre (2007) about 4.7 per cent of Australians have tried cocaine. Cocaine is a stimulant drug, pain reliever, and also highly addictive – addiction can occur quickly with a novice user.

Heroin is one of the least popular drugs in Australia with only 1.4 per cent of Australians trying the drug. Like alcohol, heroin is a **depressant** – it slows down the activity and messages from your brain to your body. Sadly, users of heroin are at a higher risk of fatal overdose.

Figure 4.6 Heroin is derived from the opium poppy plant.

Interestingly back in the 1930s, Australia was using 7.5 per cent of the world's supply of heroin. Per capita this was three times as much as Britain and fifty times as much as America. Basically, per capita, Australia was the biggest user of heroin in the world (Rowe 2005).

Sigmund Freud, one of the most well-known psychologists, used to prescribe cocaine to his patients as an antidepressant. At that time (late 1800s and early 1900s) cocaine was not an illegal drug as it is today. Freud was a regular user of cocaine himself. Critics of Freud claim that his theories are a result of his drug use. Regardless, Freud's theories are still discussed and supported by many, and his work is considered an important foundation for psychology today.

ACTIVITY 4.9 LSD, COCAINE AND HEROIN

1. What are the major differences between LSD, cocaine and heroin? (Hint: what types of drug are they?)
2. How has heroin use changed in Australia?

Where to go to for help

Lifeline
24-hour telephone counselling service
ph. 13 11 14
www.lifeline.org.au

Kids Helpline (for ages 5–18 years)
24-hour counselling service
ph. 1800 551 800
ww.kidshelp.com.au

CounsellingOnline
Free alcohol and drug counselling online 24-hours-a-day. Provides support for alcohol and other drug users, and others affected by alcohol and drug use in the community, including family members, relatives and friends.
www.counsellingonline.org.au

Headspace
Australia's National Youth Mental Health Foundation provides health advice, support and information for young people aged 12–25 on a variety of issues
www.headspace.org.au

Drug & Alcohol Information Service
24-hour service
ph. 1800 811 994 or 1800 422 599

National Drug Campaign 'Where's your head at?'
www.drugs.health.gov.au/youth

Somazone
A website created by young people for young people
www.somazone.com.au

Doing Drugs
Features Triple J's *Doing Drugs* forum with Paul Dillon – aimed at people who use drugs or are thinking about using drugs. Ask questions or read other posts.
www2b.abc.net.au/triplej/morning/drugsarchive

DID YOU KNOW?

FIVE TIPS FOR FEEDING YOUR BRAIN

1. The brain is approximately 60 per cent fat, so eating omega-3 fats is very important for our neurons. A good source of omega-3 fats is oily fish.
2. Breakfast is very important for boosting the brain – breakfast is the most important meal of the day!
3. Apples! Foods high in antioxidants fight against destruction of brain tissue. Good sources include apples (and other fruit), vegetables, legumes (e.g. beans) and cereals.
4. Eating certain foods gives you a natural dose of dopamine and the 'feel-good factor', such as yoghurt, almonds and chocolate.
5. Exercise – exercise helps your brain grow and also releases endorphins which makes you feel good, and also floods the body with blood and oxygen.

END OF CHAPTER SUMMARY

- There is a peak in grey matter in the brain just before puberty.
- White matter increases speed of neural impulses and has been linked to intelligence.
- Areas of the brain that continue to develop in adolescence include the frontal lobe, corpus callosum and hippocampus. Adolescents also use their amygdala more.
- The amygdala is linked to the fight-or-flight response and emotion recognition. The hippocampus is linked to memory and the corpus callosum is the strand of tissue between the hemispheres of the brain.
- Drugs increase the level of dopamine in our bodies and therefore may make us feel good. Drugs can also increase the number of dopamine receptors in our brain, which can cause addiction.
- As their brain is still developing, teenagers are more at risk of brain damage through drug use.
- Alcohol, nicotine and cannabis (marijuana) are the most commonly used drugs by teenagers in Australia.

END OF CHAPTER TEST

Multiple-choice questions

1 There is evidence of neurogenesis in the hippocampus. Neurogenesis is:
   A growth of neurons
   B genetics of neurons
   C reduction of neurons
   D reduction of grey matter.

2 Alcohol is a(n):
   A stimulant
   B hallucinogen
   C illicit drug
   D depressant.

3 Cannabis (marijuana) can:
   A cause hallucinations
   B cause delusions
   C cause memory problems
   D all of the above.

4 Stimulant drugs:
   A slow down activity and messages between brain and body
   B cause blackouts
   C keep a person awake or alert
   D contain THC.

5 Fighting addiction can cause dysphoria which is:
   A a depressed mood, e.g. sadness
   B a feeling of elation
   C the opposite emotion from euphoria
   D both A and C.

Short-answer questions

1 Sean has had a big argument with his parents who won't let him go to his mate's birthday party. Sean is incredibly frustrated. His parents think it's more important for him to stay at home and concentrate on his exam revision. Sean disagrees – his exam is not a priority. Using what you have learnt about the adolescent brain, what could be one explanation for the conflict between Sean and his parents?

2 Kelly is at a party and has been drinking all night. She has her P-plates and as she leaves the party her friend's parents ask her if she's right to drive. Kelly announces she's fine and the parents note that she appears to be in a fairly sober condition, and has no problems with her coordination or walking. They let her leave.
   a Is it still possible that Kelly is drunk and should not be driving? Why or why not?
   b The next day Kelly has no recollection of her conversation with her friend's parents. Why?
   c What are some other effects that alcohol will have on Kelly's body and brain?

In your dreams

CHAPTER 5

It takes a person who is wide awake to make his dream come true.

Roger Ward Babsom

Sleep A state of consciousness during which the individual is unresponsive to external stimuli and experiences a state of immobility

Clinical psychology A branch of psychology concerned with prevention, diagnosis and treatment of mental disorders and psychological problems

If you live until you are 78 years old, and **sleep** 8 hours a night on average, you will have spent 26 years of your life asleep. Despite this amazing amount of time, relatively little is known about why we sleep and why we dream. The field of psychology that investigates aspects of sleep and dreaming is known as **clinical psychology** and is relatively new. Advances in modern technology allow researchers to investigate the physiological changes that occur to the brain during sleep, furthering our understanding of why we sleep. In order to monitor sleep, volunteers spend a night in a research laboratory where psychologists track changes in their brainwaves and body movements during their sleep.

What about dreaming? Have you ever tried to analyse your dreams, or confided the contents of your dreams to a friend? For centuries people have attempted to understand why we dream and what our dreams mean. Two of the most opposing and prominent theories about dreaming are the *psychoanalytical* theory, which proposes that dreams are our unconscious thoughts and feelings coming to the surface, and the *biological* theory, which proposes that dreams are the by-product of random brain activity that occurs during a specific stage of sleep known as rapid eye movement (REM) sleep.

Throughout this chapter you will learn about your sleep–wake cycle, why you sleep, how much sleep you actually need and what you can do to improve the quality of your sleep. You will also learn about why you dream.

What is sleep?

Every night you drop into a state vastly different from when you are awake. Sleep has been described as a non-waking state of consciousness that is characterised by general unresponsiveness to the environment and physical immobility. Other than occasional tossing and turning, you are usually motionless during sleep and unresponsive to your environment.

However, despite our apparent lack of response to external stimuli, sleep is not a state of total unconsciousness. We move, we snore, we smile and we wake. We respond to the most different of stimuli – new parents may sleep through a car alarm going off outside their window, yet wake to their new born whimpering in the next room. You may even have held a conversation with someone who was asleep or perhaps you have walked in your sleep!

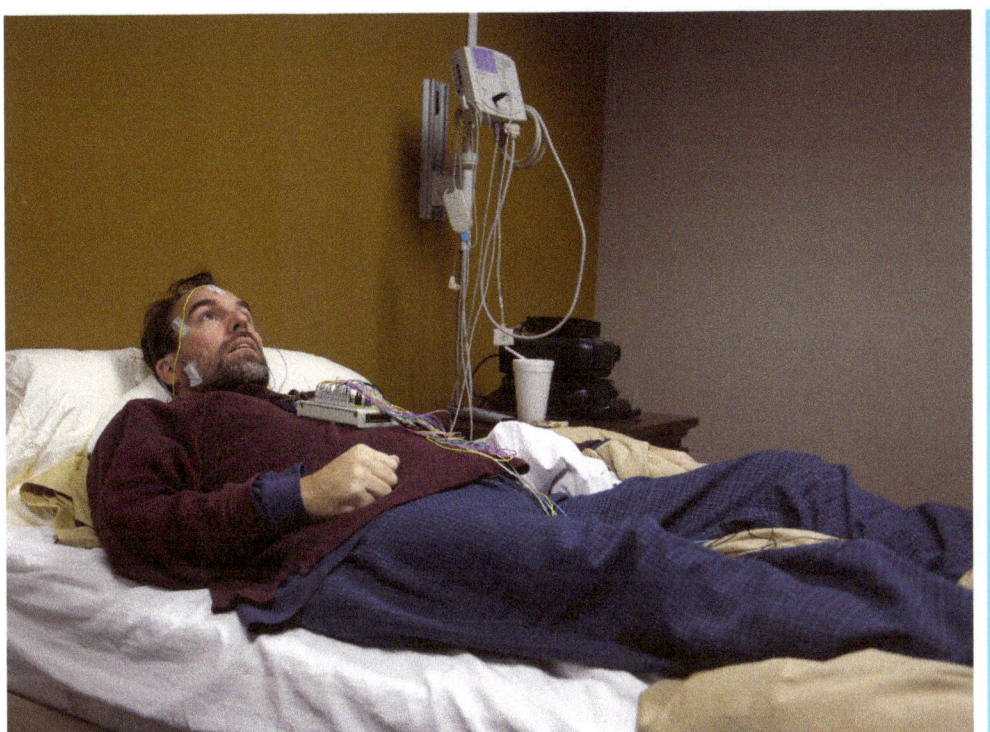

Figure 5.1 A sleeper in a sleep research laboratory

Why do we sleep when we do?

Although different animal species require different amounts of sleep, humans tend to sleep five to eight hours every night, and do so in a pattern tied to the 24-hour light–darkness cycle. This cycle is called a **circadian rhythm** (meaning 'about a day'). Other cycles considered to be circadian are attentiveness, eating, body temperature and blood pressure.

These cycles are thought to be controlled by the **pineal gland**, a structure found in the *hindbrain* (a primitive brain structure) and about the size of a pea. The pineal gland senses light and then triggers the release of a hormone that controls the activity of rhythms of the body. If this structure is damaged in animals, they tend to either sleep all day or not sleep at all.

Circadian rhythm
A naturally occurring body rhythm that occurs once in a 24-hour cycle

Pineal gland A small gland found deep within the brain and responsible for sleep and hormone development

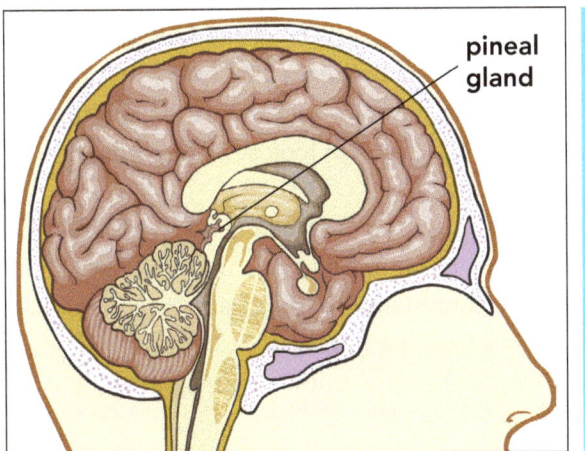

Figure 5.2 The pineal gland – a structure important in regulating sleep in animals

What happens if we are left without external cues as to the time of day, such as natural light? If this occurs, as it did with French geologist Michael Siffre – who lived in a cave for two months with no external cues to guide his sleep–wake cycle – then we tend to fall into a 25-hour cycle. Without such cues, Siffre's sleep–wake cycle increased and he slept once every 24.5 to 25 hours.

ACTIVITY 5.1 SLEEP

1. What is sleep?
2. What is REM sleep?
3. Explain what a circadian rhythm is. List any other examples of circadian rhythms that you can think of.
4. What brain structures are involved in the regulation of our sleep–wake cycle?

Why do we sleep?

All animals sleep. Dolphins have one side of their brain asleep at a time, bats sleep during the day, and even fruit flies have periods of inactivity that are considered sleep. However, the amount required by each animal varies greatly. Possums sleep for 18 hours a day while elephants sleep only 3 to 4 hours. Humans average 8 hours, while cats average 12. This difference in the amount of sleep necessary for survival has led scientists to hypothesise that body size is linked to the amount of sleep needed. Generally, the larger the animal, the less sleep it needs. This hypothesis is based on the premise that one function of sleep is to repair damage to brain cells. Smaller animals have a higher metabolic rate, which means they sustain more damage to their cells. As a result of this, they need more sleep.

Evolutionary psychology (which explains our behaviour from a perspective of progression or growth from our caveman days) explains sleep as having an adaptive purpose. Evolutionary psychologists claim that we sleep at night because that was when we were least likely to be threatened by predators out hunting. Furthermore, sleeping at night helps conserve the energy needed for daylight hours.

Basically, it appears sleep helps restore our body from the general wear and tear it sustains during the day. Evidence for this theory comes from data collected from studies in which animals were deprived of sleep. Obviously it is unethical to deprive humans of sleep, so most of what psychologists know about why we sleep and what happens when we do not have enough sleep comes from studies on animals.

One such study was conducted by psychologists Rechtschaffen and Bergman in 1995. They completely deprived laboratory rats of sleep for four weeks. Initially the rats lost a lot of weight but began eating a lot more; their core body temperature increased, as did their metabolism. After two weeks of **sleep deprivation**, the rats had lost even more weight and their body temperature became unstable. Their thyroid glands failed and their metabolic rates decreased. After three weeks, the rats' immune systems failed, and most died within four weeks. Rechtschaffen and Bergman concluded that sleep is necessary to keep the body working; without sleep it has to work extra hard and this has an effect on the metabolism and the immune system. We will look at a case study of sleep deprivation in human subjects later in this chapter.

Although most psychologists consider sleep essential for resting and repairing our bodies, it is also thought that sleep must play a more important role in our survival. The amount of energy saved by sleeping is only the equivalent of that found in a piece of toast – 50 calories. Sleep must certainly have a more pressing function.

Another way that psychologists study *why* we sleep is to investigate and study what happens *when* we sleep.

Evolutionary psychology The field of psychology that emphasises the role of adaptation, function and purpose in our development

Sleep deprivation Consistently going without adequate sleep so that tiredness is experienced during the day

What happens when we sleep?

Ancient scholar and poet Virgil (70–19 BCE) wrote that sleep is 'death's brother'. Due to advances in technology, we now know that this is not true. We are actually very active during sleep, engaging in activities such as moving and talking, and we experience vivid imagery. Sleep is generally divided into two distinct stages, REM (rapid eye movement) sleep and **non-rapid eye movement sleep (NREM)**. A device that allows researchers to investigate these two stages is the **electroencephalograph (EEG)**.

The EEG

Many different physiological activities are recorded during sleep. This is known as **polysomnography**, and often consists of monitoring eye movements, muscle tension and (most commonly) brain waves. Far from being unconscious, when we sleep our brain produces different sorts of brain waves. An EEG measures these waves and produces a read-out as a line on a roll of paper or a screen. When the peaks and troughs on the line are close together, it is described as having high frequency or being fast. When the peaks and troughs are more spaced out, it is described as having low frequency or being slow.

Some brain states produce waves with a characteristic shape, each with their own name. These are alpha, delta, theta and beta waves. Other patterns that can be detected on an EEG include **spindles** and **K-complexes**.

Non-rapid eye movement sleep (NREM) Stages 1 to 4 in the sleep cycle

Electroencephalograph (EEG) A device that detects, amplifies and records the electrical activity of the brain through electrodes placed on the scalp

Polysomnography The measurement and recording of different body functions during sleep

Spindles Short bursts of high frequency activity in brain waves

K-complexes Single sharp spikes in a low-voltage series of brain waves

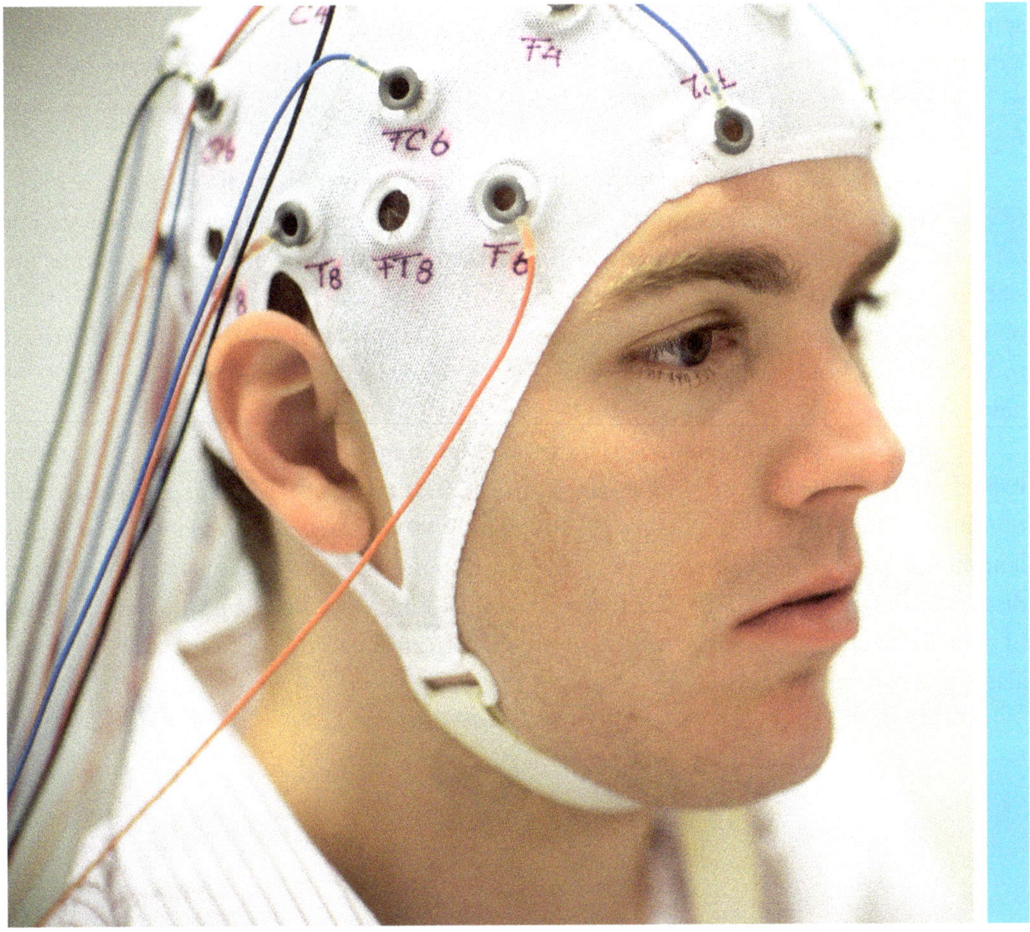

Figure 5.3 An EEG measures the electrical activity of the brain.

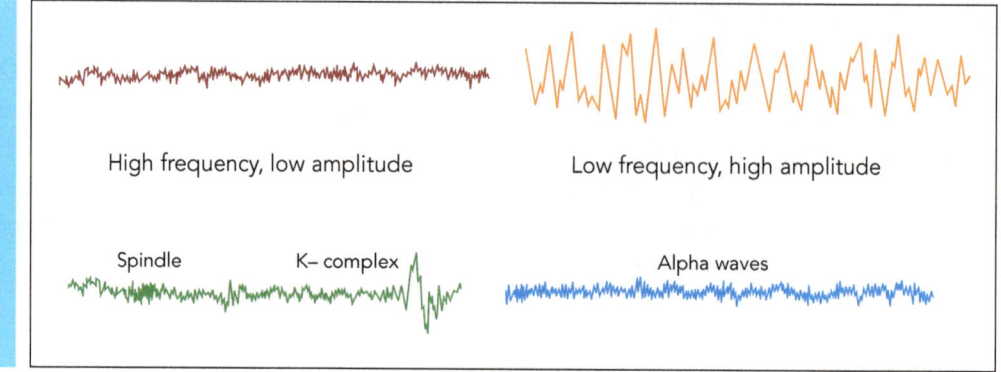

Figure 5.4 Brain waves patterns showing frequency and amplitude

Sleeping, waking and the EEG

Different readings on an EEG indicate different stages of sleep. The waking EEG shows irregular activity known as beta waves. As you become drowsy, alpha waves appear. At this point, you are still awake. When theta waves appear, you are properly asleep and have entered stage 1 of sleep.

After spending about five minutes in stage 1 sleep, you enter stage 2 and the EEG changes again. The trace now shows slightly larger waves, and spindles and K-complexes appear for the first time. Stages 1 and 2 are relatively light sleep, from which you can be woken fairly easily. Eventually you move to stage 3. Slow delta waves appear and sleep spindles diminish. After about ten minutes you enter stage 4 sleep, where the EEG shows almost all delta waves. Stages 3 and 4 are deeper types of sleep, and it is very difficult to be woken. These stages are often called slow-wave sleep (SWS) because of the slow frequency of the waves.

At various points in the night, you enter the stage known as **rapid eye movement (REM) sleep**. Here the EEG shows a trace very like that of someone who is awake, except for occasional bursts of sawtooth waves. REM stands for rapid eye movement, because the sleeper's eyes dart around quickly during this stage. If you watch a sleeping person, you can observe this happening by watching their eyelids. This stage of sleep was first identified in 1953 by psychologists Aserinsky and Kleitman, who were observing the sleep habits of newborn infants.

It takes about 45 to 60 minutes to move through stages 1 to 4 of sleep. We then move back through each stage before heading into the first cycle of REM sleep. A total cycle of non-REM and REM sleep takes approximately 90 minutes, with each cycle of REM lengthening as the night progresses, and stages 3 and 4 sleep becoming shorter and then disappearing altogether. This shortening of stages 3 and 4 of sleep, and the lengthening of your REM stages explains why you often wake from the middle of a dream when your alarm goes off in the morning.

Rapid eye movement (REM) sleep A stage of sleep characterised by quick eye movements and beta brain waves. Most dreaming occurs in REM.

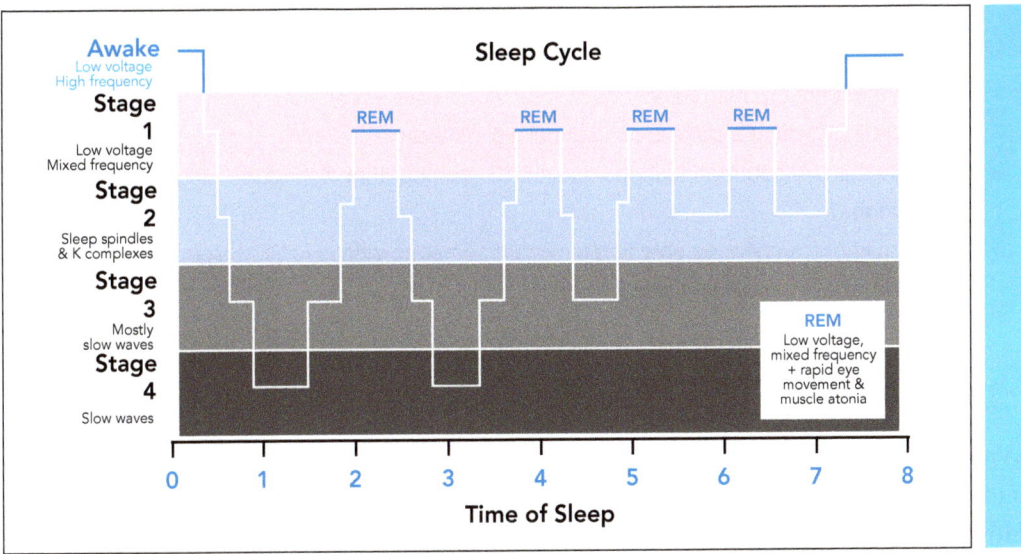

Figure 5.5 The sleep-wake cycle

Table 5.1 Summary of the stages of sleep and the characteristic brain waves associated with each stage

Stage of sleep	Type of brain wave	Description of brain waves	Illustration of brain waves
Awake and alert	Beta	Beta waves have high frequency and low amplitude.	
Awake but drowsy (in a state of deep relaxation)	Alpha	Alpha waves have medium amplitude and medium frequency.	
Stage one	Alpha and some theta	Alpha waves have medium amplitude and medium frequency. Theta waves have higher amplitude than alpha waves.	
Stage two	Theta (with sleep spindles and K-complexes)	Theta waves have a medium frequency and amplitude (although the frequency is lower than alpha waves and the amplitude is higher than alpha waves). Sleep spindles are bursts of very high frequency waves and K-complexes are a single wave of very high amplitude.	
Stage three	Theta and delta (less than 50% delta waves)	Delta waves have the lowest frequency and the highest amplitude of all the waves.	
Stage four	Theta and delta (more than 50% delta waves)	High amplitude and low frequency.	
REM	Most similar to beta waves	Fast, saw tooth waves with high frequency and low amplitude.	

ACTIVITY 5.2 SLEEP PATTERNS

1. Explain the function of an EEG.
2. Describe (in words) the pattern of a typical night's sleep.
3. What are the two common features on an EEG read out that distinguish stage 2 sleep from other stages?
4. How would researchers be able to distinguish someone who is in REM sleep from someone who is awake and alert?

Sleep phenomena

When we sleep we enter an altered state of consciousness – our thoughts are usually very jumbled (our dreams) and we are seemingly unaware of our surroundings and our actions. However, when we sleep, we are still capable of performing some behaviours, even if we are unaware of it at the time and unaware of them when we wake. The behaviours and occurrences are known as **parasomnias** and are characterised by abnormal movements, behaviour and experiences that occur whilst we are in various stages of sleep. Some examples of parasomnias are: sleep walking, sleep talking, sleep eating, REM behaviour disorder and snoring. These will be discussed in some detail below.

Parasomnias Unusual behaviour that occurs when we are asleep

Sleep walking

It is believed that up to as many as one in 20 adults experience sleep walking, a state of consciousness whereby we are half awake, half asleep. **Sleep walking** is also known as somnambulism (*somna* = sleep, *ambulism* = walking) and occurs most commonly in younger people. Sleep walking occurs most often in the deepest stages of sleep (stages 3 and 4) when the sleeper is very difficult to wake. Generally, sleep walkers rise from their beds and perform common day–to-day tasks, such as walking through their house or cleaning a room. Sometimes, however, sleep walkers are able to perform more complex tasks such as driving a car or sending emails. Recently, a Perth man was jailed for 15 years for killing his parents. He claimed that he may have done this when he was asleep.

Sleep walking A common sleep disturbance where people walk and carry out daily activities while they are asleep

Sleep eating

Sleep eating is another parasomnia that occurs during NREM sleep. It is also known as 'night eating syndrome' (or NES) and is characterised by the affected individual sleep walking into the kitchen at night and raiding their fridge or pantry. NES is thought to affect between 1 to 2 per cent of the population, and women are more likely to experience this phenomenon. According to the *International Journal of Eating Disorders* (May 1994), over 44 per cent of sufferers are overweight. Individuals with NES typically skip breakfast and consume most of their calories after dinner. Generally, they also experience other sleep difficulties, such as insomnia. Sleep eating can be quite dangerous, not least because the individual is up and moving around (with the potential to bump into things and hurt themselves), but also because of the odd combinations of foods that sleep eaters consume. Sufferers have been known to dip potato chips in peanut butter, eat raw food, or even eat non-food items, such as soap!

Sleep eating When the sleeper binge eats during sleep. They have no recollection of it upon waking.

It is necessary for medical professionals to diagnose the underlying cause of sleep eating in order to determine the treatment of it. Underlying causes could be insomnia, drug use, stress or another medical problem, such as a hepatitis or encephalitis. If the cause is psychological, treatment could consist of counselling and stress management. In the instances where sleep eating has a physiological cause, medicinal treatments that reduce motor activity during sleep have been found to be helpful.

Sleep talking

It can be very funny to listen to someone talking in their sleep – you may hear a random jumble of words and noises, or in some instances, be able to hold a conversation with them! However, as with all of these sleep phenomena, upon waking, the individual will have no or very little recollection of their strange behaviour while they were asleep. **Sleep talking** (somniloquy) is very common and can occur during any stage of sleep (REM or NREM). Indeed, it is estimated that up to 50 per cent of children will experience sleep talking at some stage, however, most will outgrow this by the time they reach puberty, although up to 4 per cent of adults still sleep talk. Girls and boys sleep talk as much as each other and there may be a familial connection. Although sleep talking is usually harmless, it can signify an underlying condition such as REM behaviour disorder, emotional stress, fever or substance abuse.

Sleep talking A common sleep phenomenon whereby the sleeper talks in their sleep. Generally, they don't make sense although some sleepers will hold conversations.

REM behaviour disorder

As you know, when we enter the stage of sleep known as REM, our body is unable to move and is in a state of paralysis, whereas our mind is very active (EEG readings show beta waves much the same as when we are awake). However, for some people who have REM behaviour disorder, this is not the case. Sufferers of REM behaviour disorder do not experience the muscle atonia (paralysis) that most people do. This causes them to act out their dreams whilst they are asleep. REM behaviour can be very dangerous to both the sufferer and the person they are sharing their bed with, particularly if they are having a violent or disturbing dream. People who have REM behaviour disorder are able to recall the dream they were having upon waking up, although they are not aware that they are carrying out the actions while they are asleep.

REM behaviour disorder can be caused by some medications and it is most common in men over the age of 60 years old. It is thought to affect approximately 0.5 per cent of the population (Olsen et al. 2000). Treatment of this disorder can involve some medications which work to suppress muscle activity.

REM behaviour disorder An uncommon disorder whereby the sleeper acts out their dreams

Snoring

Another common sleep phenomenon is that of **snoring**. Snoring occurs when the airflow through the air passages is obstructed in some way. Although anyone can snore, it is most common in people who are middle aged. Do either of your parents snore? Do you snore?

It is estimated that approximately 25 per cent of people snore every night, with about 60 per cent of men and 40 per cent of women snoring at least some of the time. Although it's generally harmless, snoring can have adverse consequences for the sufferer's bed partner (as they are constantly woken by the loud noise!). Sometimes, (in about 10 per

Snoring A common sleep disorder where the individual's airways are blocked during sleep resulting in a loud, rumbling sound

cent of cases), snorers will also suffer from sleep apnoea which is a condition in which the individual stops breathing for up to two minutes at a time throughout the night.

There are many causes of snoring, many of them are lifestyle dependent, however, even small changes to an individual's lifestyle can result an improvement in their snoring patterns. Some of the more common causes of snoring are: being obese, drinking alcohol, breathing through the mouth rather than the nose (this can be affected by colds and illnesses, and also allergies). Sometimes, if the person sleeps on their back, their tongue may fall backwards and block the airway, causing them to snore.

How can snoring be treated?

If the cause of the snoring is due to lifestyle, changes such as losing weight, lowering alcohol consumption and sleeping on your side rather than back can assist snorers. If the cause is not due to lifestyle, but rather, due to genetic factors or illness, some medical treatments are available. These include things such as: wearing a nasal mask to regulate breathing, wearing a mouth guard device to change the shape of the jaw, and widening the airways. In some severe cases, the individual could undergo surgery to unblock nasal passages and airways.

ACTIVITY 5.3 SLEEP PHENOMENON CASE STUDIES

1. Choose one of the sleep disorders described above and write a case study to accompany it. Ensure that you describe the patient and their symptoms accurately. Your case study should be approximately 100 to 150 words long.
2. Swap with the person sitting next to you, read their case study and then write a suitable treatment plan for their case study.

What happens if we do not sleep?

Tired? Grumpy? Trouble concentrating in class? If you answered yes to these, and you are an Australian teenager, chances are that you are sleep deprived. Although 95 per cent of the general population needs and gets five to eight hours sleep per night, Westernised teenagers are among the world's worst sleepers and are the group most likely to go without adequate sleep. Although the amount of sleep each individual needs depends on many things – age, level of activity (physical and mental), general health and wellbeing – teenagers should generally be getting nine to ten hours of sleep per night.

The result of sleep deprivation in rats has already been described, but what about humans? There are not many people who would volunteer to be kept awake for weeks on end, and besides, it is unethical for psychologists to conduct such a study. However, the effects of sleep deprivation can be understood a little better through the case studies of people who have gone without sleep for prolonged periods of time.

Case studies

CASE STUDY 1

As part of a school assignment in 1964 to break the world record of time without sleep, 17-year-old high school student Randy Gardner spent 264 hours (11 days) awake without any stimulants to assist him, not even coffee.

He was supervised closely by a sleep researcher and a medical officer. The effects of his prolonged sleep deprivation were intriguing. After four days he began hallucinating, at one stage believing he was a famous football player, and later mistaking a stop sign for a person. When Gardner was asked, on the eleventh day, to count backwards from 100 by sevens, he reached 65 and stopped – when asked why, he claimed he had forgotten what he was doing!

However, on his last day without sleep, Gardner spoke at a press conference in a clear and articulate manner, without stumbling over his words at all.

CASE STUDY 2

In 1959, Peter Tripp, a radio DJ, went for 201 hours (8 days) without sleep (although he drank coffee to help him stay awake). Like Gardner, Tripp had hallucinations followed by moments of clarity and normal thinking. When he was connected to an EEG, psychologists were able to determine that Tripp's patterns of hallucinations and clarity roughly followed a 90-minute cycle. Without him being aware of it, his brain was automatically drifting into sleep. When he was hallucinating, the EEG reading showed beta waves – he had drifted into REM sleep while still awake!

Also interesting was the pattern of recovery for both men. After not sleeping for 11 days, Gardner slept for 14 hours and 40 minutes before waking around 10 p.m. He stayed awake for 24 hours and then slept for a normal 8 hours. Tripp slept for 13 hours the first night, and then reduced amounts each subsequent night. This alone was an interesting study – despite missing so much sleep, they did not need to make up every hour.

Figure 5.6 Randy Gardner attempting to beat the world record time of going without sleep

> ## ACTIVITY 5.4 SLEEP DEPRIVATION CASE STUDIES
>
> 1. What is an advantage of using a case study instead of an experiment in psychological research?
> 2. Why are researchers unable to carry out many human studies into the effects of sleep deprivation?
> 3. Search online for another case study of severe sleep deprivation. Write a brief summary of this case study.

What happens if we don't get enough sleep?

Psychologist Suzanne Warner from Swinburne University of Technology conducted a study in 2008 and demonstrated that, on average, Australian teenagers miss more than 1 hour of sleep per night and are forced to wake up 2.5 hours earlier than their natural rhythms. So, what happens to us if we don't get enough sleep? Studies have shown that the brain tries to compensate for the lack of sleep by working harder. Functional magnetic resonance imaging (fMRI) technology has found that the pre-frontal cortex regions of sleep-deprived subjects display more activity when undergoing verbal tasks than subjects who are not sleep deprived, however, their temporal lobes (which are responsible for language processing), were not as activated. This suggests that some parts of the brain have to work harder, but they aren't as effective (Drummond et al. 2000).

Although the sleep deprivation experienced by Gardner and Tripp is severe, mild sleep deprivation can lead to problems such as reduced alertness, poorer memory, reduced concentration and lack of motivation. Studies have also shown that chronically sleep-deprived students are more likely to have problems with impulse control, which can lead to risk-taking behaviour. Students who are C, D or F students get, on average, half an hour less sleep per night than students who regularly get A or B grades.

As well as being detrimental to our cognitive abilities, sleep deprivation can also have adverse affects on our physical health, changing our metabolic rates and increasing the release of stress hormones. Do you feel more stressed when you don't get enough sleep?

Further, sleep deprivation can have significant long-term, and sometimes, tragic consequences. Many well-documented accidents have been attributed to sleep deprivation, such as the Exxon Valdez oil spill and the Ukrainian Chernobyl nuclear disaster (1986). Closer to home, it is estimated that up to 20 per cent of all motor vehicle accidents can be attributed to drowsiness. This equates to approximately 70 deaths per year and over 500 serious injuries on Australian roads. Staying awake for 17 hours straight is equivalent to having a blood alcohol level of 0.05 and means that a person is twice as likely to have an accident. When a driver is sleep deprived for 24 hours, the chance of them having a car accident increases to 17 times that of someone who isn't sleep deprived. The increased risk of accidents may be due to the increased occurrence of microsleeps. **Microsleeps** are episodes where someone falls into a very brief period of sleep although they seem like they are awake. People who are extremely sleep deprived will experience microsleeps although they will not be aware that they are experiencing them. Their head may nod and their eyes may close or appear droopy. EEG readings demonstrate that brainwave patterns change from alpha waves (drowsy or very relaxed) to theta waves (definite sleep).

Microsleep When a sleep deprived person falls into a quick sleep that lasts for seconds. Microsleeps can have significant consequences.

CHAPTER 5 IN YOUR DREAMS

ACTIVITY 5.5 TAC CAMPAIGNS

The details of this activity are available on the Cambridge GO website.

Just how much sleep do we need?

Throughout our lifespan we need different amounts of sleep, and the amount of sleep we need is generally related to our growth and development. Before reading on, when do you think we require the most sleep, and at which stage throughout our lifespan do you think we will require the least? Experts consider the estimates for the amount of sleep required shown in table 5.2 to be reasonable.

Table 5.2 Estimates for amounts of sleep required at different stages in life

Age	Amount of sleep (hours)
Newborn infants 0–2 weeks	16–18
Babies 14–15 weeks	14–15
Young children 3–5 years	10–12
Teenagers	9–10
Adults	7–9
Older people	6–7

Figure 5.7 Young children need much more sleep than adults.

ACTIVITY 5.6 SLEEP LOG: ARE YOU GETTING ENOUGH SLEEP?

The details of this activity are available on the Cambridge GO website. You will also find information on how you can sleep better.

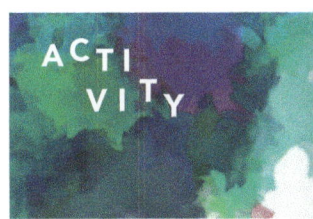

What are dreams?

Dreams The strange story-images we experience during REM sleep

Every night, during REM sleep, we experience strange stories and narratives. We call these **dreams**. Dreams are vivid, story-like images that occur when we sleep, particularly when we experience REM sleep. Dreams can be in black and white or colour, pleasant or terrifying, realistic or abstract. Yet we rarely dream in smells or tastes, and studies using imaging techniques have shown that the parts of the brain responsible for these senses are not activated when we dream.

Research has shown that the majority of our dreams occur when we are in REM sleep. Researchers know this because they have connected participants to EEGs and then woken them when they are in REM sleep. Using this technique, researchers found that 80 per cent of people report having been dreaming when they were woken, even those who claim they 'never dream'.

That is not to say that we only dream during REM sleep. We dream during the other stages of sleep, but those dreams are not as colourful, vivid or story-like. Instead, they tend to be a series of disconnected images.

As with sleep, researchers are not really sure why we dream, or what, if anything, our dreams actually mean.

Why do we dream?

There is no one definitive reason why we dream. Similar to sleep research, much of what researchers know about why we dream comes from their knowledge of what happens when we are deprived of dreaming time or REM sleep. As with sleep deprivation studies, it is not ethical to conduct such tests on human subjects, so animals are used instead.

In 1967, psychologist Michel Jouvet wanted to investigate the effect of REM deprivation in animals. He placed a cat on a small island surrounded by cold water. Every time you enter REM sleep your muscles completely relax, almost to a state of paralysis. So whenever the cat entered REM sleep, it fell off the island and into the water. The longer the cat was deprived of REM sleep, the more time it spent trying to get into REM sleep. It became more and more distressed by this and eventually died.

REM rebound The increase in the amount of time spent in REM sleep following a period of REM sleep deprivation

Studies that deprive humans of REM sleep show that the more deprived of REM sleep they are, the more attempts they make to enter REM sleep. When subjects are allowed to sleep uninterrupted, they increase the amount of time spent in REM over five days until they have recovered the lost REM sleep. Psychologists call this phenomenon **REM rebound**.

There are many theories as to why we dream. Two of the most influential theories are Freud's *psychoanalytic* theory and Hobson and McCarley's *activation–synthesis* theory.

Freud's psychoanalytic theory of dreaming (1900)

Sigmund Freud is often referred to as 'the grandfather of psychology' because he developed many influential theories about personality and how it develops. Freud's theory was called 'psychoanalytic', and he believed that dreams were the 'royal road to the unconscious'.

Freud theorised that our mind, or psyche, consists of three levels: the *conscious mind*, or everything of which we are immediately aware; our *preconscious mind*, everything we can easily recall; and our *unconscious mind*. In our unconscious mind reside all the thoughts and feelings that cause us to feel guilty or anxious. We cannot access our unconscious mind because we have pushed those feelings deep down and may not even be aware of them. Freud likened our mind to an iceberg. Why do you think this is?

We cannot access the contents of our unconscious mind because they are protected by our *ego*. This does not mean that we have a big head; this is a mechanism we employ to stop ourselves feeling negative emotions, such as guilt and anxiety. But when we dream, our ego drops its defences and we can access the contents of our unconscious mind. Freud said our dreams contain the contents of our unconscious mind, and could be interpreted by a trained psychoanalyst to reveal our deepest thoughts, wishes and desires.

However, it is not quite that straightforward. Our dreams also have different levels of content – manifest and latent content. **Manifest content** is what we remember of our dreams. These are the symbols contained in our dreams, the images we can describe to people when we share our dreams with them. **Latent content**, on the other hand, is what these symbols actually mean. The symbols need to be interpreted in order to reveal their true or hidden meanings. For more informtaion on these hidden meanings, visit the *Cambridge GO* website.

One of the biggest problems with Freud's theory of dream analysis is that there is little scientific evidence to support his claims. His patients recorded their dreams themselves, which meant they were subjective or unreliable. Further, the actual analysis was subjective as it was based on Freud's interpretation. It is very difficult to test such a theory as this.

Manifest content The content of our dreams that we remember upon waking, according to psychoanalytic theory

Latent content The true meaning of the content of our dreams, according to psychoanalytic theory

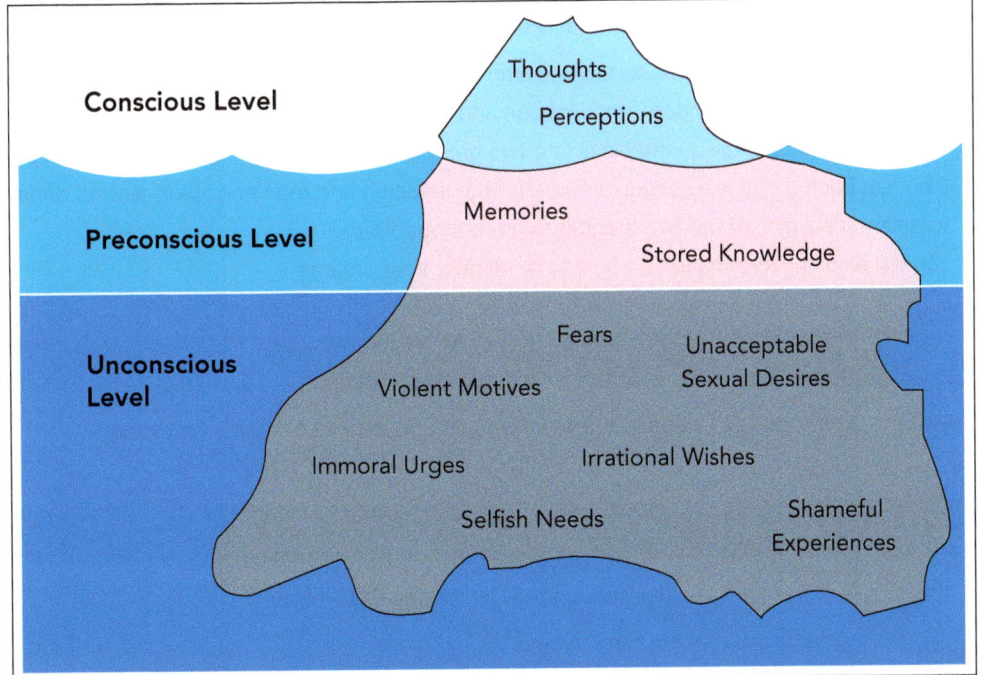

Figure 5.8 The three levels of our psyche

Hobson and McCarley's activation–synthesis hypothesis (1977)

Whereas Freud's theory is considered a *psychological* approach to understanding why we dream, Hobson and McCarley's theory is a *biological* approach. They proposed that dreams are a by-product of the random firing of neurons that occurs during REM sleep. The random activation of neurons sends information to the body to move, but because of the muscle paralysis that occurs during REM sleep, we are not able to do so.

When we enter REM sleep, our brain generates waves of electrical activity in a structure called the pons. These waves travel up to the brain and reach the areas that, if we are awake, would interpret incoming sensory information. These areas treat the activity as if it were real sensory information.

In order to interpret this information, the mind tries to form it into a coherent whole (synthesis). To make this synthesis process clearer, the brain draws on its previously stored memories. Our dreams are often strange because these brain waves activate many parts of the brain simultaneously.

The strength of the activation–synthesis hypothesis is that it correlates with what we already know about the brain waves present during REM sleep. It is also consistent with what we know about how the mind works – we try to make sense of things in the easiest way possible. Further, the fact that the visual, auditory and motor (movement) areas are activated in the brain during REM sleep, but the areas responsible for smell and taste are not, explains why we dream in the former senses but not the latter.

However, these are still just theories, and just as we have no definitive reason as to why we sleep, we also have no definitive answer as to why we dream.

ACTIVITY 5.7 DREAM THEORIES

Your task is to conduct some further research into the two dream theories discussed above: Freud's psychoanalytic theory, and Hobson and McArley's activation–synthesis hypothesis. Your teacher should divide the class into two groups and assign each group with one of the theories. Each group is to conduct some further research and then engage in a class debate to determine which of the two theories is more probable.
You will also find information on how to remember your dreams.

ACTIVITY 5.8 DREAM ANALYSIS

Visit the Cambridge GO website to see information on what our dreams may mean.

ACTIVITY 5.9 ERA: DREAM ANALYSIS

The details of this ERA are available on the Cambridge GO website.

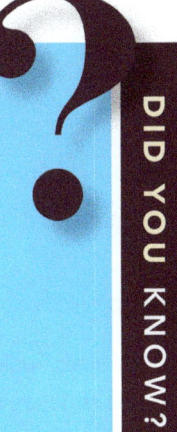

DID YOU KNOW?

Why are yawns so contagious? Psychologists Andrew and Gordon Gallup believe that we yawn in order to increase blood flow to our brains and to cool them (Hooper 2008).

They hypothesise that contagious yawning is really an evolutionary mechanism to 'maintain group vigilance'. What this means is that yawning as a group increases blood flow to the brain, which increases the amount of attention within that group. Our brain operates more efficiently when it is cool, and yawning helps enhance this brain function. So when you yawn in class, your teacher should be thanking you, as you are really making the transition from boredom to alertness!

END OF CHAPTER SUMMARY

- Sleep is a non-waking state of consciousness defined by general unresponsiveness to the environment and physical immobility.
- The sleep–wake cycle is a *circadian* rhythm as it occurs once every 24 hours.
- The most accepted theory of why we sleep is that sleep helps restore our bodies from the general wear and tear of the day. If we do not sleep, we may experience changes to our metabolism and immune system.
- Electroencephalographs (EEGs) detect, amplify and record the electrical activity of the brain during sleep. Brain waves are described by their frequency and amplitude and occur in typical patterns over the course of a night's sleep.
- Rapid eye movement sleep is known as REM sleep. During this stage, the eyes move quickly underneath the eyelids. This is a deep sleep and is when most dreaming occurs.
- Sleep deprivation can have significant consequences on both our physical and psychological health. It can also lead to tragic consequences.
- Most teenagers do not get the required nine to ten hours of sleep per night. This may have effects such as reduced alertness, poorer memory, reduced concentration and lack of motivation.
- Sleep hygiene can be improved by reducing caffeine intake, turning off electronic devices, getting adequate exercise during the day and developing a regular routine before bedtime.
- Dreams are narratives that we experience during REM sleep. If deprived of REM sleep, we experience REM rebound and try to enter REM sleep earlier.
- Sigmund Freud proposed a **psychoanalytic dream theory** in which dreams were the unexpressed contents of our unconscious minds. The manifest content was what we remember of our dreams and the latent content was the true meaning of the manifest content. There is little scientific evidence to support this theory.
- The **activation–synthesis hypothesis** by Hobson and McCarley proposes that dreams are the brain's way of making sense of the electrical activity that occurs when we dream. There is some evidence to support this theory.

END OF CHAPTER TEST

Multiple-choice questions

1. The sleep–wake cycle is thought to be controlled by a structure in the brain named the:
   A pons
   B cerebellum
   C pineal gland
   D forebrain.

2. Stage 2 sleep is characterised by theta waves and what other characteristic?
   A Delta waves
   B Spindles and K-complexes
   C Snoring
   D Eyes flickering beneath their lids.

3. Complete the following sentence. An entire sleep cycle takes approximately _____ minutes, and we experience _____ cycles per night.
   A 90; 4–5
   B 60; 6–7
   C 120; 4–5
   D 30; 7–8.

4. Sleep deprivation studies cannot use humans because:
   A everyone's sleep cycle is different, so it would be impossible to make the experiment reliable and valid
   B people enjoy sleeping so much that researchers have trouble finding volunteers to participate
   C it is impossible to keep someone awake as they will fall asleep when they are tired
   D it is unethical to do so because it causes physical and psychological harm to the participants.

5. Complete the following sentence. Although some sensory areas of the brain are activated during sleep, those responsible for _____ and _____ are not.
   A smell; taste
   B touch; hearing
   C taste; movement
   D seeing; hearing.

Short-answer questions

1. Describe the relationship between age and sleep requirements.
2. Briefly explain each stage of sleep in terms of the brain waves experienced, how long it lasts for and its characteristics.
3. Explain some of the effects of sleep deprivation.

Pursuing happiness

CHAPTER 6

Happiness comes from within.

Buddha

One of the questions we often ask ourselves, our family and friends is 'are you okay? Are you happy?' **Happiness** is one of the most important factors of success in a person's life. Those who are happiest are thought to live longer, be stronger and fulfil many (if not most) of their goals and aspirations.

A new movement in psychology called **positive psychology** aims to help people find happiness and meaning in their lives. What is happiness and what is the meaning of life? How can we be happy? And why are some people fulfilled while others are not?

Positive psychology

Psychological research has historically investigated mental illness, mental health and deviations from what is considered **normal**. Studies by psychologists have been mostly preoccupied by human suffering, illness, dysfunction and failure.

Yet psychology may now have a greater dual focus thanks to the advent of positive psychology. Not only may psychology help people cope with mental illness and **adversity**, but psychology may also now help us maintain a healthy sense of wellbeing.

In other words, positive psychology concentrates on **mental wellness**, or effective mental health.

Positive psychologists aim to determine and increase human strengths, leadership, creativity and happiness.

Rather than focus on mental illness, why not concentrate on mental wellness? This idea is not entirely new. Back in the 1940s, Abraham Maslow theorised a 'hierarchy of needs' (see figure 6.1). He believed that by studying people who are successful, intelligent and healthy, we might learn how to be successful, intelligent and healthy.

Maslow's physiological needs are our instinctive needs – the instincts of all animals. If the environment is right, people will grow and develop as they should. Beyond these basic needs are higher needs and people only progress to the next level once previous levels have been met. Therefore without the physiological needs, people cannot achieve safety needs; without safety needs, they cannot achieve belonging needs and so on.

Happiness A sense of wellbeing and satisfaction in one's life

Positive psychology The area of psychology that specialises in helping people improve their sense of wellbeing and happiness

Normal The average, custom or standard level of something. In psychology, it means being 'free' of mental or physical disorders.

Adversity An event or situation that is challenging or difficult

Mental wellness Behaviour, thoughts and emotions that help support a positive, effective and functional mental state

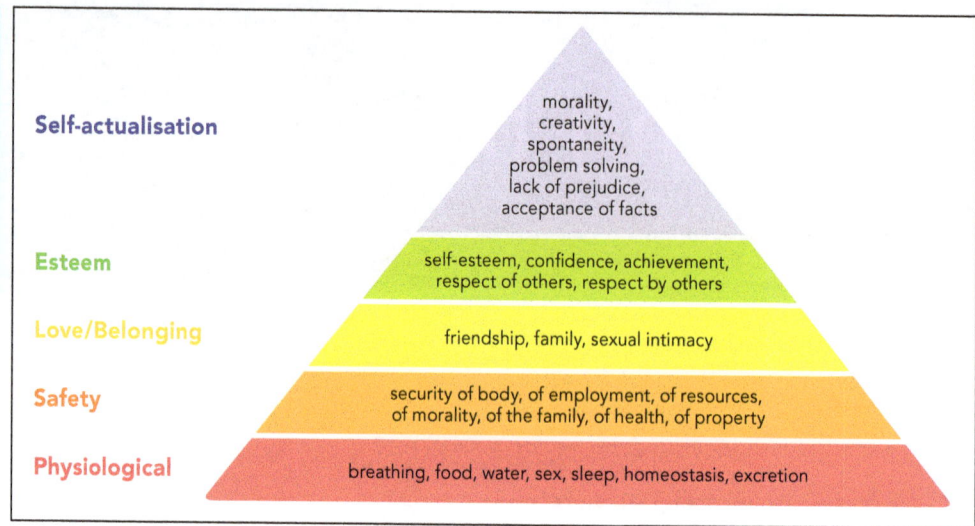

Figure 6.1 Maslow's hierarchic theory of needs

Positive psychology is a very new area of psychology, officially recognised and launched by the American Psychological Association (APA) in 2000. The president of the APA at that time, Dr Martin Seligman, is considered the 'father of positive psychology'.

Positive psychology has become increasingly popular in Australia, with universities now offering courses specialising in this area. Conferences are held on an annual basis and professional groups and companies have been created, such as the Australian Institute of Happiness. Geelong Grammar School in Victoria has established a Centre of Wellbeing, the first of its kind at any Australian school.

ACTIVITY 6.1 POSITIVE PSYCHOLOGY

1. What is positive psychology?
2. What are the main roles and responsibilities of a positive psychologist?
3. Explain Maslow's theory of needs. What needs must be met first?
4. Search online for a positive psychologist in Australia. Which organisation do they work for? What qualifications do they have? What other information does the website give you about this psychologist? Share what you find with your class.
5. a If you wanted to become a positive psychologist, what would you need to do?
   b Find a university where you could study to become a positive psychologist.

ACTIVITY 6.2 ERA: HOW HAPPY ARE YOU?

The details of this ERA are available on the Cambridge GO website.

What determines happiness?

Happiness includes all the positive parts of our life and how we feel. Positive psychologists are interested in helping people improve their happiness and wellbeing.

For us to understand what makes us happy, we have to consider what determines happiness. This chapter will consider two theories of happiness. The first is Dr Martin Seligman's formula of happiness. The second is Dr Barbara Frederikson's positivity ratio.

Formula for happiness

Psychologists have identified three major factors of happiness: circumstances, voluntary activities and a 'set point' of happiness. If we wanted to calculate happiness, we might use the following formula, created by Dr Martin Seligman:

Happiness = $S + C + V$

where S = set point
C = circumstances of life (e.g. race, sex, age, wealth, where you live)
V = voluntary activities (e.g. holidays, exercise, hobbies)

Our set point of happiness

Every person has their own different 'set point' of happiness. This level of happiness is thought to be genetically determined, and (as shown in the pie graph below) contributes to 50 per cent of our happiness. Our **set point of happiness** is thought to be relatively stable as it is genetic – we cannot change our genes! Therefore, our set point tends to remain the same throughout our lives. What does this mean in terms of our happiness? While we might have times in our lives when we have a higher or lower level of happiness, we tend to return to this set point.

As our set point is genetic, we cannot change it in order to change our happiness. Instead, we have to look at the other two contributing factors if we want to change our level of happiness.

Set point of happiness Personal level of happiness that is genetically determined and therefore unique and stable (unchanging) for each person

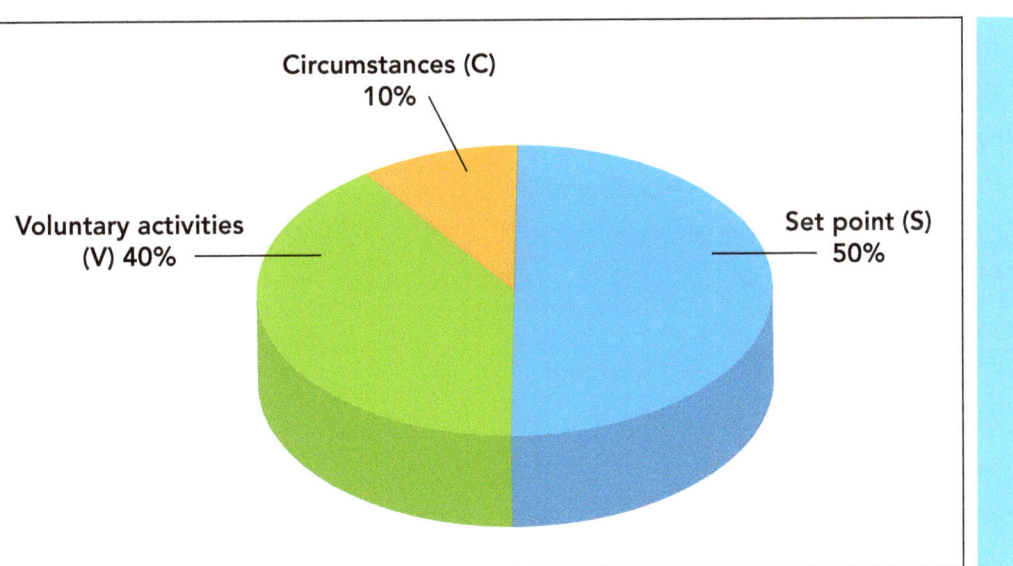

Figure 6.2 The three factors of happiness

ACTIVITY 6.3 A FORMULA FOR HAPPINESS

1. What is Seligman's formula for happiness and what are the three major factors of happiness?
2. What is our 'set point'? Why is it considered stable?
3. How much does each factor contribute to happiness? Which factor contributes the most? Which factor contributes the least?

Circumstances of life

Circumstances External life factors such as wealth, health and relationship status; one of the three factors of happiness

Culture The beliefs, values, practices and social behaviour of a particular nation or group of people

Life expectancy The average number of years we might expect someone to live, taking into account gender, race, socioeconomic status and where they live

Circumstances contribute approximately 10 per cent of our happiness and are a small but important factor. Circumstances include where we live, our age, gender and **culture**. They can also include lifestyle features, such as our jobs, income (wealth), religion, health and even if we are married or not.

Wealth

Unsurprisingly, the unemployed are generally less happy than those with jobs.

Unemployed people are also at a greater risk of depression, psychological ill-health and stress-related diseases such as heart disease. Furthermore, they have a diminished **life expectancy**.

Only 56 per cent of unemployed Australians feel happy, compared to 80 per cent of employed Australians (ABS 2007). In fact, the unemployed are the third unhappiest group of people in Australia. People who suffer from mental health issues and stress are the unhappiest. These figures can be seen in table 6.1.

Table 6.1 Australians who are happy with their lives

Category	Percentage (%)
High income earners	88
No long-term health condition	83
Partner in couple, no children	82
Married	81
Employed	80
Have a non-school qualification (e.g. uni or vocational)	78
Parents with non-dependant children	78
Middle income earners	77
Aged 18 years or over	76
Parents with children (two-parent households)	75
With a long-term health condition	75
Without a non-school qualification	73
Never married	71
Aged 85 years or over	71
Retired	68
Living alone	68
Low income earners	64
Divorced or separated	63
Single parents	60
Unemployed	56
With mental or behavourial problems	46
With high psychological distress	34

Source: adapted from the Australian Bureau of Statistics 'Life Satisfaction and Measures of Progress' (2007)

ACTIVITY 6.4 ANALYSING STATISTICS

1. Using the statistics in table 6.1, write a few sentences about who is the happiest and the unhappiest in Australia; for example, 'Three-quarters of parents with children (two-parent households) report themselves to be happy, compared to 60 per cent of single parents'.
2. What strikes you as interesting about the statistics in table 6.1? Hint: Compare 'Single parents' to 'Never married'.
3. Are there any groups missing from the statistics above? Who do you think should also be included and why?

Can happiness be bought?

As you can see, those who earn a high income are the happiest. Does this mean wealth necessarily makes us happier? Many people think that winning Tattslotto, for example, will definitely make them happier, but this may not be true. There has been a great deal of research into the effect of money on happiness and it appears that, contrary to what we might think, money *does not* guarantee happiness.

Consider the notion of 'retail therapy'. When we need some cheering up, we often tend to go shopping! We know how much fun it can be and how good we can feel when we treat ourselves.

This may be due to the pleasure we have learned to associate with shopping since we were kids. Social researcher Tony Wellington theorised that we *learn to believe* that shopping brings happiness. Australian children spend more time shopping with their parents than they do watching their parents work! Shopping is something children can participate in, while it is harder for them to help their parents work. Shopping is also a highly enjoyable activity for children as there is a sensory overload of new sights, smells and sounds. Consider the colours and contents of a toy store to understand how much they appeal to children (and some adults). Therefore, from a young age we learn to associate shopping with pleasure. This is further reinforced by any little treats or rewards we might get when shopping with our parents.

Consider as well the messages we get from advertisements. Marketing cleverly plays upon what we want. We all want to better ourselves, and advertisements promise us that we will feel better, feel happier, if we buy a product. Yet research shows that buying material items does not make us happier.

Figure 6.3 From a young age, we learn to associate shopping with pleasure.

The things we buy

Cannot decide between a new mobile phone or tickets to a concert? Take the tickets – they will make you happier. The things we buy can be classified as one of two types of purchases: **materialistic purchases** and **experiential purchases**. Experiential purchases generally make us happier than materialistic purchases.

Experiential purchases are those made with the primary intention of attaining a life experience. Examples of experiential purchases would be travelling on holidays, going to a concert or having a massage.

Materialistic purchases are those made with the primary intention of acquiring a material possession. Examples of materialistic purchases would be new clothes or furniture.

Sometimes, however, a purchase can be both experiential and materialistic. For example, Simon and Stella both buy a bike but for different reasons. For Stella the bicycle is experiential; it allows her to ride to work and explore her city on weekends. Simon, on the other hand, buys the bicycle to add to his collection of bikes. Simon's splurge is Stella's 'must-have'.

The more we follow materialistic goals, the less happy we are. In a survey of people's attitudes about shopping, researchers found that people who might say 'buying things gives me a lot of pleasure' and 'some of the most important achievements in my life include acquiring material possessions' were less happy. Similarly, people who 'have a job with a high social status' or 'buy things just because I want them' had a lower sense of wellbeing or happiness (van Boven & Gilovich 2003). Materialistic people also tend to have more debt – they are likely to have more credit cards and take out more loans.

Materialistic purchases Purchases that have the primary intention of gaining material possessions

Experiential purchases Purchases that have the primary intention of gaining a life experience

Figure 6.4 A concert ticket is an example of an experiential purchase.

Think back to the statistics described in table 6.1. If the happiest people in Australia are those on a high income, then surely money brings happiness? Consider carefully what makes us happy and what makes us unhappy. First, materialistic people tend to have more credit cards. We must acknowledge that *not* having money can cause unhappiness. For example, look at people struggling with **poverty** and **economic depression**.

Economic depression occurs when the economy declines and reduces a nation's overall income. This can lead to reduced happiness in people nationwide, or even worldwide. Consider Australian's responses to the US banks collapsing and the global economic crisis of 2008–09.

Poverty Not having enough money for basic needs such as food, clothing and housing

Economic depression Where the financial affairs of a nation or group of people are in a slump

Poverty is an awful experience. People with little or no money have to spend what they do have on basic needs. Look back to Maslow's hierarchy of needs. When physiological and safety needs are not being met, then happiness is rare. Being poor is stressful.

Nevertheless, once basic needs are met, more money does *not* lead to greater happiness.

Consider the impact of a $100 pay rise. For a poor person, the first $100 would give enormous satisfaction – it is the difference between starving and eating! But an extra $100 received by someone who has $100 000 would not be noticed. As a person's income rises, they receive *less happiness* for each pay rise.

So why are high-income earners in Australia the happiest? One thing we know is that high- and middle-income earners tend to make more experiential purchases. This is because their basic needs are met. Those with less money, in comparison, have to meet their basic needs first. Experiential purchases can make us happier, so if someone makes more experiential purchases, they might also be happier.

Interestingly, it also seems that people feel happy when they give their money away! That is, when they make a charitable donation. This is probably due to the experiential nature of giving to charity.

Australians are now eight times richer than we were a century ago. The good life has become the 'average' life. Yet we do not say we are happier, even though we all have more money. Therefore, more money does not lead to greater happiness.

Figure 6.5 This man working as a porter in Mumbai, India, may not earn enough money to pay for even his basic needs.

ACTIVITY 6.5 EXPERIENTIAL VERSUS MATERIALISTIC PURCHASES

1 What are the differences between experiential and materialistic purchases? Give an example of each.
2 What type of purchase tends to make us happier and why?
3 Why is it that high-income earners in Australia might be happier than middle- and low-income earners?

Health

Health is another circumstance that affects our happiness. Being healthy, or at least looking after our health, can be a great way to increase happiness. Research has shown that people who regularly exercise feel better, are more confident, less fearful and less depressed (Scully 1998). For minor forms of depression, a run in the park might be more effective than psychotherapy. There may also be a chemical reason for this: exercise releases **hormones** and **endorphins** into our bloodstream, and these help improve our mood. Endorphins are a great booster for our spirits – so if you have a bad day, get out there and move!

Figure 6.6 Playing sport releases endorphins, which improve your mood.

Hormones Important chemicals that act as messengers in our bodies and help regulate body functions

Endorphins Chemical substances in our brains that act as natural painkillers in times of pain or stress. Endorphins can also cause people to feel better after strenuous exercise (a runner's 'high').

Marriage

Apparently, happy people marry sooner and stay married longer. It seems that happier people are more attractive and easier to live with. However, the unhappiest people are those in unhappy marriages. Australians in unhappy marriages are less happy than Australian singles (refer back to table 6.1). Single people are also more likely to suffer from depression.

Research is finding that people in *any* good relationship are happier than single people. That is, we do not necessarily have to be married to enjoy the benefits of a relationship.

This can be reassuring for those who do not want to get married. There are other advantages to being in a relationship. The old adage 'a problem shared is a problem halved' shows how stress levels can be reduced for people in a relationship. We can also expect to live longer if we are in a relationship. Being in a relationship, therefore, is more important to happiness than money, lifestyle or work.

Sadly, however, people spend more time concentrating on work and money than concentrating on their relationships. The greatest thing we might learn from this is that we should take good care of our relationships.

Circumstances of life – a summary

It seems that those with a job are happier than the unemployed, the middle class are happier than the working class, those who are paid more are (mostly) happier than those who are paid less, those who are healthy are happier than those who are sick, and those in a relationship are happier than those who are single.

Nonetheless, circumstances only contribute approximately 10 per cent to our happiness. Also, when we have a change of circumstance – such as getting more money – we tend to get used to this and eventually return to our set point of happiness, so the new 'surge' of happiness is short lived. This is called **adaptation**.

So if the effects of changing our circumstances do not last, we should concentrate on the third major factor of happiness – voluntary activities.

Adaptation An organism's response to change; once it becomes used to the change, its response will diminish

ACTIVITY 6.6 HAPPINESS

1. Why do positive psychologists argue that money does not buy happiness?
2. How can changing our circumstances be costly? Look back at what circumstances include, such as where we live.
3. How do health and marriage (other types of circumstances) contribute to happiness?
4. Choose a class debate. Divide your class into two and research together for your side of the argument. Nominate three speakers to represent your group and present your case in a class debate.

   Class debate 1: 'Does money buy happiness?'
   Class debate 2: 'Would marriage make our generation happier?'

Voluntary activities

Voluntary activities are a large contributing factor to our happiness. They contribute 40 per cent (refer back to the pie graph) so they are very important.

What are voluntary activities?

Voluntary activities are intentional activities – things we *choose* to do. There are three types of voluntary activities: behavioural, cognitive and volitional.

Behavioural activities are activities that require us to act or do something. They might include playing sport regularly or other hobbies, such as horse riding, painting or collecting trading cards.

Cognitive activities are what we do with our mind. For example, being optimistic (looking on the bright side of situations) is a great cognitive activity. We *choose* to be optimistic, so it is a voluntary activity.

Volitional activities involve working towards personal goals. As a student, you probably have many goals including academic, sporting and social goals, which you choose to pursue.

The benefits of voluntary activities

First of all, voluntary activities are varied, and variety is the 'spice of life'. Voluntary activities keep us alert and stimulated.

Second, adaptation occurs *less* for voluntary activities. Adaptation is the way we return to our set point after a surge or decline in happiness, and occurs mostly when we change our circumstances. When we change our voluntary activities, adaptation tends *not* to occur. This is because voluntary activities help us appreciate the world.

For example, a man gets married. He has changed his circumstance (*C*), so he may be happier than if he were not married. Eventually, he might return to his set point level of happiness, but if he engages in voluntary activities (*V*), he can prolong or increase his happiness. A cognitive activity could be concentrating on the best features of his marriage, such as what he likes most about his wife. A behavioural activity could be buying his wife flowers or helping her in the kitchen. A volitional activity could be setting shared goals as a couple, such as saving up for a holiday together.

Finding a fit

What voluntary activities should we undertake? There is no single activity that will increase every person's happiness; we are all unique and have different interests. **Extroverts**, for example, may benefit more from activities involving other people than **introverts** would. So we need to find activities that suit us.

Voluntary activities are not always fun activities. Some voluntary activities are not as enjoyable as others. However, they will contribute to our happiness in the long run. *Short-term pain = long-term gain*. For example, as a student, studying for an exam may not be the happiest activity for you. But despite the short-term inconvenience and stress, the long-term benefits of passing the exam could contribute to sustainable happiness.

Voluntary activities Activities that are intentional, that an individual chooses to do

Behavioural activities Activities that require us to operate or act; a sub-type of voluntary activities

Cognitive activities Any activities that involve our thinking processes; a sub-type of voluntary activities

Volitional activities Any activities that we choose, or decide to take part in; a sub-type of voluntary activities

Extroverts People who are sociable, outgoing and confident. They tend to have interests outside their own self.

Introverts People whose thoughts and feelings are directed inward. They tend to be reserved and shy.

ACTIVITY 6.7 VOLUNTARY ACTIVITIES

1. Define voluntary activities and the three types.
2. Give an example of each of the three types of voluntary activities.
3. What are the two main benefits of voluntary activities?
4. Search the internet: On your own or as a class, create a list of strengths and positive traits and see how many apply to you or other students in the class. You can find example catalogues on the Authentic Happiness website, which is operated by Dr Martin Seligman.

The positivity ratio

The second theory of happiness is Dr Barbara Frederickson's positivity ratio. According to Frederickson, positivity opens us up. Like a lily in the sun, when we soak up positivity it tends to transform us and change the way our minds function. We are also more creative, more resilient, make better decisions and perform better.

Frederickson says that for every negative emotion we should aim to have three positive ones. This is her positivity ratio – 3:1.

Shouldn't we avoid negative emotions all together? No. According to Frederickson, we need negative emotions – to understand happiness we need to experience sadness, and to understand joy we need to experience anger. Negativity is our dose of reality which helps us to remain balanced.

Frederickson likens her ratio to a sailboat. The keel of the boat is negativity (n), whereas the rest of the ship – that is the mast and the sail – are positivity (p). The sail gives us speed, but without the keel we would be directionless (and we certainly would not be able to sail without it). Therefore, negativity is essential for us as human beings.

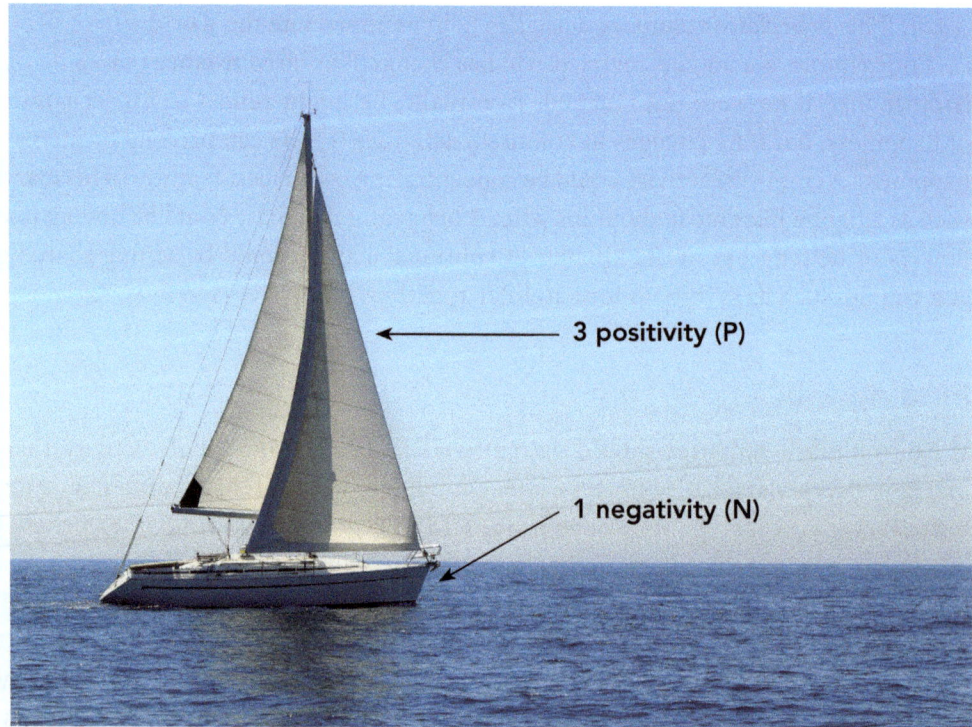

Figure 6.7 For every negative emotion we should have three positive emotions to keep us balanced, like a sailboat.

Happiness and humour

How can we achieve a positive state of mind? We might do it through happiness, love or humour.

How does humour work?

It is theorised that humour activates our brain's rewards centre. When we are amused, **dopamine** is released, which then stimulates our brain, particularly the **frontal lobe** where most of our higher-order analytical thinking takes place. Therefore, humour essentially acts as a fuel for our brain. Chapters 2 and 4 also discussed the brain.

Laughter relaxes the body, lowers blood pressure and releases feel-good endorphins much as a short burst of aerobic exercise would do. It also lowers levels of stress hormones and thus boosts the immune system. Dr Barbara Frederickson also found that students who watched a funny video (e.g. penguins playing) experienced an improvement in their thinking ability (2005).

Laughter bonds people and makes us feel closer. This is particularly true when we meet people for the first time. We may feel nervous or anxious about a person we do not know, and humour distracts us from our anxiety.

People are also 30 times more likely to laugh with their friends than they would if they were alone, even when watching the same comedy. So, if you want to laugh more, hang out with your friends!

Dopamine A hormone that plays an important role in cognitive functions, such as memory, problem solving and attention. It is also known as the 'pleasure' hormone, as it provides feelings of enjoyment and happiness.

Frontal lobe The region of the brain involved in decision making, problem solving, motor control and personality

Figure 6.8 Laughter releases endorphins, which make us feel good.

ACTIVITY 6.8 POSITIVITY RATIO

1. What is the positivity ratio? Explain the ratio.
2. Why are negatives necessary? Why don't we always just aim for positives?
3. When we laugh, which neurotransmitter is released?
4. What other physiological effects does laughter have on the body?

END OF CHAPTER SUMMARY

- Positive psychology is a new area of psychology that aims to help people find happiness and meaning in their lives.
- Positive psychology concentrates on mental wellness rather than mental illness.
- Abraham Maslow was one of the first psychologists to emphasise the importance of mental wellness and looked at how people can be successful, intelligent and healthy with his **hierarchy of needs**.
- Positive psychology was officially recognised by the APA in 2000.
- There are three major factors of happiness: set point (S), circumstances (C) and voluntary activities (V). Dr Martin Seligman's formula is Happiness = $S + C + V$.
- Our set point (S) is stable and genetic. It contributes 50 per cent towards our happiness and is something we cannot change.
- Our circumstances (C) contribute only 10 per cent, but people focus a lot on them when they should instead concentrate on voluntary activities (V).
- Our circumstances include age, gender, where we live, culture, wealth, health and marital status.
- Money does not buy happiness. However, people with money have greater freedom and are able to purchase more experiential purchases than those with less money.
- **Materialistic purchases** are those made with the intention of gaining a possession, such as CDs. **Experiential purchases** are those made with the intention of gaining experiences, such as seeing a band.
- The healthier we are, the happier we are. If you are feeling unhappy, get out and move! Stay active.
- People in relationships tend to be happier than single persons.
- Voluntary activities (V) are intentional activities. There are three types: behavioural, cognitive and volitional.
- Voluntary activities contribute 40 per cent to our happiness and are a very important way to change our happiness level. The more we do (or the greater the variety), the happier we are.
- Adaptation occurs less with voluntary activities. Adaptation is when, after a change in happiness, we return to our set point.
- The **positivity ratio** states that for every negative emotion we should have three positive ones. Negativity is necessary for us to understand what positivity is.
- Laughter activates the release of dopamine and relaxes the body.

END OF CHAPTER TEST

Multiple-choice questions

1. There are three major factors of happiness. These are:
   A health, money and circumstances
   B voluntary activities, smiling point and circumstances
   C voluntary activities, health and circumstances
   D voluntary activities, set point and circumstances.

2. Our set point of happiness is:
   A unstable and genetic
   B unstable and cultural
   C stable and genetic
   D stable and cultural.

3. Examples of materialistic purchases include:
   A going to a concert, buying clothes and a new car
   B climbing Mount Everest, scuba diving and going to concert
   C new books to read, new bike to ride and a new iPod
   D scuba diving, clothes and a new car.

4. Examples of experiential purchases include:
   A going to a concert, buying clothes and a new car.
   B climbing Mount Everest, scuba diving and going to concert
   C new books to read, new bike to ride and a new iPod
   D scuba diving, clothes and a new car.

5. The positivity ratio states that:
   A every positive emotion has three negative ones
   B a positive emotion is worth less than a negative one
   C every negative emotion should have three positive ones
   D none of the above.

Short-answer questions

Read the following scenario and then answer the following questions.

Matilda likes to keep busy. When she is not at school, she plays sport or goes to movies with her friends. Lately she has started rock climbing with her new boyfriend. At school, her teachers comment on her cheerfulness and optimism. Matilda rarely takes days off from school. She hopes to become an accountant like her father when she leaves school and is aiming to be accepted into a local university.

1. Identify the following factors from Matilda's scenario above: circumstances and voluntary activities (behavioural, cognitive and volitional).
2. What level of happiness do you think Matilda experiences? Clearly justify your answer.

Human relationships

CHAPTER 7

There is no joy except in human relationships.

Antoine de Saint-Exupery

Figure 7.1 Anger can be communicated non-verbally.

Humans are social creatures. We live in family units, we eat with others, we talk, work and play with others. These constant interactions mean that we have developed sophisticated ways to communicate our thoughts and ideas. We can speak and write, send emails or text messages, or use the fax and phone. What you may not realise is that the vast majority of our communication requires none of the above, because it is non-verbal communication.

According to some studies, we actually only speak, on average, for a total of 10 to 11 minutes a day. American anthropologist Albert Mehrabian (1971) claimed that:

- only 7 per cent of the total message we impart is verbal (i.e. the words we use)
- about 38 per cent of our communication is vocal, or dependent on the tones and volume we use
- about 55 per cent of the total message of our communication is non-verbal, consisting of gestures, expressions and postures.

This chapter will give you an insight into the different ways we communicate non-verbally – through personal space, hand gestures and facial expressions. It investigates cultural differences between these messages, as well as the differences that men and women experience when trying to communicate with each other.

How do we use our communication skills to develop our friendships and our romantic relationships?

ACTIVITY 7.1 CONVEYING THE MEANING OF A SENTENCE BY CHANGING YOUR INTONATION

The details of this activity are available on the Cambridge GO website.

Territory and personal space

There is nothing more frustrating than sitting and minding your own business, and then having a stranger sit right next to you. You look out the window, avoid eye contact, turn your body away and get as far away from that person as possible. It is an awkward shuffle and we have all experienced it at some stage or another; it is the fight to preserve our personal space and protect our **territory**.

Psychologists differentiate between territory and personal space. Territory refers to fixed spaces that somehow belong to us, or a group to which we belong. **Personal space**, on the other hand, is the amount of distance we need to maintain between ourselves and the people with whom we interact. Generally, the people we interact with adhere to the same rules as us, so we never have a problem. In the instance above, we may feel uncomfortable because someone else lives by a different set of rules. The study of these 'personal space' rules is called **proxemics**, and was developed by Edward Hall in the 1960s. The distance between two people during any social interaction depends on their relationship to each other. The difference between territory and personal space is that territory is static whereas personal space moves with you.

Territory The fixed spaces that somehow belong to us or a group to which we belong

Personal space The amount of distance we need to maintain between ourselves and the people with whom we are interacting

Proxemics The study of personal space rules

Territory

Psychologists distinguish between three different types of territory: primary, secondary and tertiary. **Primary territory** is any area used exclusively by the individual or group, usually over a long period of time. This may include things like your bedroom or your house. **Secondary territory** is used regularly by the individual or group, but is also used often by other people. This may be your favourite lunch spot at school, or the row of seats in which you sit in class. **Tertiary territory** consists of shared spaces which everyone can use. An example of tertiary territory is a public park or a shopping mall.

Like animals, we mark our various territories and we defend them when they are invaded. Psychologists refer to the way we mark our territories as **delineation**. Unlike animals, we do not do this by leaving our scent on items; instead, we have developed more sophisticated ways to demonstrate that something belongs to us. Most obviously, we delineate our territory through the use of physical barriers. Your house probably has a fence around it, and maybe a lockable gate. Visitors probably need to announce that they are 'invading' your territory by ringing the doorbell or knocking on the door. Your bedroom is an example of primary territory that belongs to you. Possibly you delineate it by putting posters on the door and walls and decorating it in a way that tells everyone that this is your room.

Psychologists have found that the more objects we use to delineate our territory, the more we convey ownership of it. Similarly, touching an object seems to convey our ownership of that object, even if temporarily. For example, think about how you signal to a waiter that you are still using your glass or your plate – by touching it lightly as they

Primary territory Any area that is used exclusively by an individual or group over a long period of time

Secondary territory Any area that us used regularly by the individual or group but is also used often by other people

Tertiary territory Shared spaces that everyone has the right to use

Delineation The way we mark our territory to separate it from another's

approach. Psychologist Carol Werner researched this idea in 1981 by observing people in a videogame arcade. A researcher either stood close to a 'Space Invaders' machine or touched the machine, but not the controls. The psychologists found that new players were significantly less likely to approach the game when the researcher was touching it.

But why do we defend our territory? And why do we create these boundaries in the first place? Psychologists try to explain territory from two perspectives: the socio-biological perspective and the socio-cognitive perspective.

Socio-biological psychology proposes that because many animal species also show territoriality, it may act as a way for us to control our resources. All animals need resources to provide food, water and shelter in order for them to breed and raise young. There is then an advantage for that animal or species if they can establish and maintain control over an area that provides these resources. One criticism of this theory is that while humans build houses as their primary territory, we may gather our food and resources from places many kilometres away. When we are burgled, or someone invades our territory, our initial concern is not whether they invaded our pantries and stole our food, but whether they took our jewellery or electronic goods. However, a supporting argument for this perspective is that territoriality is displayed by all cultures, suggesting some innate basis.

Socio-cognitive psychology argues that while territoriality in humans may have its origins in animal behaviour, we have learned when and where to apply it. This branch of psychology proposes that humans like everything to be ordered and neat. We like to simplify everything to make sense of an ever-changing world, and we do this by constructing mental models that help us understand and predict how we act. If we control our primary territory, we can predict what is likely to happen there; we also have more control over who enters it. Territory, according to this perspective, also allows us information about another person's status and personality. If you decorate your bedroom wall with posters of musicians, you are sending a clear message to all who enter about your style, interests and beliefs.

Personal space

We have all experienced someone encroaching on our personal space, leaving us feeling uncomfortable and attacked. Personal space is the little bubble of air around us that we do not like people to enter without our permission. The amount of space we are comfortable with changes from individual to individual, and depends on many other things, such as our culture and our relationship to the other person. The study of personal space is called proxemics, suggesting that it investigates the proximity we maintain when interacting socially with someone else. We try to maintain a balance between being overly familiar and encroaching, and awkwardly distant and disengaged.

Psychologist Edward Hall, the founder of the study of proxemics, suggests that there are four different **personal space zones** we try to uphold. These are *intimate distance, casual-personal distance, social-consultative distance* and *public distance*.

The intimate distance zone is 0 to 45 centimetres and is reserved for people with whom we share a very close relationship. This could be a parent's hug, or a romantic kiss. Sometimes we have to let strangers into this zone, as is often the case with doctors, dentists and hairdressers. The casual-personal distance zone is what we maintain when engaging in conversation with a friend; this ranges from 45 to 120 centimetres. The social-

---

Socio-biological psychology A branch of psychology that tries to explain people's behaviour from an evolutionary perspective

Socio-cognitive psychology A branch of psychology that tries to explain and also gives us information on people's behaviour through the thoughts and ideas that accompany it

Personal space zones The areas of space around us that we try to maintain: intimate distance, casual personal distance, social-consultative distance and public distance

consultative distance zone is 1.2 to 3.6 metres and is used when talking with a stranger or if you have a meeting of some sort. Finally, the public distance zone is maintained when we give a speech or lecture to a group of people. You might have noticed how students avoid the front row of a classroom for this very reason as it impinges on that public distance space. This zone keeps us the furthest away from those with whom we are interacting, at 3.6 to 7.6 metres away.

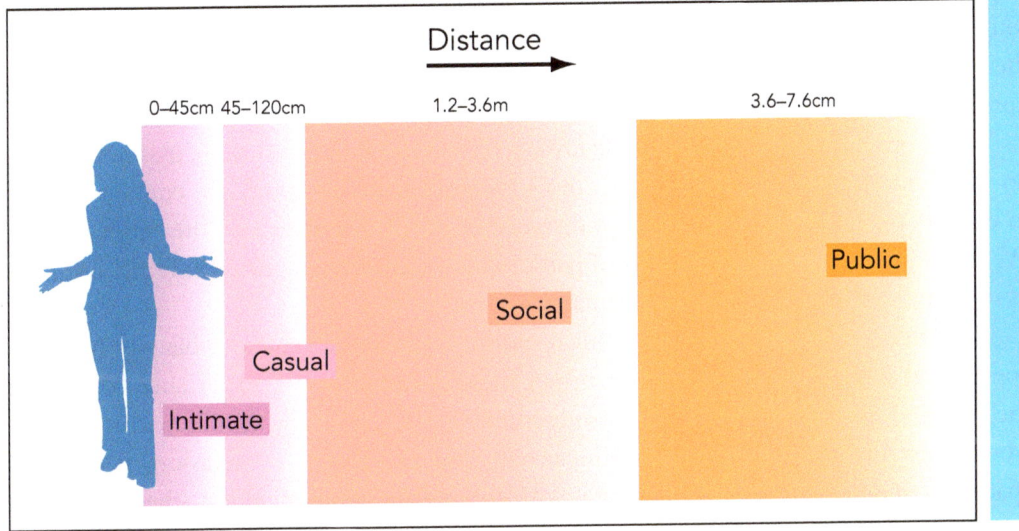

Figure 7.2 Personal spaces for social interaction

ACTIVITY 7.2 TERRITORY AND PERSONAL SPACE

1. What is the difference between territory and personal space?
2. What are the three types of territories? Briefly describe each one using personal examples.
3. What are some examples of secondary territory that you use?
4. What are some ways in which you delineate your territory? Think of your desk at school or your bedroom.
5. What are the two reasons given as to why we defend our territory? Briefly describe them and explain which is the most likely explanation.
6. During lunchtime, or at the beginning or your next class, observe different ways that people try to mark their territory. You might observe people saving seats for others in class, or people sitting in small groups.

ACTIVITY 7.3 PERSONAL SPACE DIAGRAM

In this activity you will be designing your own personal space diagram.
1. In the middle of a piece of A4 paper, draw a small circle with a sketch of yourself. Draw four concentric circles around this. Label the innermost ring 'intimate', the second ring 'casual', the third ring 'social' and the outermost ring 'public'.
2. Where do you think each person you know belongs in your diagram? Write out a list of people you know and put them in the appropriate circle. Include people who are close to you, such as your parents, siblings, boyfriend or girlfriend and your friends, as well as casual acquaintances and even complete strangers.

Autonomic nervous system A subdivision of the peripheral nervous system that contains the sympathetic and parasympathetic nervous system

Fight-or-flight response Physiological response to threat or intense excitement; causes the release of adrenalin in the body

Agoraphobia The irrational fear of public or open spaces

The amount of personal space we require depends partly on individual culture and societal rules. For example, Americans generally require more personal space than people from Mediterranean and Latin American cultures, and more than men in Middle Eastern cultures. Typically, people from rural areas require more space than people from urban areas. However, psychologists are beginning to believe that these rules might be very deeply ingrained. In 2007, researchers observed the avatars (digital representations of the humans who control them in video games) in Second Life, a virtual reality game. They found that some avatar behaviour supported studies that had previously shown how humans protect their personal space. The unspoken rules we follow in our normal waking life were being upheld in a virtual reality, despite the fact they were merely pixels on a screen.

When our personal space is invaded, we tend to react in a predictable manner. Rarely do we 'fight back' or ask someone to move away; instead we avoid eye contact, retreat to corners (as in an elevator) and put distance between ourselves and the other person. We may even experience a moment of panic, which can activate our **autonomic nervous system** and our **fight-or-flight response**.

One change we experience when this response is activated is that our bladder becomes constricted and we cease producing urine; more specifically, we experience a delay in the onset of and a decrease in the production of urine. A study conducted by Dennis Middlemist in 1976 investigated urine production in relation to invasion of personal space. Setting up in a male public toilet with three urinals and a cubicle, the researchers waited until an unsuspecting participant entered the toilet and began using a urinal. The confederate would then position themselves either at the adjacent (closest) urinal, or at the one furthest away (moderate distance) and time the onset and duration of urination. In the control condition, the participants were left undisturbed. As was predicted, when the confederate was right next to the participant, their average time to onset increased and their duration of urination decreased, suggesting that invasion of personal space leads to an increase in anxiety levels.

This increase in anxiety levels can be completely normal, or it can escalate to a more severe problem, resulting in an individual trying to avoid all circumstances where they might come into contact with strangers, such as the anxiety disorder agoraphobia. **Agoraphobia** is the irrational fear of public or open spaces, causing sufferers to avoid being in settings where they feel out of control. This may lead them to avoid people too.

Our interpretation of invasions of our personal space generally depends on the context. For example, we accept our space being invaded during peak hour on public transport, but it is very uncomfortable if a stranger sits next to you in an uncrowded movie theatre.

ACTIVITY 7.4 PERSONAL SPACE

1. What is the name for the study of personal space?
2. What are three sorts of people we are likely to allow into our intimate distance zone? Why do you think we let these people in?
3. What were the dependent variables in Middlemist's 1976 study?
4. What were the independent variables?
5. Think of some problems encountered by people of different cultures when they are trying to communicate. Can this problem be fixed? How?
6. Try it yourself. This afternoon on the tram or bus, sit next to someone you do not know and see their reaction. What happened?

ACTIVITY 7.5 ERA: PERSONAL SPACE

The details of this ERA are available on the Cambridge GO website.

Gestures

As mentioned earlier, approximately 55 per cent of our communication is non-verbal.

It is estimated that there are 100 000 words in the English language, and the average person has a vocabulary of 30 000 to 60 000 words. However, we have at our disposal approximately 750 000 non-verbal symbols! This vast number of gestures means that we can convey many things for which we may not have the words, adding to the richness of our communication. One way we do this is through the use of hand gestures.

Gestures are any movement of the forearm, hand, wrist or finger used solely for communication. Groups of gestures are called clusters and they always need to be read together. On their own they can be misinterpreted. For example, someone rubbing their nose may not necessarily be lying; they may just have an itchy nose!

So why use hand gestures when we could just speak? There are more nerve connections between our hands and brain than in any other part of the body. This means our hands are able to produce small and dexterous movements that would be impossible if we were to use our feet instead! If we redesigned the human body so that it was proportionate to the amount of cortical space (brain space) allocated to each part of our body, we would look something like the following diagram.

Gesture Any movement of the forearm, hand, wrist or finger for communication

Figure 7.3 The creature in the diagram is called a sensory **homunculus**. Note its disproportionately large hands, lips and tongue.

Homunculus Latin for 'little human'; a representation of a person used to illustrate the proportions of cortical space allocated to each body part

Psychologists believe that spoken language evolved from gesture. Studies of different primates, bonobos and chimps, have shown that they employ 31 gestures as well as 18 facial or vocal signals, and that although their facial signals are the same, the same gesture was used in many different contexts both between and within species. Researchers believe that human gestures evolved to become more facial (moving our mouths, lips and tongue) and therefore vocal, and less manual (hand movements), so that we could use our hands for other activities such as carrying and making tools. Further evidence of this is that orang-utans also gesture to increase effective communication.

Today, we often use our hands to signal our emotional state. The more excited or animated we become, the more likely we are to use large, expressive hand movements. Gestures also act as 'punctuation marks' to regulate the taking of turns in a conversation. By opening up your hands in a forward movement, you signal to the other person that it is their turn to contribute to the conversation. Think about what it is like communicating with someone who uses very few gestures. Do you feel that they are not engaged?

ACTIVITY 7.6 CLASS ACTIVITY

Turn to the person next to you and tell them about your weekend. You are not allowed to use your hands at all. Was this easy or difficult? Discuss this with the class.

ACTIVITY 7.7 CLASS ACTIVITY

The details of this activity are available on the Cambridge GO website.

Hand gestures also help us remember information. Researchers have found that they amplify the impact of spoken words. People recall more of what is said if the speaker communicates with *relevant* gestures. In a 2003 study, New Zealand psychologists Cross and Franz asked 120 college students to view three blocks of 27 video clips of a woman saying phrases like 'peel the banana' and 'the square box'. There were three conditions in this study: the speaker used gestures that *matched* the content; the speaker used gestures that *did not match* the content; or the speaker used *no* gestures at all. The volunteers had to name as many phrases as they could remember after each block. The psychologists found that people were able to recall more phrases that were spoken with relevant gestures, than when there were no gestures. Recall was worst when the phrase was accompanied by an irrelevant gesture.

Cross-cultural differences in gestures

The world is getting smaller. Advances in technology allow us to travel abroad with relative ease; we can jump online and chat to friends overseas, or watch videos from Japan on YouTube. A potential problem with this is that gestures and non-verbal communication are not the same worldwide.

Just like the amount of personal space we require, the meaning of gestures varies wildly from country to country and misinterpretation could be rather embarrassing! Table 7.1 shows three common hand gestures and what they may mean.

Table 7.1 Three common hand gestures and their meanings

Name	Gesture	Australian meaning(s)	Other meanings
Thumbs up		This is a common gesture that means a few different things. Often it is used when you want to signal that everything is 'okay' or 'good'. If you have ever water-skied, then you know that it is used to signal to 'go faster'. Similarly, scuba divers use it to signal 'go up'. How do you signal to someone that you would like a lift? This is a gesture commonly used by hitchhikers.	In Greece this sign, with the thumb thrust forward, means 'get lost'; it can also mean 'number one', or 'number five', depending on where you begin counting. You can demonstrate that someone is 'under the thumb' by holding it upside down, which also means that something is 'bad'.
The ring		We generally use this gesture to symbolise that something is 'okay' or 'good'. We may also use it to portray 'nothing' or 'zero'.	In France and Belgium, this also means 'zero', or signifies that something is 'worthless'. In Japan this means 'money', in Greece it symbolises that someone is homosexual. In Arabic countries, it is very rude and insulting.
The V sign		When this sign is used with the backs of the fingers facing out, it is generally considered rude. However, if it is used as it appears in this photo, then it means 'peace' or 'victory'.	In some parts of Europe, the rude version of the gesture means 'victory'; it also may mean 'number two'.

ACTIVITY 7.8 HAND GESTURES

1. What are groups of gestures called?
2. Provide an example where a gesture could be taken out of context.
3. Look at the diagram of the homunculus on page 95 and explain why it has large lips, mouth and tongue. What survival advantages are there in this?
4. Think of five phrases, other than 'the square box' and 'peel the banana,' that could be used in an experiment on gestures. Pool these with the class responses and conduct the experiment yourself!
5. What are some other common gestures? Think of three and then list alternative meanings for them. Are they the same in every country?

ACTIVITY 7.9 FACIAL EXPRESSIONS

Visit the Cambridge GO website for information on facial expressions and emotions as well as the details of this activity.

Putting it all together: human relationships

The whole reason for non-verbal signals is that we have information we want to communicate to someone. As mentioned at the beginning of this chapter, human beings are social animals; we like to engage and interact with other people. The signals we send out allow us to formulate and develop these relationships with others; this enhances our survival, particularly if it is a romantic relationship that we are engaging in.

This section looks at the signals we employ and the ways in which we develop two very different types of relationships – friendships and romantic relationships.

Friendship

With the advent of social networking sites, such as MySpace and Facebook, it seems as though everyone has hundreds of friends at their disposal. Indeed, a recent study suggests that 300 friends is the optimal number of friends to have on such a site – any more and you appear desperate! However, you probably do not come into contact with most of those people on a daily basis. What constitutes a friend? Someone you see every day? Someone you can share your deep, dark secrets with? Or just a bunch of mates who like to get together and have a good time?

Friendly interactions develop early in life. Recent research suggests that peer pressure can begin as young as 9 months old, with babies craving attention and interaction with each other. Australian psychologists Professor Ben Bradley and Dr Jane Selby (2003) videotaped 25 groups of three 9-month-old infants and found that they communicated with each other through play, touching, gestures and giggling.

Differences in the communication style exhibited by the different sexes are also seen from a very early age. Female babies only a few hours old are attracted to human faces and maintain eye contact two to three times longer than male babies. Male babies are attracted to objects. At 12 weeks old, girls are able to identify pictures of family over strangers, whereas boys are not. Preschool-age girls remember more about people and their emotions, whereas preschool-age boys remember more about objects and their shapes.

This difference in communication styles from an early age shapes the way we communicate with our friends in later life. Women tend to talk about relationships and feelings with their friends; they discuss personal issues, such as marriage, children, shopping and their other friendships. Men, on the other hand, tend to talk about things and events, such as sports, electronic devices and cars.

The way we develop these friendships is also different. Women usually develop friendships by sharing pieces of information that may make them vulnerable; they ask their friends for advice as a way to signal their trust.

Men, on the other hand, often tease and provoke embarrassment in their mates as a way of developing an intimate relationship. It shows that they like this person enough to include them in a personal joke of some sort.

Embarrassment is usually demonstrated by people looking down, awkwardly smiling, and gazing to the left. In about 25 per cent of cases they will touch their face. This embarrassment gesture acts as a social apology. As with male relationships, it signals the initial dominance and then acceptance of a new member into the group.

Another way we promote friendships is through 'mirroring'. There are specialised neurons (nerve cells) in our brains called **mirror neurons** that are involved both in physical

---

Mirror neurons
Specialised neurons in your brain that fire when you perform an action but also when you view that action being performed by someone else

actions and observations of actions. When we watch an action, these neurons can activate the parts of our brain that would activate if we performed that action ourselves. When we sit near someone we like, or someone that we know well, we have a subconscious tendency to mirror their actions. We may cross our arms if theirs are crossed, or we may play with our hair if they play with theirs. The point of this mirroring behaviour is that it makes us feel at ease and it builds rapport with the other person. It also shows that we agree with the person and what they say.

Figure 7.4 Mirroring behaviour

It has been suggested that the reason mirroring behaviour is 'hardwired' into the brain is that it leads to better cooperation, which leads to more and better resources, such as food, medicine and shelter. Interestingly, women are four times more likely to mirror another woman than a man is to mirror another man. Mirror neurons may also explain why women are more perceptive than men at reading social situations. When shown short films with the sound turned off, women were able to read the situation accurately 87 per cent of the time, whereas men only read it correctly 42 per cent of the time.

ACTIVITY 7.10 FRIENDSHIP

1. Explain the function of embarrassment from an evolutionary perspective.
2. What are some gender differences you know of in the playing behaviour of children who are of kindergarten age?
3. What are mirror neurons?
4. Explain another function that mirror neurons might perform.
5. What are some qualities that you look for in a friend?
6. How do you think friendships are maintained over time?
7. What effect might social networking sites have on communication in friendships?

ACTIVITY 7.11 MIRRORING

Get into pairs and sit opposite each other. One person is the 'leader' and slowly moves their body. Maintaining eye contact, the 'follower' mimics their movements, mirroring their actions. The aim is to stay together as closely as possible. Then change leaders.

Was this easy or difficult?

Try to do the same by pulling different facial expressions. Did making the same face as your partner change the way that you felt? Write a brief reflection on this activity.

Romantic relationships

We subconsciously send out signals that tell people around us how we are feeling and what we are thinking, all without saying a word. But how do we send out and detect the signals that suggest that someone is interested in us as more than a friend?

Humans are incredibly adept at reading these signals, without even knowing that we are doing so. Look at the two pictures below and choose which is more attractive.

Figure 7.5 Which picture is more attractive?

Chances are that you chose the picture on the left. Without even realising it, we read signals that show someone is interested in us. When we are attracted to someone our pupils dilate (get bigger) as if to see 'more' of them. And if we appear attractive to someone, *their* pupils dilate, which means they appear more attractive to us.

Interestingly, men's pupils dilate more when they look at photos of women, but women's eyes dilate the most when they look at pictures of mothers and babies.

Flirting

Think about some famous movie love scenes – how do you know that the characters are interested in each other? Chances are that they engage in **flirting**. Flirting can be described as the non-verbal signals that suggest you are ready to engage in some form of exchange with the other person. For women, typical flirting signs include tilting the

Flirting Non-verbal signals that suggest you are ready to engage in some form of exchange with another person

head to the side or exposing the neck or wrist. They are presenting themselves as slightly vulnerable, which endears them to the other person. Men flirt by positioning their bodies in an open stance, or holding their hands on their waist to draw attention to their belt line and make themselves appear bigger. Evolutionary psychologists believe these signals indicate that we are non-threatening and not going to run away.

Flirting appears to be biologically ingrained. In the 1960s, women from African tribes were filmed and it was found that they tilted their heads and stared longer than usual while smiling at the object of their affections, just as Western women do.

Recent research suggests that married people flirt just as much as single people. It makes sense that single people would flirt, since they are trying to attract a mate. But why do married people flirt? Psychologist Arthur Aron claims that flirting is a way for married people to 'test the value' of their spouse, as if checking whether there is an alternative possibility to their partner that might be better (Luscombe 2008). It sounds unromantic, but it makes sense from a biological perspective – if your life partner dies, you need to know that other options are available. Further, flirting can act as a social lubricant, and it might allow practical benefits – you may flirt to get out of a speeding fine or obtain a discount on your latest purchase.

Table 7.2 Ways in which men and women flirt

Men	Women
• Assume open body position	• Assume open body position
• Raise eyebrows upon initial meeting	• Raise eyebrows upon initial meeting
• Lean forward	• Lean forward
• Glance sideways and for longer than usual	• Glance sideways
• Smile	• Smile
• Adopt a posture that emphasises chest and crotch	• Adopt a posture that emphasises hips and breasts
• Feet or knees point to other person	• Feet or knees point to other person
• Spread legs wide, hands on hips	• Tilt head to one side, exposing vulnerable neck
• Hands spread and in belt loops, thumbs down	• Play with hair, toss or flick it
	• Lick lips
	• Touch lightly on the hand or arm
	• Wrist may go limp, or may be exposed to other person
	• Play with glass, ring, keys, etc.

Kissing

Kissing is a non-verbal gesture that signals our interest in someone, or is used as a greeting. However, unlike the facial expressions discussed earlier, the custom of kissing is different in many countries. Western countries tend to kiss on the lips for romance, and on the cheeks for a greeting. It is common for people in Vietnam and Thailand to rub noses with their lover, while in Siberia, India and the South Pacific, nose rubbing is used as a greeting for some cultures. The 'Malay kiss' used by Maoris, Mongolians and Tongans is a combination of nose rubbing and sniffing, and is the equivalent of our 'French kiss'.

There is still no definitive explanation as to why we kiss, but there are many theories. Evolutionary psychologists believe it might be a remnant of the ancient ritual of a mother chewing food before feeding it to her offspring, in much the way that birds do. Sigmund Freud related it to breastfeeding as an infant. Christopher Nyrop, a nineteenth century Danish scholar, proposed that kissing was a way to 'taste' the person, a symbolic attempt of recognition and affection.

Marriage

Although it is often cited that one in three marriages ends in divorce, 91 per cent of people still get married. Prior to marriage, people will most likely go through three stages of emotion identified by psychologists: lust, infatuation and attachment.

Lust occurs in the early stages of romantic attraction; it involves physical and non-verbal gestures displayed by both partners, indicating their interest in each other. Infatuation, the second stage, is often referred to as 'the honeymoon period'; this is the stage where you focus on your partner's good qualities, think about them constantly and want to spend all your time with them. During this stage, the brain releases chemicals such as dopamine, which makes you feel good; phenylethylamine, which increases excitement; and serotonin, which gives you a feeling of emotional stability. The part of your brain responsible for this is the ventral tegmental area (VTA) at the base of the brain. This stage lasts, on average, six months.

After this stage, people often break up, or develop their relationship to the third stage, attachment. During this stage, a cooperative bond is formed, partly because the brain also releases a chemical called oxytocin, which is responsible for developing feelings of attachment (new mothers produce a lot of oxytocin when their baby is born to promote their bonding), and partly because other areas of the brain, the caudate nuclei located on either side of the head, are responsible for habit. It seems this part of the brain makes loving someone a hard habit to break.

Marriage appears to have many benefits. Married people have lower rates of suicide and mental health problems and they live longer, perhaps in part because they are less likely to smoke or drink heavily. They are also less likely to experience stress, although married men are nearly 20 per cent more likely to be overweight than unmarried men. Obviously the marriage needs to be a good one in order to reap these benefits; research shows that the stress of a bad marriage can be very detrimental.

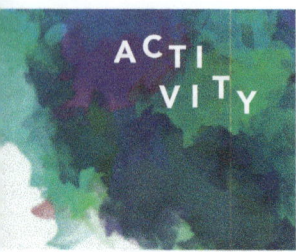

ACTIVITY 7.12 FLIRTING AND KISSING

1. When we expose our wrists and necks during flirting, we make ourselves vulnerable. Why is this so?
2. Suggest another reason why people might flirt.
3. Research and propose another reason why we kiss.

ACTIVITY 7.13 ROLE-PLAY

Construct a role-play demonstrating successful and unsuccessful flirting techniques.

Heartbreak

Grief can be devastating; unrequited love, a break up with a boyfriend or girlfriend, or the death of a family member can all leave you feeling incomplete and indeed, heartbroken. Unfortunately, this feeling of heartbreak is a part of life. There is a Spanish proverb which, when translated, reads 'where there is love, there is pain'.

Whilst feelings of heartbreak generally subside, they can result in a major depressive episode. Results from a study into the brain activity of nine women who were experiencing acute grief because of a relationship breakup showed that there is an increase in activity levels in the parts of the brain, such as the cerebellum and brainstem, which are typically related to sadness. More interestingly, fMRI results from the same study show that there is a decreased level of activity in the left hemisphere which is responsible for our logical and analytical thought processes (Najib et al. 2004). The more acute the women's grief, the greater the decrease in activity.

What can I do to heal my broken heart?

There is another saying that 'time heals all wounds'. This may be true, but in the meantime, it may be useful to write your thoughts and feelings down on paper. A study conducted in 2002 found that undergraduate students who were required to write about a relationship breakup experienced less respiratory illnesses, less tension and fatigue than participants who were in the control group and were required to write in a non-emotional way about impersonal relationship topics (Lepore & Greenberg 2002).

END OF CHAPTER SUMMARY

- The majority of our communication with others is non verbal. Seven per cent of the total message is verbal (words only), 38 per cent is vocal (intonation, volume, etc.) and 55 per cent is non-verbal (gestures, posture and expressions).
- Territory is the fixed space that belongs to us, and can be defined as primary, secondary or tertiary. We define territory through fences, doors and personalising our spaces. We can also do this by touching items to claim them.
- Personal space is the area surrounding us and, unlike territory, it moves with us. There are four different zones of personal space: intimate distance, casual-personal distance, social-consultative distance and public distance. The study of personal space is also known as **proxemics**.
- Gestures are movements of the forearm, hand, wrist or finger used solely for communication. Groups of gestures are called clusters.
- Gestures may mean different things in different countries and cultures.

END OF CHAPTER SUMMARY

- Facial expressions are outward displays of internally experienced emotions, and are thought to have evolved over many years to what we recognise today.
- Paul Ekman designed the first set of scientifically valid studies into facial expressions and found that anger, fear, surprise, disgust, sadness and happiness are displayed the same way by members of all cultures, which means they are innate and not learned.
- Further evidence for Ekman's theory comes from babies who are born blind – they display the same facial expressions as babies with normal vision, meaning that facial expressions are not learned.
- There is growing evidence that expressions of other human emotions: elevation, interest, pride and confusion may be universal also.
- We demonstrate that we like someone by mirroring or copying their body language. Mirror neurons in our brain are responsible for this.
- Flirting is the sum of non-verbal signals that suggest you are ready to engage in contact with another person. Flirting may be innate.
- There are three stages of romantic attraction: lust, infatuation and attachment.
- Heartbreak results in physiological changes in the brain that may affect our logical thinking. However, heartbreak can be eased by writing about the experience.

END OF CHAPTER TEST

Multiple-choice questions

1. Any areas used exclusively by an individual or group over a period of time are referred to as:
   A primary territory
   B secondary territory
   C tertiary territory
   D personal space.

2. You have a part-time job at a supermarket. A customer comes up to you and asks you where they could find the eggs. They stand about 1.5 metres from you. This distance is known as:
   A intimate distance
   B casual-personal distance
   C social-consultative distance
   D public distance.

3. Groups of gestures are called:
   A bunches
   B groups
   C crowds
   D clusters.

4. When we are attracted to someone, what physiological change occurs?
   A Our pupils constrict.
   B Our pupils dilate.
   C Our nose gets bigger.
   D Our nose gets smaller.

5. Which of the following chemicals is not released during the attachment stage?
   A dopamine
   B phenylethlamine
   C serotonin
   D oxytocin.

Short-answer questions

1. Imagine you are at a party. You notice two of your friends talking to each other. Describe the behaviours you might see that tell you they are flirting with each other.

2. Describe the three stages of attachment by writing a case study about a couple that has been married for 20 years.

The darker side of human nature

CHAPTER 8

There is so much good in the worst of us, and so much bad in the best of us, that it behoves all of us not to talk about the rest of us.

Robert Louis Stevenson

What is it that makes people good or makes people bad or evil? Are people born bad or do they become that way? And more importantly, in every good person is there an element of bad? This chapter will explore what it is about our human nature that sometimes leads us to behave in ways that are antisocial and destructive. We will first look at psychopathy (a personality disorder) and then later on in the chapter we'll look at why some good people do bad things.

Psychopathy

Did you know that about 1 per cent of the world's population is thought to be psychopathic? This is a surprising figure, as most people associate 'psychopath' with a person to be feared. Should we fear one out of every 100 people? There are many stereotypes about psychopaths. People believe, for example, that all prisoners must be psychopaths or that all psychopaths are violent and psychotic. These are generalisations, and are not fair or accurate.

What does 'psychopath' mean?

A **psychopath** is someone who shows certain personality traits and behaviours.

A psychopath suffers from psychopathy, a type of personality disorder that occurs across all cultures. Psychopaths tend to make good first impressions and often strike people as being relatively **normal**. Yet they are dishonest and undependable and engage in reckless and inappropriate behaviour for no reason other than they think it is fun.

Importantly, psychopaths seem to experience little empathy or guilt.

Furthermore, they have **dysfunctional** relationships as they have difficulty loving others or expressing their love. Psychopaths are impulsive and rarely learn from their mistakes. Psychopaths are more likely to be male, although the reason for this gender difference is unknown. Also, a person needs to be over the age of 18 years to be diagnosed as psychopathic.

Psychopath A person who suffers from psychopathy. They tend to be impulsive and reckless, and show little remorse or guilt for antisocial behaviours.

Normal The average, custom or standard level of something. In psychology it means being 'free' of mental or physical disorders.

Dysfunctional Working abnormally or incorrectly

105

Psychotic An abnormal condition of the mind; a generic psychiatric term for a mental state often described as involving a 'loss of contact with reality'

DID YOU KNOW?

Psychopathy does not mean **psychotic**. They are two separate types of psychological illness. Psychopathy is a personality disorder, while psychosis is a mental illness where a person loses their sense of reality and cannot function effectively in everyday life. Psychopaths, by comparison, are rational and understand (but simply do not care) that their actions are wrong in the eyes of society.

It might be possible for a psychopath to also be psychotic, or for a psychotic person to suffer from psychopathy. But we can not assume that the two go hand in hand, as it is rarely the case.

ACTIVITY 8.1 PSYCHOPATHY

1. What is psychopathy?
2. What are some characteristics of psychopathy?
3. What does it mean to be psychotic?
4. How is psychopathic different from psychotic?

How to measure psychopathy

Psychopathy Checklist Revised (PCL-R)
A diagnostic tool for measuring psychopathy; created by psychologist Robert Hare

Interpersonal is a person's ability to relate to and connect with other people.

Affective relates to emotional state. An 'affect' is another way of describing an emotion.

Lifestyle How a person usually behaves, their way of living

Antisocial Voluntary behaviour which breaks social norms and has no benefit to others, or shows disregard for others

Psychologists continue to argue the definition of psychopathy and how it could be measured. There are two diagnostic tools that psychologists can use to measure psychopathy. One is the the **Psychopathy Checklist Revised (PCL-R)**, created by psychologist Robert Hare in 2003. The other is the Psychopathic Personality Inventory (PPI). Both are valuable diagnostic tools, and have many similarities.

The PPI was the first tool to be created, and is based on the work of psychologist Hervey Cleckley, who was the first to study psychopathy in the 1940s. The simplest tool for measuring psychopathy, however, is Hare's PCL-R, which we will study in this chapter. Hare's model argues that psychopathy is a personality disorder with antisocial tendencies, and has four dimensions:

1. **Interpersonal** for example, cunning, conniving, manipulative/charismatic, pathological lying, glib/superficial, grandiose self-worth
2. **Affective** for example, callousness/lack of empathy, failure to accept responsibility, lack of remorse or guilt, shallow affect (shallow emotion)
3. **Lifestyle** for example, impulsive, irresponsible, parasitic, lack of realistic goals, stimulation seeking
4. **Antisocial** for example, early behavioural problems, juvenile delinquency, poor behavioural control, persistent rule breaking, criminal versatility.

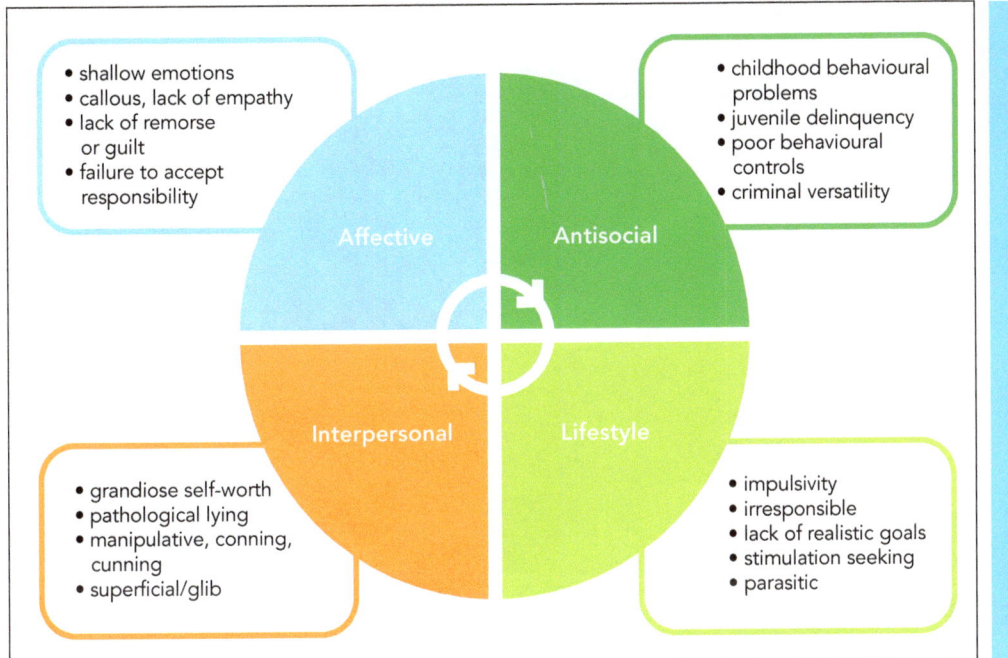

Figure 8.1 The four dimensions of PCL-R

It is thought that about 25 per cent of prisoners in Australian prisons meet the criteria for psychopathy. It would be wrong, however, to say that all psychopaths are criminals, or that all criminals are psychopaths. Psychopathic people can live a normal life and never commit crimes. In fact, criminal psychopaths are the minority – psychopaths in the normal world, such as the workplace, are the majority (Clarke 2005).

Executive psychopaths

Psychopaths are more likely to be living a normal, non-violent life. They harm their victims in non-violent ways. The most common psychopath is one in the workplace.

Psychopaths in the workplace can initially be very successful. Many psychopathic characteristics can be mistaken for leadership qualities – their cool decisiveness, fondness for the fast lane, charisma and cunning can be seen by employers as highly valuable characteristics. Yet psychopaths in the workplace can also be highly destructive, as they tend to lie and exploit others in order to get what they want. One in ten workplaces has a psychopathic colleague who functions effectively in normal society but victimises their colleagues, creating a toxic workplace (NZPA 2009).

Our own behaviour

We can probably *all* admit to behaving in a way characterised by one of the four dimensions of the PCL-R. We might manipulate others (e.g. when playing poker or selling cars), act impulsively (e.g. run a yellow light when driving) or be callous (e.g. push through others at a sale). And we have all been guilty of lying.

Figure 8.2 We all act impulsively at times.

So what distinguishes our questionable behaviour from psychopathy? It is that a psychopath *consistently* demonstrates psychopathic characteristics. It is also not just the characteristics that are present that make a psychopath, it is also what is absent or missing. A psychopath might be antisocial (a present characteristic) but they will also have little to no **prosocial** behaviour; that is, prosocial characteristics are missing. A normal person might have antisocial moments, but still understands the importance and value of acting prosocially, such as helping others.

Prosocial Voluntary behaviour intended to benefit another, such as helping, sharing and comforting others

Figure 8.3 Prosocial behaviour, such as helping, is not common in psychopaths.

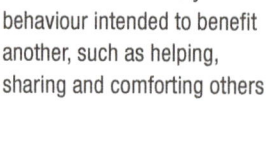

ACTIVITY 8.2 MEASURING PSYCHOPATHY

1. How can psychopathy be measured? Mention two well-known tools.
2. What are the characteristics of each of the four dimensions of the PCL-R?
3. Are all criminals psychopathic? Why or why not?
4. Are all psychopaths criminals? Why or why not?
5. Can you find an example of a psychopath who is not criminal? What about them suggests they could be psychopathic?
6. What is the difference between prosocial and antisocial behaviour? In your answer, give examples of each.

ACTIVITY 8.3 ERA: THE EFFECT OF LABELLING YOUNG PEOPLE AS PSYCHOPATHIC

The details of this ERA are available on the Cambridge GO website.

DID YOU KNOW?

In 1993 a gene called MAOA, located on the X chromosome was discovered. Nicknamed the 'warrior gene', MAOA is thought to be responsible for antisocial behaviour. The gene essentially cleans up our brain by producing a protein that breaks down neurotransmitters that have outlived their usefulness, such as dopamine. If the gene is not working properly then an increase of these neurotransmitters can cause abnormal mood and behaviour.

However, is this a myth to be busted? We need to be critical of how we think about research. Although having the gene makes it more likely one could be aggressive, could there be many other factors involved in the appearance of aggression? Environmental factors, such as smoking, appear to be a trigger for the gene to express itself (Yong 2010). Nature and nurture both seem to play a role.

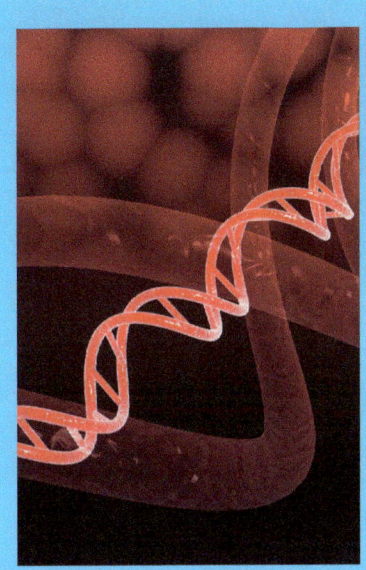

Figure 8.4 Is there such a thing as dangerous DNA?

Abu Ghraib and the Lucifer Effect

How do good, ordinary people do bad or evil things? Dr Phillip Zimbardo, a famous social psychologist and researcher, believes that whilst most people are good, they can be persuaded to engage in antisocial destructive behaviour. Zimbardo's theory is that people might behave badly due to what he calls the 'Lucifer Effect'.

The **Lucifer Effect** is the transformation of a person's character from good to bad. Zimbardo named his psychological theory based upon the story of the angel Lucifer, who became the Devil as he disobeyed God and was proud of his defiance.

For the rest of this chapter we will look at what occurred at the now infamous prison Abu Ghraib in Iraq, and how the Lucifer Effect can be used to explain the terrible behaviour shown by US soldiers towards Iraqi prisoners.

Lucifer Effect The transformation of a person's character causing good people to commit bad behaviour

Background to Abu Ghraib

Abu Ghraib is a prison located near Baghdad and was built in the 1950s. In October 2002, Saddam Hussein, President of Iraq, gave **amnesty** to all prisoners in Iraq. Once empty, Abu Ghraib was looted and vandalised, and nearly all official documentation of what occurred there was destroyed. It was rumoured that the prison already had a dark history of abuse and death of prisoners. Then the US invaded Iraq.

Amnesty A government pardon for past misdeeds

Figure 8.5 Saddam Hussein, President of Iraq in 2002

Figure 8.6 Abu Ghraib is a prison located near Baghdad, Iraq

Figure 8.7 George W Bush, US President during the Abu Ghraib scandal

The US invaded Iraq in 2003 as part of their 'war against terror' and reprisal for the attacks in New York on 11 September 2001. President Saddam Hussein went into hiding. The US occupation forces (also known as the US coalition) began using Abu Ghraib as a detention facility.

ACTIVITY 8.4 THE LUCIFER EFFECT AND ABU GHRAIB

1. Robert Louis Stevenson is a famous author who wrote *Treasure Island* and *The Strange Case of Dr Jekyll and Mr Hyde*. Look back at the quote at the beginning of the chapter by Robert Louis Stevenson – what do you think he meant when he said this?
2. What is the Lucifer Effect?
3. What is Abu Ghraib? In your answer give a brief outline of its history.

What happened at Abu Ghraib?

In January 2004 the US Army appointed Major General Antonio Mario Taguba to investigate allegations of abuse at Abu Ghraib.

At the centre of the allegations was the 800th Military Police (MP) Brigade of the US Army. They were in charge of Tier 1A at Abu Ghraib. Tier 1A was a block reserved for prisoners who were thought to possess Iraqi intelligence regarding the whereabouts of Saddam Hussein or the location of weapons of mass destruction.

One detainee was forced to stand on a box, with a hood over his head and wires attached to his body. The prisoner was led to believe that if he fell off the box he would die from electrocution. In fact, the electrodes were false and aimed at creating anxiety and fear, rather than death. When questioned about this particular incident, an officer replied that their job was to keep them awake and that 'MI (military intelligence) wanted to get them to talk' (Taguba 2004, p. 18).

Figure 8.8 Anti Abu Ghraib protest

There were also reports of other abuse, such as detainees being forced to denounce their religious beliefs and force-fed pork and alcohol (Higham & Stephens 2004).

Specifically, Major General Taguba found evidence (which he included in his report) of many other horrific acts, some of which included:

a Punching, slapping and kicking detainees; jumping on naked feet
b Forcing detainees to remove their clothing and remain naked for days
c Arranging naked detainees into a pile and jumping on them
d Pouring cold water on naked detainees
e Beating detainees with a broom handle or a chair
f Videotaping and photographing naked detainees
g Male detainees forced to wear female underwear
h Placing a dog chain around detainees' necks and forcing them to behave like an animal
i Taking photos of dead detainees
j Using military working dogs (without muzzles) to intimidate and frighten detainees with the threat of an attack, and in one instance, a military dog biting and wounding a detainee
k Breaking chemical lights and pouring the phosphoric liquid onto detainees
l Threatening detainees with charged pistols.

(Taguba 2004).

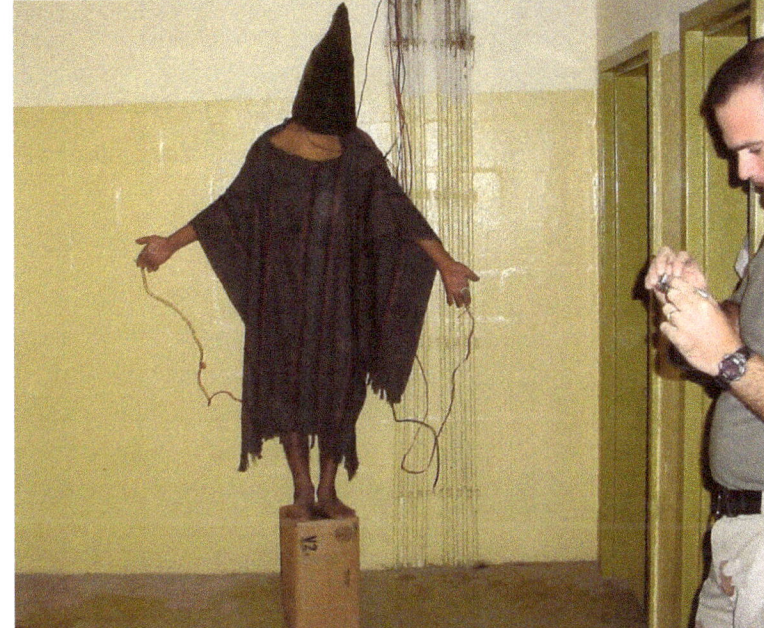

Figure 8.9 This hooded detainee believed that he would die from electrocution.

Major General Taguba also found that the facilities of Abu Ghraib were overwhelmed. The prison was holding more prisoners than it was built for – there were more than 5000 prisoners. It was over-capacity and therefore overcrowded. He also found that the prison was significantly under-resourced and under-manned. These problems contributed to poor living facilities, lack of accountability by officers, and escapes and riots by detainees.

ACTIVITY 8.5 MAJOR GENERAL TAGUBA

1. Who is Major General Taguba and why was he at Abu Ghraib?
2. What did Major General Tabuga find that was evidence of abuse of detainees at Abu Ghraib?
3. What were some other issues Major General Taguba discovered about the conditions at Abu Ghraib?
4. How do you think these conditions might have affected the detainees at the prison?
5. How do you think these conditions might have affected the soldiers working at the prison?

The consequences of Abu Ghraib

Photos of the abuse (taken by the soldiers themselves as 'trophies') were eventually leaked to the media, leading to the investigation in 2004. The then-President George Bush claimed he had been unaware of the issue. He blamed lower-level officials, particularly those who were at Abu Ghraib at the time. Brigadier General Janis Karpinski, who was in charge of Abu Ghraib, was forced to resign. Furthermore, Major General Taguba who originally investigated the incidents at Abu Ghraib was also forced to resign.

Figure 8.10 Letter from the US Army informing Brigadier General Karpinksi to stand down from her position in Iraq

Abu Ghraib is a violation of the Geneva Convention

Figure 8.11 The United Nations in Geneva where the Geneva Convention was agreed to by nations.

Under the **Geneva Convention**, it is illegal to humiliate prisoners. Clearly, prisoners were humiliated several times at Abu Ghraib. It is also illegal to torture or kill prisoners, but furthermore, it is also illegal under the Geneva Convention to *threaten* to kill or torture prisoners. But history tells us that torture has been practised for hundreds and thousands of years. Is there ever a time that torture can be allowed or is excusable?

Geneva Convention
A set of agreements between nations of the treatment of victims of war. The agreements were negotiated in the aftermath of World War II.

ACTIVITY 8.6 CLASS DEBATE

Is torture ever allowed or excusable? Imagine a terrorist has planted a bomb in Melbourne – thousands of lives are at stake. Do that individual's rights override the right of thousands? Divide the class into two groups to discuss both sides of this debate.

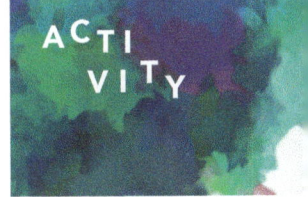

Why do good people do bad things?

To understand what happened at Abu Ghraib we need to consider what the officers and personnel were like *before* they took up their roles at the prison. Were they already 'bad apples' before they were at Abu Ghraib?

Zimbardo argues that rather than the soldiers being bad apples, perhaps the situation they had been put in was a 'bad barrel' (Zimbardo 2008). In other words, what happened at Abu Ghraib was due to the environment the soldiers were working in. According to the Lucifer Effect, a good bunch of soldiers had become transformed into bad soldiers. Their characters were transformed by the environment and conditions at Abu Ghraib.

Past history – the Stanford Prison Experiment

Zimbardo was asked to act as an expert witness in defence of one of the officers at Abu Ghraib. The US Army saw similarities between what occurred at Abu Ghraib and what happened in Zimbardo's Stanford Prison Experiment.

Figure 8.12 Zimbardo's famous simulated prison study was conducted in the basement of one of the buildings at Stanford University.

In the basement at Stanford University in the USA in 1971, Zimbardo conducted a study with 24 university students who volunteered to participate. Participants were given roles of either 'prison guard' or 'prisoner'. Zimbardo described them all as 'good apples' prior to the experiment. After six days, Zimbardo was forced to terminate the experiment due to the trauma experienced by the students who were playing the 'prisoners'. The students playing the 'guards' had become antisocial, carrying out humiliating acts. Afterwards Zimbardo admitted that he and his team of researchers had failed to provide constraints to prevent prisoner abuse, and that instead the 'good apples' had been encouraged by the procedures of the study to act in creatively bad ways.

ACTIVITY 8.7 ABU GHRAIB AND THE STANFORD PRISON EXPERIMENT

1. According to the Geneva Convention, what sort of behaviour towards prisoners is considered illegal?
2. What do you think Dr Phillip Zimbardo means by the soldiers of Abu Ghraib being from a 'bad barrel' (rather than being 'bad apples')?
3. How can the Lucifer Effect be applied to soldiers at Abu Ghraib?
4. What was the Stanford Prison Experiment? (You can also search online for more information at http://www.prisonexp.org/.)
5. What were some of the similarities between the Stanford Prison Experiment and what happenedAbu Ghraib?

Abu Ghraib – the social and environmental features

Let us now consider some of the social and environmental features that may have influenced soldiers' behaviour at Abu Ghraib:

1 **Training**
   Officers claimed they had no training prior to Abu Ghraib. When they arrived in Iraq they participated in a 45-minute lesson on cultural awareness. They also further claimed they had little supervision by their superior officers.

2 **Nonstop work**
   The prison was under-manned. This meant that military officers were overworked. There were rarely rostered days off. Such a pattern was considered usual at the time. However, fatigue and stress were common results.

3 **Living conditions at Abu Ghraib**
   There were poor living conditions – both for detainees and officers. The prison had no sewage system – only portable toilets and holes in the ground. As they were not regularly emptied, they overflowed. The prison had inadequate shower systems and water was rationed. Furthermore, electricity failed regularly due to inadequate electricity generators.

4 **The broader context: Occupation of Iraq**
   Abu Ghraib was the focus of nightly mortar attacks by Iraqi groups who were furious about the US occupation of Iraq. Soldiers slept inside the walls of the prison following deaths of comrades. The continuing attacks created fear amongst soldiers.

5 **Prisoner riots and the fear factor**
   Detainees often rioted due to poor living conditions and the poor food. They would often riot when there were mortar attacks, as soldiers would have more to handle and cope with. Detainees would create weapons or get weapons smuggled in, and officers therefore worked in a situation of uncertainty and fear.

6 **Breakdown in military order**
   The Commander Brigadier General Janis Karpinski stayed at Camp Victory near Baghdad Airport, not at Abu Ghraib so she was off-site. She was also told Tier 1A was a 'special site' under supervision by military intelligence and so she never visited it. Therefore, as Karpinski was never allowed to be fully in charge, soldiers often disregarded her command. This led to a breakdown in military order.

7 **Anonymity of authority**
   Military personnel often did not wear ID or identify themselves, and they directed officers to not address each other by their names. Therefore they all became anonymous and lacked accountability for their actions.

8 **Obedience to authority**
   Superior officers encouraged mental and physical abuse of detainees. Officers claimed that they were directed to 'Loosen this guy up for us ... make sure he has a bad night ... make sure he gets the treatment' (Taguba 2004).

ACTIVITY 8.8 REFLECT

1 Out of the eight features listed, which do you think are the four most influential features? Why?
2 Which do you think are the two least influential features? Why?

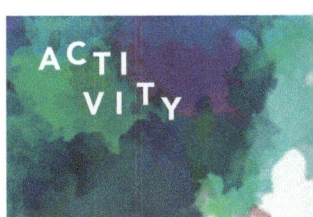

The social-psychological concepts at play

There were socio-psychological concepts at play at Abu Ghraib. These included groupthink, conformity, obedience to authority, deindividuation and dehumanisation.

Groupthink is where group members behave in the interest of group harmony. People tend to make decisions and opinions that match the group consensus. Therefore, if one officer decided to act in a certain way, the others may have followed as part of 'groupthink'. **Conformity** is where people feel pressure to act a particular way as everybody around them is acting that way. Peer pressure is an example of conformity. Therefore, soldiers who observed other soldiers behaving in an antisocial way (and encouraged and praised by their superiors) may have felt pressure to do the same. **Obedience to authority** is common in the army due to the chain of command. Soldiers are trained to be obedient and to follow orders from their superiors. The superior officers at Abu Ghraib encouraged and praised the behaviour of their soldiers. One solider reported that MI said, 'Good job, they're breaking down real fast. They answer every question. They're giving out good information … and keep up the good work.' (Taguba 2004, p. 19).

Two of the most influential factors for antisocial behaviour, however, are deindividuation and dehumanisation.

Groupthink Where people make decisions and behave in accordance with the group consensus, to maintain group harmony

Conformity Where people behave in a way that is considered normal and acceptable by group standards. Peer pressure is an example of conformity.

Obedience to authority Where in a hierarchical society, people obey the instructions from people above them in status, e.g. army

What are deindividuation and dehumanisation?

Deindividuation occurs when people are anonymous, resulting in that person feeling they have lost their sense of self or identity. People who are deindividuated are more likely to commit antisocial or aggressive acts. As soldiers in Tier 1A did not wear ID badges, or call each other by their names, they felt anonymous. The sense of anonymity resulted in a lack of accountability for actions and therefore a greater likelihood of antisocial acts being committed. This may also explain why they took photos of their abuse. They may have had a moral disengagement about what they were doing due to their anonymity.

Dehumanisation is when people of an 'out group' are considered to not be human, and instead are seen as objects or animals. Essentially, dehumanisation applies to any processes that make people appear less human. Examples of dehumanisation at Abu Ghraib included the officers making detainees act like dogs, or putting bags on their heads, or calling them by non-human names. These acts would have made the detainees appear less human to the soldiers. By dehumanising the detainees, officers would have found their acts of abuse easier to carry out.

Deindividuation Where people lose their sense of self and feel anonymous, can lead to more antisocial behaviour due to people feeling a lack of responsibility and accountability

Dehumanisation Where people of an 'out group' are considered to not be human, and instead are seen as objects or animals

What do you think?

Do you think the soldiers at Abu Ghraib behaved the way they did because they were already bad? Or did they become that way due to the situation they were in? Furthermore, if this is the case, is it an appropriate excuse for their behaviour?

Zimbardo's testimony as an expert witness did not sway the legal system. The officers involved in the abuse were sentenced to prison. Zimbardo felt that the punishment for the individual soldiers was a marketing exercise by the US government who wanted to save their reputation, but also did not want to take responsibility for what occurred.

Figure 8.13 Dehumanising is where people are not considered human and not treated as human beings.

ACTIVITY 8.9 COMPREHENSION

1. Name the five psychological concepts that may have influenced the soldiers at Abu Ghraib.
2. Define the terms 'groupthink', 'conformity' and 'obedience to authority'.
3. Do you think there was evidence of groupthink, conformity and obedience to authority at Abu Ghraib? What evidence is there?
4. Define the terms 'deindividuation' and 'dehumanisation'.
5. What evidence was there of these two factors at Abu Ghraib?
6. Do you think the actions of soldiers at Abu Ghraib were due to the Lucifer Effect? Why or why not?
7. Do you think the punishment of soldiers at Abu Ghraib was justified? Why or why not?

Researchers showed a short film to babies aged between six months and one year. In the film a circle with eyes tries to climb a hill while a triangle tries to force it down. A square tries to help the circle up the slope. After the film, researchers observed which shape the babies favoured the most by timing how long they looked at a picture of each shape. Eighty per cent of the babies chose to look at the square over the triangle. It appears that some sense of good and evil may be innate (*Telegraph*, London, 2010).

END OF CHAPTER SUMMARY

- A psychopath suffers from psychopathy, a personality disorder.
- Psychosis is a mental state often described as a loss of contact with reality and can include hallucinations and delusions.
- Robert Hare's checklist, PCL-R, outlines four dimensions of psychopathy, including interpersonal, affective, lifestyle and antisocial.
- Most psychopaths live a normal life, e.g. executive psychopaths.
- The Lucifer Effect is the transformation of a person's character from good to bad.
- Social and environmental factors affecting soldiers at Abu Ghraib included context, living conditions, prisoner riots, breakdown in military order, training, nonstop work, anonymity of authority and obedience to authority.
- The major psychological factors at play at Abu Ghraib included dehumanisation and deindividuation.

END OF CHAPTER TEST

Multiple-choice questions

1. Hare's PCL-R describes four dimensions. The **affective dimension** includes:
   A lying, grandiose self-worth and cunning
   B lack of empathy and guilt, failure to accept responsibility
   C juvenile delinquency, persistent rule breaking
   D impulsiveness and irresponsibility.

2. At Abu Ghraib officers did not wear ID at Tier 1A. This is an example of:
   A anonymity of authority
   B context
   C fear factor
   D boredom.

3. Dehumanisation is:
   A peer pressure
   B conformity
   C making humans appear less human
   D losing identity, becoming anonymous.

4. Not wearing ID and not calling each other by their names is also an example of:
   A fear
   B deindividuation
   C dehumanisation
   D conformity.

5. Placing detainees on a leash or putting bags over their heads caused:
   A deindividuation
   B dehumanisation
   C anonymity
   D breakdown in military order.

Short-answer questions

1. One of your friends says that someone who has hallucinations is psychopathic. Are they accurate? Why or why not? Explain.

2. Do you think the soldiers at Abu Ghraib behaved the way they did because they were already bad? Why or why not?

3. Place yourself in the shoes of a US soldier at Abu Ghraib. What would you have done in their circumstances? How would you have behaved? Discuss as a class.

Conduct and misconduct: the right or wrong of ethics

CHAPTER 9

The meaning of good and bad, of better and worse, is simply helping or hurting.

Ralph Waldo Emerson

A primary goal of psychology and psychiatry is to improve people's lives and to help them. To do this, however, sometimes research is required. Or in the case of caring for patients, psychologists and psychiatrists have to choose treatment for people. These decisions require a great deal of responsibility and duty of care. Professionals have to treat people with respect and explain to them their rights.

Ethics – what are they?

Ethics are moral guidelines, or rules of conduct. They protect patients, research participants, the profession itself (whether it be psychology or psychiatry, for example), and they also protect the professional themselves (the psychologist or psychiatrist). Ethics help us distinguish right from wrong.

Ethics for psychologists and psychiatrists

Across the world, professions in each country have their own regulatory boards and codes of ethics that professionals must abide by. In Australia, psychologists and psychiatrists are registered through the **Australian Health Practitioner Regulation Agency (AHPRA)**. AHPRA is responsible for the registration and accreditation of ten health professions in Australia, including psychology, medicine, nursing and dental. In Australia, psychiatrists follow the medical code of ethics (that all doctors must follow) as well as the **Royal Australian and New Zealand College of Psychiatrists (RANZCP)** Code of Ethics. Psychologists must abide by the **Australian Psychological Society (APS)** Code of Ethics.

Ethics are moral guidelines, or rules of conduct, that help us distinguish right from wrong.

Australian Health Practitioner Regulation Agency (AHPRA) Responsible for the registration and accreditation of ten health professions across Australia, including psychology, medicine, nursing and dental

Royal Australian and New Zealand College of Psychiatrists (ANZCP) Psychiatrists in Australia abide by their code of ethics

Australian Psychological Society (APS) Psychologists in Australia abide by their code of ethics.

There are similarities between their codes of ethics and some of the main principles are shown in the following table.

Table 9.1 Comparison of the RANZCP and APS codes of ethics

RANZCP Code of Ethics (Psychiatrists) 2010	APS Code of Ethics (Psychologists) (2007)
Psychiatrists shall: • respect the humanity and dignity of every patient • provide the best psychiatric care for patients • maintain confidentiality of patients and their families • seek valid consent from their patients before undertaking treatment	A: Respect for the rights and dignity of persons. This includes: justice, respect, informed consent, privacy, confidentiality, release of information to clients and collection of client information from associated parties
Psychiatrists shall: • not misuse their professional knowledge and skills • shall comply with ethical principles	B: Propriety. This includes: competence, record keeping, professional responsibility, collaborating with others, accepting clients of other professionals, psychological assessments and research.
Psychiatrists shall: • not exploit patients • uphold the integrity of the medical profession	C: Integrity. This includes: reputable behaviour, communication, non-exploitation, authorship, financial arrangements, ethics investigations and concerns.

Why do we need codes of ethics?

Although most of us would like to think we know the difference between right and wrong, not everybody is in agreement. What might be seen as the 'right thing to do' by one person might horrify another.

Therefore, **codes of ethics** have been written so that regardless of someone's personal opinion, they *must follow the rules*. If the code of ethics is broken, they *have broken the rules – regardless of their personal moral judgment*. If a professional breaks their code of ethics, they can be deregistered and no longer able to practise.

This chapter will now consider one of the greatest ethical scandals in Australia.

Code of ethics A set of ethical guidelines that act as rules that professionals must abide by. If they breach the code they can be deregistered.

CHAPTER 9 CONDUCT AND MISCONDUCT: THE RIGHT OR WRONG OF ETHICS

> **ACTIVITY 9.1 CODES OF ETHICS**
>
> 1. What are ethics?
> 2. What is AHPRA and what does it do?
> 3. What do RANZCP and APS stand for?
> 4. The APS has three main principles of ethics: what are they?
> 5. To whom does the APS Code of Ethics apply – psychologists or psychiatrists?
> 6. To whom does the RANZCP Code of Ethics apply – psychologists or psychiatrists?
> 7. Choose two principles of ethics from the RANZCP and APS codes, and explain them.
> 8. Why do professionals have a code of ethics?

Dr Harry Bailey and the Chelmsford Hospital scandal

Dr Harry Bailey practised as a psychiatrist in New South Wales from the 1950s until the 1980s. He later became known as the 'Jekyll and Hyde' psychiatrist of the Chelmsford Private Hospital (Chandler & MacDonald 1991). A **Royal Commission** was established in 1988 to investigate his practices and Bailey was found to be responsible for the death of 24 patients and the resulting suicides of another 19 patients.

The beginning

Dr Harry Bailey was born in NSW in 1922, and was a pharmacist's assistant before getting married. He eventually went to university to complete a medical degree. Bailey specialised in psychiatry and, before his downfall, was one of the most reputable psychiatrists in NSW.

In 1954 Bailey won a fellowship to study with eminent psychiatrists Dr Ewan Cameron in Canada and Dr William Sargent in London. At this time **psychosurgery** was a popular form of treatment for mental illness. Sargant and Cameron favoured treatments such as **deep sleep therapy** and **lobotomy**. For Sargant and Cameron, they believed that the one way to beat mental illness was through electricity, drugs and chemically induced sleep. Their perspective and practices greatly influenced Bailey.

What was 'deep sleep therapy'?

In deep sleep therapy (DST) patients were sedated with drugs until they were unconscious and then kept in this state of unconsciousness for an extended period. In other words, it was an induced coma through the use of drugs such as **narcotics**. Sometimes deep sleep was also referred to as 'narcosis'. A common narcotic used was **barbiturates**. Barbiturates were favoured by Bailey when he induced comas on his patients at Chelmsford Hospital in NSW. Often patients were kept for up to three months in a state of deep sleep, being woken up long enough for bouts of other therapies such as **electroconvulsive therapy (ECT)**.

As we learnt in the first chapter, if administered correctly, ECT is a safe and successful treatment. However, chillingly, psychiatrists such as Bailey, Cameron and Sargant, tended to use DST to overcome patients' *refusal* to have ECT. Furthermore, they misused ECT – it was administered more frequently and at higher and more dangerous doses.

Royal Commission A major government public inquiry into an issue

Psychosurgery ny surgery on the brain for the purpose of assisting symptoms of mental illness

Deep sleep therapy (also known as DST) Where a person is in a coma (unconscious state) induced by drugs

Lobotomy (also known as frontal lobotomy) Surgery that disconnects the nerves from the frontal lobe from the rest of the brain

Narcotics Any drugs that induce sleep or decrease sensitivity to pain, such as opiates

Barbiturates Depressant drugs that act as sedatives, and are highly addictive

Electroconvulsive therapy (ECT) A form of medical therapy where low levels of electrical impulses are applied to an anesthetised patient's skull (and brain)

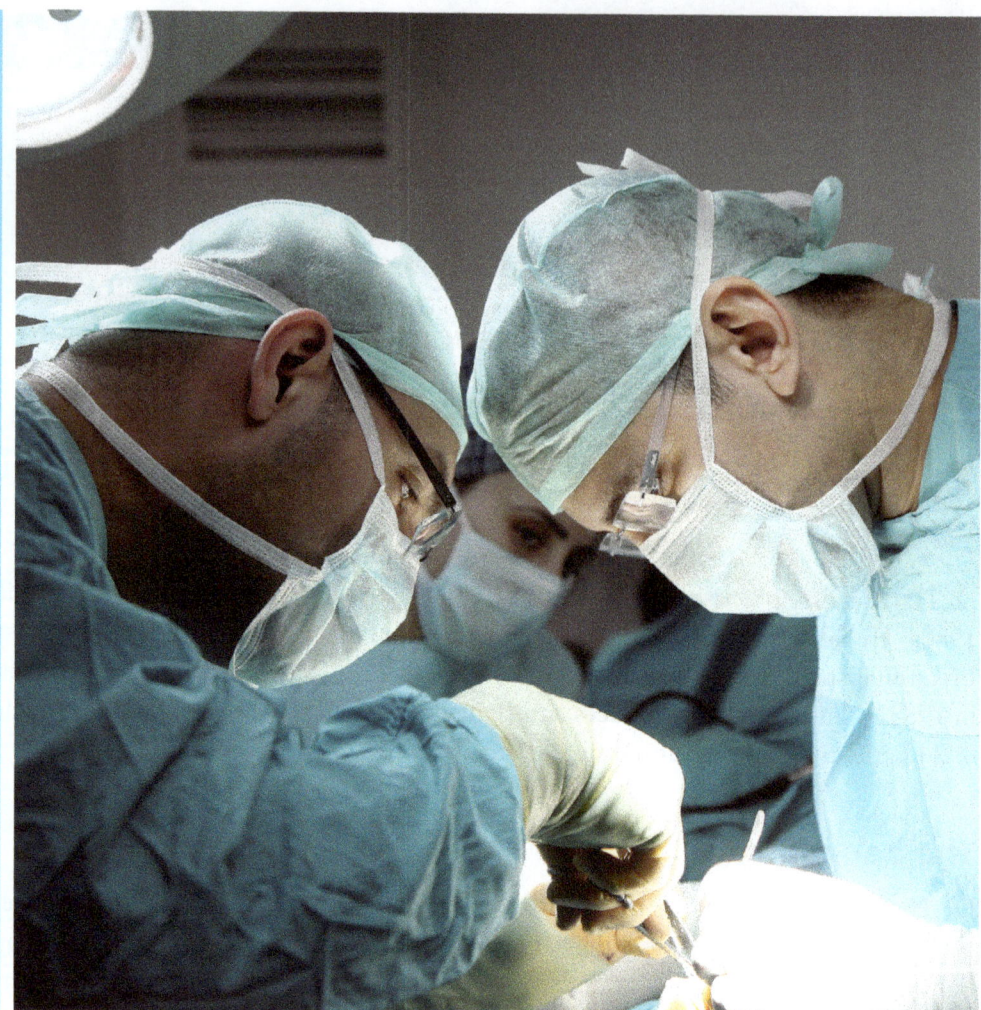

Figure 9.1 A lobotomy is surgery where nerves from the frontal lobe are disconnected from the rest of the brain.

The risks of DST

There were many risks for patients in being given DST. As patients were kept in constant sedation, they had weakened immune systems and were more vulnerable to contracting other illnesses. Being unconscious and immobile further increased complications. After treatment those who survived reported hallucinations and significant muscle weakness (Walton versus Gardiner 1993).

Bailey used DST to treat patients with depression, anorexia nervosa, schizophrenia and drug addiction. In his first two years at Chelmsford Hospital, five patients died during DST. More deaths followed until an inquest was held in 1967 (four years after Bailey began at Chelmsford). The coroner, however, did not find Bailey culpable and instead was impressed by the reputable psychiatrist.

The Citizens Committee on Human Rights, a part of the Church of Scientology, received information from a nurse about Bailey's mistreatment. They campaigned for years for a Royal Commission to be held to investigate Bailey's practices at Chelmsford.

In 1974, an investigation by the ABC television programme *Four Corners* further fuelled public concern about Bailey's practices. The ABC reported on Bailey's use of lobotomies. By that stage he had conducted 150 **leucotomies** – a type of lobotomy (Mitchell 2002).

Leucotomy (also known as frontal leucotomy) Surgery that cuts through the white matter in the prefrontal lobe in the brain. In practice, there is little difference between a leucotomy and a lobotomy.

The death toll increased

Bailey closed down his practice at Chelmsford in 1979 due to the growing pressure and scrutiny he was under by both the media and the government. By this time 24 patients had died during DST at Chelmsford. The year before, Sharon Hamilton, Bailey's patient and lover, died. She sadly committed suicide, and left Bailey as one of the beneficiaries of her estate. Bailey's reputation was damaged further by this. It was felt he may have influenced Hamilton and therefore exploited her.

Bailey clearly misused his professional power on many levels. His colleagues knew of his sexual relationships with female patients and other staff at the hospital. Additionally, despite receiving criticisms for some of his written articles and research, Bailey often talked up his achievements.

Regardless of all this, Bailey's wife remained incredibly loyal, as did some of Bailey's past lovers and colleagues. He was described by many as handsome and charming.

Complaints were made to Sir Henry Roth who was at the time the Professor of Psychiatry at Cambridge University. Sir Henry acknowledged that what had occurred was inhumane, but also urged that the issue be kept confidential for the time being (Chandler & MacDonald 1991).

In 1983 Bailey was finally charged with manslaughter, but this charge was dismissed in 1985. By this stage the media pressure was intense.

Bailey was informed that a Royal Commission was to be established to investigate reports of unethical medical treatment at the hospital. He contacted his old mentor Dr William Sargant in London, and asked if he would testify at the Commission in Bailey's favour. They had continued a strong relationship throughout the years, and Bailey had often spoken to his colleagues about the morbid competition between the two to see 'who could keep their patients in the deepest coma without killing them'.

Figure 9.2 Dr Harry Bailey

Sargant, however, disappointed Bailey. Sargant destroyed all communication he had between himself and Bailey, and also destroyed communication from Dr Ewan Cameron as well. Sargant was fearful. His response to Bailey's request to testify was that he would testify but that 'I should have found myself supporting the prosecution and not the defence'. (Streatfield 2006, p. 255)

On 8 September in 1985, Bailey overdosed on barbiturates – the medication he had favoured when inducing comas in his own patients. He wrote in his suicide note, 'Let it be known that the Scientologists and the forces of madness have won. (Chandler & MacDonald 1991).

The whistleblowers

Tensions between Scientologists and psychiatrists were strong at the time in Australia. Scientology was criticised by many around the world, particularly psychiatrists, who were concerned about their practices. So strong was the criticism that Australia did not recognise the Church of Scientology as a religious faith until 1973.

Scientology was one of the main whistleblowers on Chelmsford Private Hospital. It was alleged by media that Scientologists were upset about Australia not recognising their religion until 1973, and that they had focused on prominent psychiatrists as part of a 'witch hunt' (Chandler & MacDonald 1991). So rather than the Church of Scientology's claim against Chelmsford being altruistic, they may have had hidden motives.

Regardless of the motivations, the practice of deep sleep therapy was unethical and had to be addressed.

The Royal Commission

The Royal Commission heard evidence from October 1988 until July 1990 and found that 1127 patients received DST at the Chelmsford Hospital for a variety of complaints, including depression, anorexia nervosa, stress, drug and alcohol problems, neuroses and schizophrenia. Of these patients, 24 people had died at the hospital due to Bailey's deep sleep therapy. An additional 24 people survived the treatment, but of those, 19 committed suicide within a year of being released from the hospital. Sadly for those who survived, there were a number of cases of brain damage and other physical injury (*Walton v. Gardiner* (1993)).

The Royal Commission found evidence not just of medical negligence, but also obstruction of justice and fraud. Firstly, there was evidence to suggest that many patients had not signed consent forms. Further, employees at the hospital had destroyed the unsigned consent forms prior to the Royal Commission being held. Secondly, there was also evidence that Dr Harry Bailey had signed fraudulent death certificates that did not accurately state the cause of death. In this way, Dr Bailey avoided coroner's inquests. It turned out that out of the 24 patients who had died, 17 of these had false death certificates (*Walton v. Gardiner* (1993)).

ACTIVITY 9.2 COMPREHENSION

1. Who is Dr Harry Bailey?
2. What is DST?
3. Why is DST also referred to as 'narcosis'?
4. Is ECT dangerous? Carefully consider what you have read in this chapter as well as in Chapter 1.
5. When did Dr Bailey close down his practice at Chelmsford? How many patients had died?
6. Who are Dr William Sargant and Dr Ewan Cameron?
7. What other criticisms did the Royal Commission make of Dr Bailey?
8. What is a Royal Commission? Have there been any recent Royal Commissions in other issues that you are aware of? Discuss as a class.

The unethical behaviour of Dr Harry Bailey

Was Dr Harry Bailey's treatment of patients unethical? It is useful now to consider the ethical principles outlined by the RANZCP and APS as stated at the beginning of this chapter.

1 **Psychiatrists shall provide the best attainable psychiatric care for their patients (RANZCP 2010)**

   Despite criticisms by his peers, and the death of other patients, Dr Bailey continued to use the dangerous practice of DST and misuse ECT. Due to his misuse of ECT he also contributed to ECT gaining a bad reputation amongst the general public.

2 **Informed consent**

   Informed consent is where the nature, risks and purpose of a treatment are explained to a patient in plain language. Further, the person's rights need to be explained, such as their right to **confidentiality**. For both psychologists and psychiatrists, this is a very important ethical principle to abide by. It respects the rights and dignity of all people. Dr Harry Bailey not only did not gain informed consent from his patients, he also was found to have used DST to avoid refusal to ECT. This was a terrible action. Further, he was later found to have destroyed any evidence of his failure to gain informed consent.

Informed consent Consent given where a person understands the nature, risks and purpose of treatment or research

Confidentiality A person's right to have their name withheld and their information kept private

Figure 9.3 Confidentiality is a right of patients that should be explained to people prior to them giving informed consent.

Multiple relationships (also known as 'dual relationships') When a psychiatrist or psychologist has a patient that is also their friend/colleague/student/trainee/intimate

3 Conflict of interests and exploitation of patients

Professionals, such as psychologists and psychiatrists, should avoid engaging in **multiple relationships** that may impair their effectiveness, objectivity and competence. In Australia, a psychiatrist or psychologist may not have a relationship with a patient or former patient until two years has passed since treatment ended.

Dr Harry Bailey was known for having relationships with his patients and staff that were of a dual nature. He was also known for exploiting patients and employees by embarking on sexual relationships. For example, Sharon Hamilton, who sadly died, left him as a beneficiary of her will.

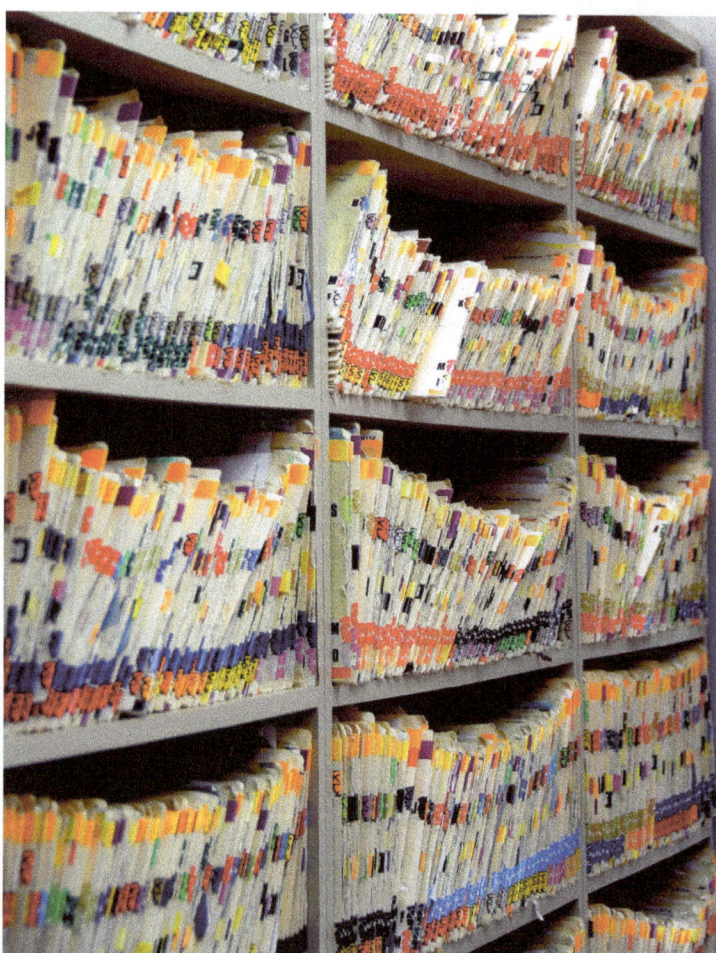

4 Recordkeeping

In Australia, health professionals must keep accurate records for a minimum of seven years. For people under the age of 18, records must be kept until they are at least 25 years of age. Dr Harry Bailey did not do this, and was also found guilty of destroying paperwork.

5 Reputable behaviour

Psychiatrists and psychologists must avoid engaging in disreputable behaviour that reflects poorly upon themselves and also on their profession. Not only did Dr Harry Bailey bring himself into disrepute, he also tainted the reputation of the Chelmsford Hospital and its employees. Dr Bailey's behaviour also tarnished the reputation of other psychiatrists, as well as the still-used treatment ECT, which is used safely and successfully in Australia.

Figure 9.4 Records must be kept for a minimum of seven years in Australia.

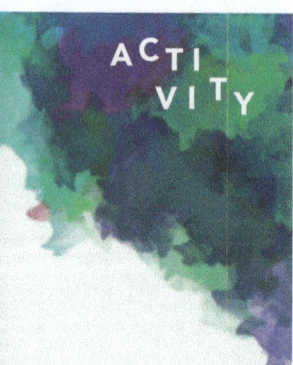

ACTIVITY 9.3 DR BAILEY

1. Choose two of the ethical principles from the above list that Dr Bailey breached and explain them.
2. Are there any other ethical principles you think Dr Bailey may have also breached that are not listed above? Name them and explain why.
3. What surprised you the most about Dr Bailey's behaviour?
4. What do you think would have been the consequences for Dr Bailey had he appeared in front of the Royal Commission?

DID YOU KNOW?

Dr Ewan Cameron, one of Dr Harry Bailey's mentors, became infamous for his use of DST and another therapy called 'psychic-driving'. **Psychic-driving** later became known as 'brainwashing' or mind control. Cameron was attempting to 'wipe the patients' minds clean' and then reprogram them (Ross 2006).

In the first stage of treatment patients would be placed in **sensory deprivation** (dark rooms, no interaction with others), and then into a very deep sleep by DST. The deep sleep reduced them to a vegetative state. They would then be given high doses of ECT and drugs. The second stage of the therapy was 'psychic-driving'. This was where hundreds of hours of tape would be played into the patient's ears through headphones or a special helmet. The tape would be of either a negative or positive type. For example, 'There's something wrong with you, nobody likes you' or 'People like you. You like people.' (Streatfield 2006, pp. 227–8).

Cameron's treatment of patients was highly unethical and a violation of human rights. The CIA in America became very interested in Cameron's techniques and they funded some of his research, Cameron accepted and became part of CIA's notorious MKULTRA project.

Want to know more? Search for 'MKULTRA' on the internet.

Psychic-driving A method used by Dr Ewan Cameron to reprogram the mind of a sedated patient by playing them hours of commands on tape. This method also became known as brainwashing.

Sensory deprivation A person is placed in a room with no sensory stimulation, e.g. dark empty rooms, or bright white rooms with no windows or people, etc.

ACTIVITY 9.4 PSYCHIC-DRIVING

1. What is psychic-driving and how is DST used in it? Outline the steps of psychic-driving.
2. What does 'sensory deprivation' mean?
3. Give an example of what a negative psychic-driving tape would say compared to a positive psychic-driving tape.
4. Why is psychic-driving nicknamed 'brainwashing'?
5. Why was Cameron's treatment of patients considered unethical? Refer to the principles he breached in your answer.

ACTIVITY 9.5 RESEARCH ASSIGNMENT

Dr Jayant Patel was charged in 2010 with three counts of manslaughter charges and one count of grievous bodily harm for surgery he had completed whilst working at Bundaberg Hospital in Queensland. Search online to find out exactly what Dr Jayant Patel (also dubbed 'Dr Death' by the media) committed.

1. What ethical principles did Dr Patel break whilst working at the Bundaberg Hospital as Director of Surgery?
2. Do you think the charges against Dr Patel's were fair? Why or why not? Share your answer and discuss your thoughts with your classmates.

What are our rights as patients?

If someone you know is recommended to have psychosurgery what are their rights?

Psychosurgery is any operation on the brain in order to treat mental illnesses. It is usually only used when other treatments have not been successful. In Victoria for example, all psychosurgery has to be approved by an independent board called the Psychosurgery Review Board.

A person's rights

In Australia, patients have the right to refuse treatment. A person also has the right to a second opinion. A person has the right to be fully informed about the nature of psychosurgery and what is being recommended to them. Furthermore, they have a right to seek legal advice or have someone represent them, or be with them when they are informed about the treatment.

What is informed consent?

A person who is recommended to have psychosurgery must be told the nature, risks and purpose of a treatment in plain language. Further, the person's rights need to be explained. When the person understands all these points and agrees to continue with psychosurgery, only then can they sign a consent form.

Figure 9.5 A psychosurgery patient must be told the risks of the treatment.

What if a person changes their mind after giving consent?

Fortunately, if they change their mind after signing the consent form, they can withdraw their consent and the surgery would not proceed.

> **ACTIVITY 9.6 PSYCHOSURGERY**
> 1. What is psychosurgery?
> 2. Can a person refuse psychosurgery?
> 3. What other rights does a person have if they are recommended psychosurgery?
> 4. What does informed consent involve?
> 5. Does it matter if someone changes their mind after signing a consent form?

What does it mean to be an 'involuntary' patient?

To be an involuntary patient means that a person's treatment is out of their control, and it has been deemed necessary that, for their benefit, others (such as their doctor and the state) take care of them.

For involuntary treatment to apply to a person, an **involuntary treatment order** needs to be placed, that is, a recommendation by a doctor. For a person to be subject to an involuntary treatment order, they must show the following:
1. They require treatment immediately.
2. Their treatment is necessary for their own personal health and safety, or for the protection of others.
3. The person has refused or is unable to consent to treatment.
4. There are no suitable alternative treatments.

Within 24 hours of the order being placed, a psychiatrist will often assess the person. If the person fits the criteria, the psychiatrist will confirm the order. The person will then be placed either in a mental health service as an **inpatient** or in a **community treatment order** (CTO). A CTO means that the person can receive involuntary treatment whilst they continue to live in the community.

A person who is receiving involuntary treatment in a mental health service and is an inpatient has rights. What are they?
1. The person's wishes and preferences for their treatment will be considered. However, the psychiatrist will have the final say.
2. The patient will receive a copy of the treatment plan.
3. Staff are to discuss with the patient their diagnosis and progress on a regular basis.
4. The patient may have a friend or **advocate** with them when planning treatment.
5. The patient has a right to a second opinion and rights to documents relating to them under freedom of information laws.

A person who is receiving involuntary treatment has some entitlements including:
- Leave of absence: the patient may apply for a leave of absence to visit family and friends, if approved by psychiatrist.
- Letters and telephone calls: the patient can contact people via phone and letters.

Involuntary treatment order A recommendation by a health professional (usually a doctor) for a person to be taken care of by the state as they either refuse treatment for their mental illness or are unable to look after themselves

Inpatient The term given to a person who must stay in an institution to receive involuntary treatment, and are not allowed to leave unless discharged

Community treatment order (also known as a CTO) Where a person is allowed to live in the community whilst they receive involuntary treatment

Advocate Someone who can support or defend a person

What about the use of seclusion and restraint with inpatients?

Seclusion is when a person is kept alone in a room where all the windows are doors are locked from the outside. This occurs when it is necessary to protect the person or others from risk to their health and safety.

Restraint is when a device is used to restrict a person's freedom to move. Restraint may be used to allow the person to be treated medically, to prevent the patient hurting themselves or others, or from destroying property.

If a person is placed in seclusion or restraint they have rights including:
- nurses must check on them at least every 15 minutes, and a doctor must examine them every four hours (unless a psychiatrist deems that less frequent examinations are OK). If restrained, the patient must be checked continuously.
- staff must provide appropriate food, drink, clothing, toileting and bedding.

Seclusion is the process by which a person is placed in a room by themselves where the windows and doors are locked on the outside.

Restraint Process by which a person's freedom to move is restricted

Discharge as an inpatient

Discharge allows an inpatient to leave the hospital. When a psychiatrist believes that the person no longer fits the criteria of inpatient, the patient will be discharged. The patient will be free to leave.

If a person wants to be discharged and a psychiatrist will not approve this, they can appeal to the Mental Health Review Board. The board will review the person's appeal within eight weeks of their initial entry as an inpatient, and then every 12 months after that.

Discharge When an inpatient has been deemed by their psychiatrist to no longer fit the criteria of inpatient, and is now free to leave the institution

ACTIVITY 9.7 INPATIENTS

1. If someone is an 'inpatient', what does this mean?
2. What is a CTO?
3. Name and explain three rights an inpatient has that you think are important.
4. Name and explain two entitlements an inpatient has.
5. Explain 'seclusion' and 'restraint'.
6. Is an inpatient free to leave an institution whenever they wish?
7. How does an inpatient get discharged?
8. Do you think that inpatients have adequate rights? Explain and discuss with your classmates.

ACTIVITY 9.8 ERA: ETHICAL DILEMMAS

The details of this ERA are available on the Cambridge GO website.

CHAPTER 9 CONDUCT AND MISCONDUCT: THE RIGHT OR WRONG OF ETHICS

END OF CHAPTER SUMMARY

- Ethics are moral guidelines or rules of conduct.
- Psychologists and psychiatrists are registered through the AHPRA and follow their professional society's code of ethics.
- Dr Harry Bailey breached many ethical guidelines with his therapies whilst practicing at the Chelmsford Private Hospital in NSW.
- One of Bailey's mentors, Dr Ewan Cameron, became famous worldwide for his unethical psychic-driving (brainwashing).
- In Australia, we have certain rights if we are to undergo psychosurgery, including a right to a second opinion, a right to refuse, a right to informed consent and a right to withdraw.
- If classified as an 'inpatient' a person has fewer rights.
- Seclusion and restraint can be used with inpatients if deemed necessary for their welfare and safety.
- Inpatients can only be discharged by approval of their psychiatrist.

END OF CHAPTER TEST

Multiple-choice questions

1. The three main principles of the APS Code of Ethics are:
   A integrity, propriety and confidentiality
   B respect for persons, exploitation and research
   C voluntary activities, health and circumstances
   D integrity, propriety, respect for rights and dignity of persons.

2. By having relationships with his patients, Dr Harry Bailey was guilty of:
   A exploiting his patients
   B misusing his professional power
   C conflict of interests
   D all of the above.

3. Informed consent is where:
   A the nature, purpose and risks of treatment are explained
   B the patient signs a consent form
   C the patient's privacy is maintained
   D none of the above.

4. An inpatient is someone who:
   A requires treatment immediately
   B has refused or is unable to consent to treatment
   C has no alternative treatments available
   D all of the above.

5. An inpatient needs their psychiatrist's approval to:
   A have a leave of absence
   B be discharged
   C change their treatment
   D all of the above.

Short-answer questions

1. One of your friends is incredibly frightened. They have been admitted into a local care facility as an inpatient. They're distressed as they do not understand what it all means and think they have no rights. What would your response be? Explain.

2. You read in a newspaper article about a research study that investigated the effect of a sports drink on elite-level athletes at an Australian sports institute. The athletes involved are named in the article, and it also appears that they were not aware they were part of a research study. What ethical guidelines have been breached by the researcher? Explain.

glossary

abstinence avoidance, in terms of addiction, avoidance of a drug

acetylcholine a neurotransmitter that plays a large role in learning

adaptation an organism's response to change; once it becomes used to the change, its response will diminish

addiction also known as dependence, this is when someone compulsively takes drugs. Addiction has been linked to high levels of dopamine in the blood.

adrenalin a hormone that is released when the fight-or-flight response is triggered

adversity an event or situation that is challenging or difficult

advocate is someone who can support or defend a person

affective emotional; an 'affect' is another way of describing an emotion

alcohol a depressant drug that is legal and the most commonly used drug in Australia.

alcohol dependence one of the most common Substance Dependence disorders for adolescents/teenagers

Alzheimer's a progressive neurological disease of the brain that leads to the irreversible loss of neurons and dementia, ultimately leads to death

amenorrhea the absence of three consecutive menstrual cycles

amnesia a form of memory loss

amnesty a government pardon for past misdeeds

amygdala an almond-shaped piece of tissue sitting above the brainstem in the temporal lobe responsible for triggering the fight-or-flight response. There is an amygdala in each hemisphere of the brain.

anorexia nervosa an eating disorder characterised by a refusal to maintain minimum body weight

antisocial voluntary behaviour which breaks social norms and has no benefit to others, or shows disregard for others

antisocial personality disorder is a personality disorder characterised by antisocial behaviour, and cannot be diagnosed until after the age of 18 years

anxiety feeling of fear, nervousness, and a lack of control, a sense of impending doom

Australian Health Practitioner Regulation Agency (AHPRA) is responsible for the registration and accreditation of 10 health professions across Australia including psychology, medicine, nursing, and dentals.

Australian Psychological Society (APS) psychologists in Australia abide by their code of ethics

autonomic nervous system a subdivision of the peripheral nervous system that contains the sympathetic and parasympathetic nervous system

axon a cable-like extension from the cell body of a neuron that sends messages to other neurons

barbiturates are depressants that act as sedatives and are highly addictive

behavioural activities activities that require us to operate or act; a sub-type of voluntary activities

binge a larger than normal amount of food is eaten in a short time period until the individual is uncomfortably or painfully full

binge-drinking ingesting several drinks at the one time, for men five to seven drinks is considered a binge and for women three to five

binge-eating disorder an eating disorder characterised by binge-eating with no compensatory behaviours; sufferers are usually overweight

biomarkers a substance or a gene, or characteristic that indicates the presence of a disease or condition

blackouts a small period of amnesia experienced (when using alcohol) that occur when you're awake

body image how you perceive, feel and think about your body

brain bank an organisation that collects, organises, handles and distributes brain tissue

bulimia nervosa an eating disorder characterised by binge-eating followed by compensatory behaviours; sufferers are usually a normal weight

cannabis or marijuana is the second most used drug in Australia for adolescents. Also known by many other names such as reefer or hash.

catatonia when muscles in the body go partly rigid, and the person remains in the same position they are in. It is also associated with muteness (no speech) and withdrawal from their environment.

central nervous system a subdivision of the human nervous system that contains the brain and spinal column

cerebrospinal fluid (CSF) the fluid that surrounds and protects the brain

circadian rhythm a naturally occurring body rhythm that occurs in a 24-hour cycle

circumstances external life factors such as wealth, health and relationship status; one of the three factors of happiness

cocaine a stimulant drug that is less commonly used and has a high risk of addiction

code of ethics a set of ethical guidelines that act as rules that professionals must abide by. If they breach the code they are deregistered.

cognitive activities any activities that involve our thinking processes; a sub-type of voluntary activities

collection of data this can be used to describe any method of collecting information such as experiments, surveys, tests, and observations

community treatment order, also known as CTO, is where a person is allowed to live in the community whilst they receive involuntary treatment

compensatory behaviour behaviours that follow a binge trying to reverse its effects such as purging, fasting or excessive exercise

conduct disorder is a mental illness characterised by antisocial behaviour including aggressive conduct, non-aggressive conduct, deceitfulness or theft, and serious violations of rules.

confidentiality is a person's right to have their name withheld and their information kept private

conformity where people behave in a way that is considered normal and acceptable by group standards. Peer pressure is an example of conformity.

construction of theories psychological theories are constructed when observing behaviour or processes in an attempt to understand the underlying reasons

contralateral on opposite sides of the body

controlled environment an environment where external factors, such as temperature and hygiene, are strictly controlled. Controlled environments are important for reliable research

corpus callosum nerve tissue connecting the two hemispheres of the brain

correlated variables are described as being correlated if a change in one variable appears to occur at the same time as another (however, sometimes a third unknown variable may be causing the changes)

cortex outer layer of the brain where most processes take place, such as 'thinking'

cortisol a hormone that is released when a person is stressed. It can be very helpful in fighting stress but too much cortisol (from long periods of stress) can weaken the immune system making people vulnerable to illness.

culture the beliefs, values, practices and social behaviour of a particular nation or group of people

deep sleep therapy (DST) is where a person is in a coma (unconscious state) induced by drugs

dehumanisation is where people of an 'out group' are considered to not be human, and instead are seen as objects or animals

deindividuation is where people lose their sense of self and feel anonymous, can lead to more anti-social behaviour due to people feeling a lack of responsibility/accountability

delineation the way we mark our territory to separate it from another's

delusions mistaken beliefs, thoughts, thinking processes such as paranoia and conspiracies

dendrites branch-like extensions at the front end of a neuron that receive messages from other neurons

depressant any substance that slows down the central nervous system and reduces brain activity

depressant drug a drug that slows down the body and brain, and inhibits metabolism

depression a mental disorder characterised by sadness, loss of interest and pleasure in life, and other negative emotions

discharge is when an inpatient has been deemed by their psychiatrist to no longer fit the criteria of inpatient, and are now free to leave the institution

diuretic a drug that elevates the rate of urination

dopamine a hormone and neurotransmitter that plays an important role of cognitive functions such as memory, problem solving and attention. It is also known as the 'pleasure' hormone, as it provides feelings of enjoyment and happiness.

dreams are the strange story images we experience during REM sleep

DSM-IV-TR is the version of the Diagnostic and Statistical Manual of Mental Disorders that gives guidelines and criteria for classifying and diagnosing mental illnesses. In 2012, the fifth edition will be published.

dysfunctional working abnormally or incorrectly

dysphoria a depressed mood such as sadness, the opposite of euphoria

economic depression where the financial affairs of a nation or group of people are in a slump

ecstasy is also known as 'E', 'X' or love drug. It is an amphetamine-type substance, and produces a sense of euphoria.

electroconvulsive therapy (ECT) is a form of medical therapy where electrical impulses are applied to an anesthetised patient's skull (and brain).

electroencephalograph (EEG) a device that detects, amplifies and records the electrical activity of the brain through electrodes placed on the scalp

empiricism the collection of information (data) through direct observation or experience, tends to also be systematic

endorphins chemical substances in our brains that act as natural painkillers in times of pain or stress. Endorphins can also cause people to feel better after strenuous exercise (a runner's 'high')

enema where liquid is forced into the colon to encourage elimination

enkephalin a powerful opiate/painkiller created by the human nervous system

ethics are moral guidelines, or rules of conduct that help us distinguish right from wrong

euphoria a heightened mood such as joy, the opposite of dysphoria

evolutionary psychology the field of psychology that emphasizes the role of adaptation, function and purpose in our development

experiential purchases purchases that have the primary intention of gaining a life experience

extroverts people who are sociable, outgoing and confident. They tend to have interests outside their own self

fight-or-flight response the automatic response of the physiological systems of the body to deal with a threat by either fighting or fleeing from the danger

flirting non-verbal signals that suggest you are ready to engage in some form of exchange with another person

foetal alcohol syndrome (FAS) injuries and defects inflicted on a foetus in the womb and caused by the pregnant woman's consumption of alcohol, which has a significant impact on the brain

foetus a developing human being, in the womb before childbirth

frontal lobe the region of the brain involved in decision making, problem solving, motor control and personality

generalised anxiety disorder (GAD) an anxiety disorder that is more common amongst adolescents, with fear of their performance at school and concerns of catastrophic events for example

geneva convention this is a set of agreements between nations of the treatment of victims of war. The agreements were negotiated in the aftermath of World War II.

gesture any movement of the forearm, hand, wrist or finger for communication

glial cells cells that support neurons and are involved with neural transmission

grey matter the cell bodies (soma) of neurons

groupthink where people make decisions and behave in accordance with the group consensus, to maintain group harmony

hallucinations mistaken perceptions, illusions; experiencing something that is not real. Hallucinations can be visual, auditory or tactile

hallucinogen a drug that causes hallucinations

happiness a sense of wellbeing and satisfaction in one's life

hemisphere half of a sphere; in psychology, the left or right half of the brain

heroin a depressant drug that is the least popular drug of choice in Australia. Users have a high risk of fatal over-dose.

hippocampus a mirror-like brain structure that has one half in each hemisphere of the brain, and is involved in memory formation

homunculus Latin for 'little human'; a representation of a person used to illustrate the proportions of cortical space allocated to each body part

hormones important chemicals that act as messengers in our bodies and help regulate body functions

hypothesis an estimated 'guess' or statement predicting the results of a study, or relationship between two variables. Hypotheses are tested through research.

illicit illegal, or against the law

informed consent is where a person understand the nature, risks and purpose of treatment or research

inpatient this is where a person must stay in an institution to receive involuntary treatment, and are not allowed to leave unless discharged

insomnia a sleeping disorder where a person cannot fall asleep or has trouble staying asleep

interpersonal a person's ability to relate to and connect with other people

introverts people whose thoughts and feelings are directed inward. They tend to be reserved and shy

involuntary treatment order is a recommendation by a health professional (usually a doctor) for a person to be taken care of by the state as they either refuse treatment for their mental illness or are unable to look after themselves

K-complexes single sharp spikes in a low-voltage series of brain waves

latent content the true meaning of the content of our dreams, according to psychoanalytic theory

laxative a substance that to induce bowel movements

leucotomies also known as frontal leucotomies, are surgery that cuts through the white matter in the prefrontal lobe. In practice, there is little difference between leucotomies and lobotomies.

life expectancy the average number of years we might expect someone to live. taking into account gender, race, socioeconomic status and where they live

lifestyle how a person usually behaves, their way of living

lobe a clearly obvious division of an organ, such as the brain or ear

lobotomies also known as frontal lobotomies, are surgery that disconnects the nerves from the frontal lobe to the rest of the brain

LSD a hallucinogen that is usually taken with other drugs to heighten effects

Lucifer Effect the transformation of a person's character causing good people to commit bad behaviour

manifest content the content of our dreams that we remember upon waking, according to psychoanalytic theory

materialistic purchases purchases that have the primary intention of gaining material possessions

membrane a sheet of tissue that covers or connects organs

meninges the layers of membrane under the skull surrounding the brain

mental health problem affects how a person behaves, feels, thinks, but is less severe than a mental illness and tends to be a temporary reaction to the stresses of life.

mental illness (or mental disorder) is a problem that significantly affects how the person behaves, feels, thinks, and is clinically diagnosed according to criteria.

mental wellness behaviours, thoughts and emotions that help support a positive, effective and functional mental state

meth/amphetamine a stimulant drug that tends to energise users but can cause psychosis. Also known as 'speed', 'base', 'ice', and 'crystal meth'.

microsleep occur when a sleep deprived person falls into a quick sleep that lasts for seconds. Microsleeps can have significant consequences.

mirror neurons specialised neurons in your brain that fire when you perform an action but also when you view that action being performed by someone else

motor neuron disease (MND) a disease where motor neurons fail to work properly and leading to muscles weakening and wasting, can lead to death

multiple relationships are also known as 'dual relationships' where a psychiatrist or psychologist has a patient that is also their friend/colleague/student/trainee

myelin sheath fatty white insulating tissue that surrounds the axons of neurons

narcotics are any drug that induces sleep or decreases sensitivity to pain, such as opiates

neuroblasts primitive cells that develop into neurons

neurogenesis the growing of new neurons

neuroimpulses the messages that travel along a neuron

neurons nerve cells in our body. They have three major parts – a cell body, an axon and dendrites.

neuroscience a term applied to any discipline that studies the nervous system, any specialist can be a neuroscientist if they research the nervous system

neurotransmitters chemical messengers by the axon that travel across the synapse and deliver messages to neighbouring neurons. Well-known neurotransmitters include acetylcholine, dopamine and endorphins.

nicotine substance found in tobacco that is addictive.

non-rapid eye movement sleep (nREM) stages 1-4 in the sleep cycle

normal the average, custom or standard level of something. In psychology, it means being 'free' of mental or physical disorders

obedience to authority where in a hierarchical society, people obey the instructions from people above them in status, e.g. army

occipital lobe a region of the brain involved with vision

onset beginning point, when something begins

parasomnias are unusual behaviors that occur when we are asleep.

parietal lobe a region of the brain involved in processing information from our sensory organs such as the skin

Parkinson's disease a disorder of the central nervous system caused by the breakdown of motor neurons in the body. Symptoms include tremors and lack of motor control.

peripheral nervous system a subdivision of the human nervous system that contains the autonomic, somatic, sympathetic and parasympathetic nervous systems

personal space the amount of distance we need to maintain between ourselves and the people with whom we are interacting

personal space zones the areas of space around us that we try to maintain: intimate distance, casual personal distance, social-consultative distance and public distance

pineal gland a small gland found deep within the brain responsible for sleep and hormone development

polysomnography the measurement and recording of different bodily functions during sleep

positive psychology the area of psychology that specialises in helping people improve their sense of wellbeing and happiness

poverty not having enough money for basic needs such as food, clothing and housing

primary territory any area that is used exclusively by an individual or group over a long period of time

prosocial voluntary behaviour intended to benefit another, such as helping, sharing and comforting others

proxemics the study of personal space rules

psychiatry a specialised area of medicine where doctors focus on mental illnesses

psychic-driving a method used by Ewan Cameron to reprogram sedated patients minds by playing them hours of commands on tape, this method also became known as brainwashing

psychology a science that studies behaviour and mental processes of human beings. This books looks at certain areas of psychology.

psychomythology misinformation or misconceptions about psychology that lay people (general population) believe

psychopath a person who suffers from psychopathy. They tend to be impulsive and reckless, and show little remorse or guilt for antisocial behaviours

psychopathy a personality disorder characterised by impulsive and reckless behaviour, and little remorse or guilt for antisocial behaviours

Psychopathy Checklist-Revised (PCL-R) is a diagnostic tool for measuring psychopathy created by psychologist Robert Hare

psychosis a state of mind that results in delusions, hallucinations and bizarre behaviour

psychosurgery is any surgery on the brain with the purpose of assisting symptoms of mental illness

psychotic an abnormal condition of the mind; a generic psychiatric term for a mental state often described as involving a 'loss of contact with reality'

rapid eye movement (REM) sleep a stage of sleep characterised by quick eye movements and beta waves

REM behaviour disorder an uncommon disorder whereby the sleeper acts out their dreams.

REM rebound the increase in the amount of time spent in REM sleep following a period of REM sleep deprivation

replicated the process of duplicating research to see if the results can be repeated, and are therefore reliable

restraint is the process by which a person's freedom to move is restricted

Royal Australian and New Zealand College of Psychiatrists (RANZCP) psychiatrists in Australia abide by their code of ethics

royal commission is a major government public inquiry into an issue

schizophrenia a severe psychotic disorder characterized by distorted thought and language, and social withdrawal

seclusion is the process by which a person is placed in a room by themselves where the windows and doors are locked on the outside

secondary territory any area that us used regularly by the individual or group but is also used often by other people

sensory deprivation is where a person is placed in a room with no sensory stimulation – e.g. dark empty rooms, or bright white rooms with no windows or people etc

sleep a state of consciousness during which the individual is unresponsive to external stimuli and experiences a state of immobility

sleep deprivation is experienced when an individual does not get enough sleep

sleep eating occurs when the sleeper binge eats during sleep. They have no recollection of it upon waking.

sleep talking is a common sleep phenomenon whereby the sleeper talks in their sleep. Generally they don't make sense although some sleepers will hold conversations.

sleep walking is a common sleep disturbance where people walk and carry out daily activities while they are asleep.

snoring is a common sleep disorder where the individual's airways are blocked during sleep resulting in a loud, rumbling sound.

socio-biological psychology a branch of psychology that tried to explain people's behaviour from an evolutionary perspective

socio-cognitive psychology a branch of psychology that tries to explain and also gives us information on people's behaviour through the thoughts and ideas that accompany it

soma the cell body of a neuron, containing its nucleus and DNA

spatial neglect damage to one hemisphere of the brain that results in a loss of awareness for the contralateral (opposite side) of the body dwell

spindles short bursts of high frequency activity in brain waves

stimulant drug a substance that speeds up messages going to and from the brain keeping a person awake and alert

substance a drug of abuse, a toxin or a medication

substance dependence a mental disorder characterised by addition to a drug, such as alcohol, and showing tolerance and withdrawal symptoms to the drug

swearing taboo words in society, or 'bad language'

synapse a minute gap between neurons

temporal lobe a region of the brain involved with hearing, speech and memory

territory the fixed spaces that somehow belong to us or a group to which we belong

tertiary territory shared spaces that everyone has the right to use

THC a psychoactive ingredient in cannabis

tolerance a need to increase the amount of drugs for desired effect

variable a factor in research that may be manipulated or controlled by the experimenter (the independent variable) or factor that changes as a result (dependent variable)

volitional activities any activities that we choose, or decide to take part in; a sub-type of voluntary activities

voluntary activities activities that are intentional, that an individual chooses to do

white matter the axons of neurons insulated by fatty white myelin sheath

withdrawal reduction of use of drug leads to significant distress or impairment

zygote an egg that has been fertilised by a sperm

references

'Activating the feeling of being followed', *New Scientist*, 2006, 191(2570), 16.

Adams, WL 2008, 'Terra incognita: When half the map is missing – and you don't notice', *Psychology Today*, 41(1), 32.

Altschuler, EL, Wisdom, SB, Stone, L, Foster, C, Galasko, D, Llewellyn, DME & Ramachandran, VS 1999, 'Rehabilitation of hemiparesis after stroke with a mirror', *The Lancet*, 353 (9169), 2035–6.

American Psychiatric Association 2000, *Diagnostic and Statistical Manual of Mental Disorders*, 4th edition, Text Revision, American Psychiatric Association, Washington, DC.

American Psychiatric Association 2010, 'What is the DSM and what is it used for?', retrieved on 6 June 2010 from **http://www.psych.org/MainMenu/Research/DSMIV/FAQs/WhatistheDSMandwhatisitusedfor.aspx**.

Amit, P, Boyle, LN, Tippin, J & Rizzo, M 2005, 'Variability of driving performance during microsleeps', *Proceedings of the Third International Driving Symposium on Human Factors in Driver Assessment, Training and Vehicle Design*, retrieved 5 August 2010 from **http://ppc.uiowa.edu/drivingassessment/2005/final/papers/04_AmitPaul_LBoyleformat.pdf**.

Anderson, JT 2005, 'Recurring dreams', *Jane Teresa Anderson's Dream Sight*, retrieved 5 August 2010 from **http://www.dream.net.au/library/recurring_dreams.cfm**.

Anxiety BC 2010, *Generalised Anxiety*, retrieved 1 July 2010 from **http://www.anxietybc.com/parent/generalized.php**.

APS 2007, *The Australian Psychological Society Ltd Code of Ethics*, retrieved 16 July 2010 from **http://www.psychology.org.au/Assets/Files/Code_Ethics_2007.pdf**.

Ash, J & Gallup, GG 2007, 'Paleoclimatic variation and brain expansion during human evolution', *Human Nature*, 18, 109–24.

Australian Bureau of Statistics 2006, *Alcohol Consumption in Australia: A Snapshot, 2004-05*, Federal Government of Australia, Canberra, retrieved 12 June 2010 from **http://abs.gov.au/AUSSTATS/abs@.nsf/mf/4832.0.55.001/**.

Australian Bureau of Statistics 2007, *Life satisfaction and measures of progress*, No. 1301.0, Canberra, Australian Capital Territory, retrieved 15 August 2008 from **http://www.abs.gov.au/Ausstats/abs@.nsf/0e5fa1cc95cd093c4a256811**.

Australian Bureau of Statistics 2007, *National Survey of Mental Health and Wellbeing: Summary of results*, ABS Cat No. 4326.0. Canberra, ABS.

Australian Bureau of Statistics 2009, *Australian Social Trends – March 2009*, retrieved 6 June 2010 from **http://www.abs.gov.au/AUSSTATS/abs@.nsf/Lookup/4102.0Main+Features30March%202009**.

Australian Bureau of Statistics 2010, *Mental Health of Young People 2007*, retrieved 20 July 2010 from **http://www.abs.gov.au/AUSSTATS/abs@.nsf/ProductsbyReleaseDate/4F1F32379D2B0214CA25776200151B61?OpenDocument**.

Australian Health Practitioner Regulation Agency 2010, *Who we are*, retrieved 24 July 2010 from **http://www.ahpra.gov.au/About-AHPRA/Who-We-Are.aspx**.

Australian National Centre for Classification in Health 2010, retrieved 8 June 2010 from **http://nis-web.fhs.usyd.edu.au/ncch_new/2.aspx**.

BBC News 2007, 'No sleep means no new brain cells', 10 February, retrieved 5 August 2010 from **http://news.bbc.co.uk/2/hi/health/6347043.stm**.

Bernstein, DA, Roy, E, Srull, TK & Wickens, CD 1988, *Psychology*, Boston, Houghton Mifflin Company.

Bernstein, L 2009, 'Brain drain: alcohol can mess up your mind', *Current Health 2*, 35(6).

Better Health Channel 2008, *Electroconvulsive therapy*, retrieved 6 June 2010 from **http://www.betterhealth.vic.gov.au/BHCV2/bhcarticles.nsf/pages/Teenagers_theme_page?OpenDocument**.

REFERENCES

Boccaccini, MT, Murrie, DC, Clark, JW & Cornell, DG 2008, 'Describing, diagnosing, and naming psychopathy: How do youth psychopathy labels influence jurors?', *Behavioral Sciences & The Law*, 26, 487–510.

Bourke, L & Geldens, PM 2007, 'Subjective wellbeing and its meaning for young people in a rural Australian centre', *Social Indicators Research*, 82, 165–87.

Buchanen, M 2008, 'Skull flex may explain mystery brain injuries', *New Scientist*, 199(2678), 11.

'Bush admits waterboarding 9/11 mastermind, says he'd do it again', *New York Times*, 4 June 2010, r18 July 2010 from **http://www.nypost.com/p/news/national/bush_admits_waterboarding_mastermind_QNLOLVfzOsic0sJSnVBBNJ**.

CBC News 2007, 'A few bad apples', retrieved 18 July 2010 from **http://www.cbc.ca/fifth/badapples/index.html**.

Chandler, J & MacDonald, J 1991, 'The battle to control the mind', *The Age*, 22 April 1991, p. 11, retrieved 4 July 2010 from **http://newsstore.theage.com.au/apps/viewDocument.ac?page=1&sy=age&kw=the+battle+to+control+the+mind&pb=age&dt=selectRange&dr=entire&so=relevance&sf=text&sf=headline&rc=10&rm=200&sp=nrm&clsPage=1&docID=news910421_0258_6329**.

Chicurel, M 2001, 'Windows on the brain', *Nature*, 412, 266–8.

Clarke, J 2005, *Working with Monsters*, Random House Australia, Sydney.

Code of Ethics July 2010, 4th edition, retrieved 16 July 2010 from **http://www.ranzcp.org/images/stories/ranzcp-attachments/Resources/College_Statements/code_ethics_2010.pdf**.

Cohen, A, Medlow, S, Kelk, N & Hickie, I 2009, 'Young people's experiences of mental health care: Implications for the headspace National Youth Mental Health Foundation', *Youth Studies Australia*, 28(1), 13–20.

Conference notes 2010, *Happiness and its Causes: Conference proceedings*, 5–6 May 2010, Conference notes by Meg Mulcahy within booklet of readings printed by Vi Conferences.

Cunningham, A 2008, 'Baby in the brain', *Scientific American Mind*, 19(2), 16.

Davies, S 2006, 'Cannabis use in young people', *Primary Health Care*, 16(4), 8.

Department of Health and Ageing 2007, *National Mental Health Report 2007: Summary of Twelve Years of Reform in Australia's Mental Health Services under the National Mental Health Strategy 1993-2005*, Commonwealth of Australia, Canberra.

Department of Health and Ageing 2010, National mental health strategy brochure, *What is an anxiety disorder?*, retrieved from website on 6 June 2010 from **http://www.health.gov.au/internet/main/publishing.nsf/Content/mental-pubs**.

Diener, E 2006, *Understanding scores on the satisfaction with life scale*, retrieved 1 October 2008 from http://www.psych.uiuc.edu/~ediener/.

Diener, E, Emmons, RA, Larson, RJ & Griffin, S 1985, 'The satisfaction with life scale', *Journal of Personality Assessment*, 49 (1), 71–5.

Doidge, N 2007, *The brain that changes itself*, Carlton North, Victoria, Australia, Scribe Publications.

Drummond, PA, Stricker, JL, Wong, EC & Buxton, RB 2000, 'Brain activity is visibly altered following sleep deprivation', *UC San Diego Heatlh System*, retrieved 5 August 2010 from **http://health.ucsd.edu/news/2000_02_09_Sleep.html**.

Eating Disorders Foundation of Victoria Inc 2009, *Eating disorders and adolescents*, retrieved 18 June 2010 from **http://www.eatingdisorders.org.au/eating-disorders/eating-disorders-and-adolescents-2.html**.

Edens, JF, Poythress, NG, Lilienfield, SO & Patrick, CJ 2008, 'A prospective comparison of two measures of psychopathy in the prediction of institutional misconduct', *Behavioral Sciences & The Law*, 26, 529–41.

Eggen, D 2008, 'House defends CIA's use of waterboarding in interrogations', *The Washington Post*, Thursday 7 July 2008, retrieved 18 July 2010 from **http://www.washingtonpost.com/wpdyn/content/article/2008/02/05/AR2008020502764.html**.

Farndon, J 2000, *The Complete Book of the Brain – all about the body's control centre*, Suffolk, UK, Roger Coote Publishing.

Ferber, D 2008, 'Laugh your arse off', *Australian Women's Health*, July, 78–81.

Fergusson, D, Horwood, J & Ridder, E 2005, 'Show me a child at seven: The consequences of conduct problems in childhood for psychosocial functioning in adulthood', *Journal of Child Psychology & Psychiatry*, 46(8), 837–49.

Flatley, C & Barbeler, D 2010, 'Jury convicts "Dr Death" Patel', *The Age*, 30 June 2010, retrieved 24 July 2010 from http://www.theage.com.au/national/jury-convicts-dr-death-patel-20100629-zj9u.html.

Fleming, N 2008, 'A helping hand for early dementia', *New Scientist*, 198 (2656), 26.

Frederickson, BL 2009, *Positivity: Top-notch research reveals the 3-to-1 ratio that will change your life*, Random House, New York, from http://www.austlii.edu.au/au/cases/cth/HCA/1993/77.html.

Gardner, PD, Tapper, AR, King, JA, DiFranza, JR & Ziedonis, DM 2009, 'The neurobiology of nicotine addiction: Clinical and public policy implications', *The Journal of Drug Issues*, 38(4), 417–41.

Geddes, L 2010, 'How many states of consciousness are there?', *New Scientist*, (2754), 30.

Gilbert, DT, Tafarodi, RW & Malone, PS 1993, 'You can't not believe everything you read', *Journal of Personality and Social Psychology*, 65(2), 221–33.

Gillespie, NA, Kirk, KM, Evans, DM, Heath, AC, Hickie, IB & Martin, NG 2004, 'Do the genetic or environmental determinants of anxiety and depression change with age? A longitudinal study of Australian twins', *Twin Research*, 7(1), 39–53.

Goudarzi, S 2008, 'One hemisphere two hands', *Scientific American Mind*, 19(2), 9.

Graham-Rowe, D 2006, 'Artificial limbs wired direct to the brain', *New Scientist*, 192(2573), 30–31.

Greenfield, SA 1996, *The human mind explained*, Canada, The Reader's Digest.

Griffiths, T 2007, 'Do our brains work like Google?' *New Scientist*, 196(2633), 27.

Gruen, R 2010, 'Sleep deprived cabbies are driving themselves to death', 21 April, retrieved 5 August 2010 from http://www.smh.com.au/opinion/society-and-culture/sleepdeprived-cabbies-are-driving-themselves-to-death-20100420-srnw.html.

Haidt, J 2006, *The happiness hypothesis: Finding modern truth in ancient wisdom*, New York, Basic Books.

Hare, R 2003, *Hare psychopathy checklist –Revised manual*, 2nd edition, Toronto, MHS.

Hassett, J & White, KM 1989, *Psychology in Perspective*, 2nd edition, New York, Harper & Row.

'Heavy, long-term pot smoking linked to brain shrinkage', *New Scientist* 2008b, 198 (2659), 7.

Henderson, M 2008, 'Spending on others brings happiness', (electronic version), *The Australian*, retrieved 1 October 2008 from http://www.theaustralian.news.com.au/story/0,25197,23413115-5001942,00.html.

Higham, S & Stephens, J 2004, 'New details of prison abuse emerge', *Washington Post*, Friday 21 May 2004, p. A004, retrieved 4 July 2010 from http://www.washingtonpost.com/wp-dyn/articles/A43783-2004May20.html.

Hoag, H 2008, 'Sex on the brain', *New Scientist*, 199(2665), 28–31.

Holmes, B 2008, 'Why blind brains never stop seeing', *New Scientist*, 198(2656), 14.

Hooper, R 2007, 'Yawning may boost brain's alertness', *New Scientist*, (2610), 14.

'How cocaine hijacks the craving brain', *New Scientist 2006a*, 190(2557), 23.

Hutson, M 2007, 'Brain trainers', *Psychology Today*, 40(1), 18.

Hutson, M 2008, 'Hold me back', *Psychology Today*, 41(4), 33.

Immordino-Yang, MH 2008, 'Strange lessons', *New Scientist*, 199(2664), 44–5.

Johnston, JE 2006, *The Complete Idiot's Guide to Psychology*, 3rd edition, New York, Penguin.

Kaas, JH 2008, 'Phantoms of the brain', *Nature*, 391, 331–3.

Klein, S 2006, *The science of happiness: How our brains make us happy – and what we can do to get happier*. Carlton North, Victoria Australia, Scribe Publications.

Kluger, J 2006, 'Why we worry about the things we shouldn't ... and ignore the things we should', *Time*, 48, 40–5.

Langmore, K 2008, 'Come on, get happy', *Vital Health*, 16–18.

Lawton, G 2007, 'Mind tricks: Six ways to explore your brain', *New Scientist*, (2622), 34–41.

Lefton, LA 2000, *Psychology*, 7th edition, Boston, Allan & Bacon.

Lemonick, MD & Park, A 2007, 'The science of addiction', *Time*, 28, 40–6.

Lewin, R 2006, 'The brain's own opiate', *New Scientist*, 192(2578), 21.

Lilienfield, SO & Andrews, BP 1996, 'Development and preliminary validation of a self-report measure of psychopathic personality traits in non-criminal populations', *Journal of Personality Assessment*, 66, 488–524.

Lilienfield, SO & Arkowitz, H 2008, 'What "psychopath" means', *Scientific American Mind*, 18(6), 80–1.

Lilienfield, SO, Lyn, AJ, Ruscio, J & Beyerstein, BL 2010, *50 Great Myths of Popular Psychology: Shattering widespread misconceptions about human behaviour*, Wiley-Blackwell, Sussex, UK.

Lima, JE, Reid, MS, Smith, JL, Zhang, Y, Huiping, J, Rotrosen, J & Nunes, E 2009, 'Medical and mental health status among drug dependent patients participating in a smoking cessation treatment study', *Journal of Drug Issues*, 1 April, 293–312.

Lovett, R 2008, 'The best way to start the day', *New Scientist*, 195(2617), 30–3.

Lovett, RA 2006, 'Jog your brain', *Psychology Today*, 39(3), 55–6.

Lunn, S 2010, 'Youngsters stressed over school and worried about body image', The Australian, 17 November 2010, 33

Malim, T & Birch, A 1998, *Introductory psychology*, Macmillan, London.

Marks, P 2008, 'Rise of the rat-brained robots', *New Scientist*, 199(2669), 22–3.

Maslow, A 1954, *Motivation and personality*, New York, Harper.

Matsumoto, D 2000, *Culture and Psychology: People Around the World*, 2nd edition, Australia, Wadsworth Thomson Learning.

McClernon, FJ & Kollins, SH 2008, 'ADHD and smoking: From genes to brain to behaviour', *Annals of the New York Academy of Sciences*, 1141, 131–147.

McNeill, P 2005, 'Scandals in medicine', MEHL Lecture Notes [pdf], retrieved 20 July 2010 from **http://www.med.unsw.edu.au/SPHCMWeb.nsf/resources/CMED3001_Lecture_9-1.pdf/$file/CMED3001_Lecture_9-1.pdf**.

Mehl, M, Vazire, S, Ramirez-Esparza, N, Slatcher, RB & Pennebaker, JW 2007, 'Are women really more talkative than men?' *Science*, 317(5834), 82. : 10.1126/science.1139940.

Mitchell, N (writer), *The Legacy of the Lobotomy* (radio broadcast episode 3 February 2002), retrieved 3 June 2010 from **http://www.abc.net.au/rn/allinthemind/stories/2002/468539.htm**. In N. Mitchell (Producer) *All in the Mind*. Melbourne, Australia, ABC National Radio.

Morris, SA, Eaves, DW, Smith, AR & Nixon, K 2010, 'Alcohol inhibition of neurogenesis: a mechanism of hippocampal neurodegenration in an adolescent alcohol abuse model', *Hippocampus*, 20, 596–607.

Morritz, C 2008, 'Direct from brain to muscle', *New Scientist*, 199(2669), 23.

Morse, G 2004, 'Executive psychopaths', *Harvard Business Review*, 82(10), 20–2.

Motluk, A 2005, 'Seeing without sight', *New Scientist*, 185(2484), 37–9.

Myers, D & Diener, E 1995, 'Who is happy?', *Psychological Science*, 6, 10–19.

'Naked dreams' 2010, *Dream Moods*, retrieved 5 August 2010 from **http://dreammoods.com/cgibin/nakeddreams.pl?method=exact&header=dreamid&search=nakedintro**.

National Advisory Council on Mental Health 2009, *A Mentally Healthy Future for all Australians: A Discussion Paper*, Dept of Heath and Ageing, Canberra.

National Drug & Alcohol Research Centre 2007, *Illicit drug use in Australia:Epidemiology, use patterns and associated harm*, 2nd edition. Ed. Joanne Ross. National Drug & Alcohol Research Centre, Commonwealth of Australia, Canberra, retrieved 12 June 2010 from http://www.health.gov.au/internet/drugstrategy/publishing.nsf/content/17b917608c1969abca257317001a72d4/$file/mono-63.pdf.

Neumann, CS, Hare, RD & Newman, JP 2007, 'The super-ordinate nature of the psychopathy checklist-revised', *Journal of Personality Disorders*, 21(2), 102–117.

'New brain cells will die unless they have a job to do', *New Scientist 2006b*, 191(2565), 17.

NSW Government, Legislative Assembly 1991, *Chelmsford Private Hospital Patient Compensation*. Item 19 of 26, retrieved 20 July 2010 from http://www.parliament.nsw.gov.au/prod/parlment/hansart.nsf/V3Key/LA19911202019.

NZPA 2009, 'Office psychos create toxic workplace', retrieved 18 May 2010 from http://news.theage.com.au/breaking-news-world/office-psychos-create-toxic-workplace-20090922g02o.html.

Olson, EJ, Boeve BF & Silber, MH 2000, 'Rapid eye movement sleep behaviour disorder: demographic, clinical and laboratory findings in 93 cases', *Brain*, (123), 331–9, retrieved 5 August 2010 from http://www.ncbi.nlm.nih.gov/pubmed/10648440.

Papadakis, M 2003, 'Shut off from shut-eye', *The Herald Sun*, 1 June 2003, 19.

'Phantom of the operation', *Psychology Today* 1996, 29(2), 11.

Philips, H 2006, 'Exercise the little grey cells', *New Scientist*, 190 (2554), 40–1.

Philips, H 2006, 'What's on your mind?', *New Scientist*, 191 (2565), 32.

Pink, DH 2006, 'A whole new mind: Why right-brainers will rule the future', *New PsyBlog* 2009, *Why you can't help believing everything you read*, retrieved 4July 2010 from www.spring.org.uk/2009/09/why-you-cant-help-believing-everything-you-read.php.

Ramachandran, VS & Ramachandran, DR 2008, 'How blind are we?', *Scientific American Mind*, 18, (2), 16–17.

Ramachandran, VS & Ramachandran, DR 2008, 'Right side up', *Scientific American Mind*, 18(2), 22–5.

Ramachandran, VS & Ramachandran, DR 2008, 'Touching illusions', *Scientific American Mind*, 18(2), 60–3.

Range, A & Schatz, C 2008, 'Top 75 questions of science', *Discover*, Spring, 26–62.

RANZCP (2010). *The Royal Australian and New Zealand College of Psychiatrists*

Ratey, J 2001, *A user's guide to the brain*, London, Abacus Book.

Robson, D 2010, 'Maxed out', *New Scientist*, 17 April, 36.

Ross, CA 2006, *The C.I.A. Doctors: Human Rights Violations by American Psychiatrists*, Chapter 12: Dr Ewan Cameron (121–30). Manitou Communications, Texas.

Rowe, J 2005, 'From deviant to disenfranchised: the evolution of drug users in AJSI', *Australian Journal of Social Issues*, 40(1), 107–22.

Roxburgh, A, Hall, WD, Degenhardt, L, McLaren, J, Black, E, Copeland, J & Mattick, RP 2010, The epidemiology of cannabis use and cannabis-related harm in Australia 1993–2007', *Addiction*, 105, 1071–9.

Sargant, W & Slater, E 1972, *An Introduction to Physical Methods of Treatment in Psychiatry*, 5th edition, Edinburgh, Livingstone, pp. 89–96 as cited on http://en.wikipedia.org/wiki/William_Sargant#cite_ref-23.

Sawyer, MG, Arney, FM, Baghurst, PA, Clark, JJ, Graetz, BW, Kosky, RJ, Nurcombe, B, Patton, GC, Prior, MR, Rapphael, B, Rey, J, Whaites, LC & Zubrick, SR 2000, *Mental Health of Young People in Australia. Child and Adolescent Component of the National Survey of Mental Health and Well Being*, Commonwealth of Australia, Canberra.

Schenck, C H & Mahowald, MW 1994, 'Review of Nocturnal Sleep-Related Eating Disorders', *International Journal of Eating Disorders*, 4(15), 343–56.

REFERENCES

Schkade, D 2005, 'Pursuing happiness: The architecture of sustainable change', *Review of General Psychology*, 9(2), 111–131.

Searight, HR, Rottnek, F & Abby, SL 2001, 'Conduct disorder: Diagnosis and treatment in primary care', *American Family Physician*, 63(8), 1579–89.

Seligman, MEP 2002, *Authentic happiness*, New York, Free Press.

Shreeve, J 2005, 'Beyond the brain', *National Geographic*, March, 2–31.

Siegel, M 2003, 'Why we sleep: the reasons we are becoming less enigmatic', *Scientific American*, 92–7.

Simons, JA, Irwin, DB & Drinnien, BA 1987, 'Maslow's hierarchy of needs', *Psychology – The search for understanding*, New York, West Publishing Company.

Simonton, DK & Baumeister, RF 2005, 'Positive psychology at the summit', *Review of General Psychology*, 9(2), 99–102.

'Sorting the true memories from the false ones', *New Scientist 2007*, 196(2629), 22.

Steven, A & Eshleman, JR 1998, 'Marital status and happiness: A 17-nation study', *Journal of Marriage and the Family*, 60(2), 527–37.

Slack, G 2007, 'Source of human empathy directly observed', *New Scientist*, 196(2629), 12.

Sleep Disorders Australia 2007, *Snoring*, South Australia, retrieved 5 August 2010, http://www.sleepaus.on.net/fs08.pdf.

Sleep Eating 2010, *Talk About Sleep*, Minnesota, retrieved 5 August 2010, http://www.talkaboutsleep.com/sleep-disorders/archives/parasomnias_sleepeating.htm.

Smith, AM, Longo, CA, Fried, PA, Hogan, MJ & Cameron, I 2010, 'Effects of marijuana on visuospatial working memory: an fMRI study in young adults', *Psychopharmacology*, 210, 429–38.

Smith, M, Jaffe-Gill, E & Segal, J 2010, 'Generalised anxiety disorder' retrieved on 1 July 2010 from http://helpguide.org/mental/generalized_anxiety_disorder.htm.

Spinney, L 2007, 'The science of swearing', *New Scientist*, 196(2635/2636), 51–3.

State Government of Victoria 2009, *Involuntary patients: About your rights*, Mental Health and Drugs Division, Department of Health, Melbourne, Victoria.

State Government of Victoria 2009, *Psychosurgery: About your rights*, Mental Health and Drugs Division, Department of Health, Melbourne, Victoria.

Stilwell, F & Jordan, K 2007, 'Economic inequality and (un)happiness' *Social Alternatives*, 26(4), 16–21.

Streatfield, D 2006, *Brainwash: The Secret History of Mind Control*, Hodder & Stoughton, Great Britain.

Sutherland, S 1995, *The Macmillan Dictionary of Psychology*, 2nd edition, Macmillan, London.

Taguba, AM 2004, Article 15–6 'Investigation of the 800th Military Police Brigade', retrieved 4 July 2010 from http://www.cbsnews.com/htdocs/pdf/tagubareport.pdf.

'Talking in Your Sleep', *Web MD*, retrieved 5 August 2010 from http://www.webmd.com/sleep-disorders/excessive-sleepiness-10/talking-in-your-sleep?page=2.

Tan, K 2005, 'Step by step, your brain mimics his moves', *Psychology Today*, 38(4), 26.

The Age, 'Patel jailed for seven years', *The Age*, 4 July 2010, retrieved from http://news.theage.com.au/breaking-news-national/patel-jailed-for-seven-years-20100701-zndg.html.

The Telegraph, 'Babies may be smarter than Freud thought', retrieved 10 May 2010 from http://www.theage.com.au/lifestyle/lifematters/babies-may-be-smarter-than-freud-thought-20100509-ulwq.html.

The Transport Accident Commission 2010, *Fatigue Campaign History*, Australia, retrieved 5 August 2010 from http://www.tacsafety.com.au/jsp/content/NavigationController.do?areaID=13&tierID=2&navID=3A68DA0D7F0000010006FFEB827AD586&navLink=null&pageID=390.

Thomas, H 2010, 'Hedley Thomas broke the Jayent Patel story to the world', *The Sunday Mail*, retrieved 3 July

2010 from **http://www.couriermail.com.au/sunday-mail/hedley-thomas-broke-the-jayant-patel-story-to-the-world/story-e6frep2o-1225887486330**.

Van Boven, L 2005, 'Experientialism, materialism, and the pursuit of happiness', *Review of General Psychology*, 9(2), 132–42.

Van Boven, L & Glovich, T 2003, 'To do or to have? That is the question.' *Journal of Personality and Social Psychology*, 85, 1193–1202.

Van Gucht, D, Van den Bergh, O, Beckers, T & Vansteenwegen, D 2010, 'Smoking behaviour in context: When and where do people smoke?', *Journal of Behavioural Therapy and Experimental Psychiatry*, 41, 172–7.

Walker, Burnham & Borland 1994, *Psychology*, 2nd edition, Queensland, John Wiley and Sons.

Walton v Gardiner 1993, HCA 77; 177 CLR 378; 112 ALR 289; 67 ALJR 485, retrieved 13 July 2010.

Wellington, T 2007, *Happy? Exposing the cultural myths about happiness*, Tinbeerwah, Queensland, Beaut Books.

White, A 2002, Substance use and adolescent brain development, *Youth Studies Australia*, 22(1), 39–45.

Whittington, S 2007, 'An inquiry into the nature and causes of the happiness of nations, *Policy*', 23(4) 44–6.

New Scientist 2008a, 'Why alcohol makes you loosen up and lash out', *New Scientist*, 198 (2654), 17.

Williams, C, Gosline, A, Lawton, G & Thomson, H 2009, 'The five ages of the brain', *New Scientist*, 4 April, 26–31.

World Health Organisation 2009. Mental health, resilience and inequalities (compiled Friedle, Lynne), retrieved 6 June 2010 from **http://www.euro.who.int/__data/assets/pdf_file/0012/100821/E92227.pdf**.

Yong, E 2010, 'Dangerous DNA', *New Scientist*, 10 April, 34–7.

Yurgolen-Todd, D 2002, *Frontline* interview 'Inside the Teens Brain' as cited in Spano, S. 2003, 'Adolescent brain development' *Youth Studies Australia*, 22(1), 36–8.

Zimbardo, P 2008, *The Lucifer Effect: Understanding How Good People Turn Evil*, Random House Inc, New York.

Zvolensky, MJ, Johnson, KA, Cougle, JR, Bonn-Miller, MO 2010, Marijuana use and panic psychopathology among a representative sample of adults, *Experimental and Clinical Psychopharmacology*, 18(2), 129–34.

index

Abu Ghraib, 109-117, ch 8 *passim*
    Baghdad, 109-110
    Bush, George W, 110
    conformity, 116
    dehumanisation, 116
    deindividuation, 116
    environmental features, 115
    Geneva Convention, 113
    groupthink, 116
    Hussein, Saddam, 109-110
    Karpinski, Brigadier General, 112-115
    obedience, 116
    social features, 115
    Taguba, Major General, 110-115
acetylcholine, 18
adaptation, 84
addiction, 37-38, 50-51
adrenalin, 49
adversity, 77
advocate, 129
affective, 106-107
agoraphobia, 94
alcohol, 36, 37, 38, 51-53
    binge drinking, 52
amenorrhea, 4149
amnesty, 109
amygdala, 23, 49-51
anorexia, *see* eating disorders
antisocial, 106-107
antisocial personality disorder, 35
anxiety, 35-36
apnoea, 67
autonomic nervous system, 94
axon, 18
axon terminals, 18
alzheimer's disease, 12
Australian Health Practitioners Regulation Agency, 14, 119
Australian Psychological Society, 119-120
AHPRA, *see* Australian Health Practitioners Regulation Agency
ALS, *see* motor neuron disease

APS, *see* Australian Psychological Society
Baghdad, 109-110
Bailey, Harry, 121-127
barbiturates, 121, 123
behavioural activities, 85
binge, 41
binge eating, *see* eating disorders
binge drinking, *see* alcohol
blackouts, 52
body image, 32, 38
    code of, 39
brain, ch 2 and ch 4 passim
    amygdala, 23, 49 - 51
    brain banks, 27
    cerebellum, 22
    change blindness, 26
    corpus callosum, 23, 49
    connections within, 19
    contralateral, 24
    cortex, 22, 48
    functions of, 22-23
    glial cells, 28
    Google, 19
    grey matter, 48
    hallucinations, 27, 54
    hemispheres, 23
    hippocampus, 4, 23, 49
    lobes, 22, 49
    mass, 17
    membranes, 21
    meninges, 21
    messages, 19
    myelin sheath, 48
    neurogenesis, 4, 49
    neurons, 3-4, 16-20, 48
    neurotransmitters, 18, 50-51
    protective mechanisms, 21
    smell, 23
    spatial neglect, 25
    taste, 23
    white matter, 48
brainwashing, *see* psychic-driving
brain waves, 65
bulimia, *see* eating disorders
Bush, George W, 110

Cameron, Ewan, 121, 127
cannabis, see marijuana
catatonia, 6, 7, 9
causes, mental illness, 42
central nervous system, 17
cerebellum, 22
cerebrospinal fluid, 19
change blindness, 26
Chelmsford Hospital, 121-127
cigarettes, *see* nicotine
circadian rhythm, 61
circumstances, 80
clinical psychology, 60
cocaine, 56
cognitive activities, 85
cognitive behaviour therapy, 43
community treatment order, 129
compensatory behaviours, 41
conduct disorder, 33 - 34
confidentiality, 125
conformity, 116
contralateral, 24
controlled environment, 19
corpus callosum, 23
correlation, 4
cortex, 22
cortisol, 51, *see* stress
culture, 80, 96-97
CBT, *see* cognitive behaviour therapy
CSF, *see* cerebrospinal fluid
data collection, 3
da Vinci, Leonardo, 24
deep sleep therapy, 121-127
dehumanisation, 116
deindividuation, 116
delineation, 91
delusions, 54
dendrites, 18
depression, 36-37
Di Mauro, Catena, 41-42
discharge, 130
diuretics, 41
dopamine, 27, 50, 87
dreams, 72-74
drugs, 42, ch 4 *passim*

addiction, 37-38, 50-51
  alcohol, 36, 37, 38, 51-53
  cocaine, 56
  depressants, 52, 56
  ecstasy, 55-56
  hallucinogens, 56
  help, 57-58
  heroin, 56
  illicit, 53
  LSD, 56
  marijuana, 9, 42, 53-54
  meth/amphetamines, 55
  nicotine, 54-55
  stimulants, 55
dysfunctional, 105
dysphoria, 51
DSM-IV-TR, 33
DST, *see* deep sleep therapy
eating disorders, 38-42
  Butterfly foundation, 46
  compensatory behaviours, 41
  Di Mauro, Catena, 41-42
  types of, 40-41
ECT, *see* electroconvulsive therapy
EEG, *see* electroencephalograph
ecstasy, 55-56
economic depression, 82
Einstein, Albert, 28
electrochemical, 20
electroconvulsive therapy
  definition, 6
  mental illness, 43
  misuse, 121-127
  myths of, 7
electroencephalograph, 63
empiricism, 2
endorphins, 18, 83
enemas, 41
enkephalin, 18
ethics, 120, ch 9, *passim*
  advocate, 129
  AHPRA, 119
  APS, 119-120
  Bailey, Harry, 121-127
  barbiturates, 121, 123

Cameron, Ewan, 121, 127
Chelmsford, 121-127
code, 120
community treatment order, 129
confidentiality, 125
deep sleep therapy, 121-127
definition of, 119
discharge, 130
fraud, 124
Hamilton, Sharon, 123
informed consent, 125
inpatient, 129
involuntary treatment order, 129
lobotomy, 121-122
multiple relationships, 126
narcotics, 121
Patel, Jayent, 127
psychic-driving, 127
psychosurgery, 121, 128
restraint, 130
rights, 128-130
Roth, Sir Henry, 123
Royal Commission, 121-127
RANZCP, 119-120
Sargent, Wiliam, 121, 123
Scientology, 122-124
seclusion, 130
sensory deprivation, 127
euphoria, 55
evidence, *see* empiricism
evolutionary psychology, 62
executive psychopaths, 107
experiential purchases, 82
extroverts, 85
fight-or-flight, 49, 94
flirting, 100-101
foetal alcohol syndrome, 7
foetus, 16
fraud, 124
Frederickson, Barbara, 78, 86-87
Freud, Sigmund, 57, 72-73
friendship, 98-99
frontal lobe, 22, 49, 87
FAS, *see* foetal alcohol syndrome

Gardner, Randy, 69
Geelong Grammar School, 78
generalised anxiety disorder, *see* anxiety
Geneva Convention, 113
gestures, 95-97
glial cells, 28
grey matter, 48
groupthink, 116
Hall, Edward, 92
hallucinations, 27, 54
hallucinogens, 56
Hamilton, Sharon, 123
happiness, ch 6 *passim*
  adaptation, 84
  adversity, 77
  behavioural activities, 85
  circumstances, 80-84
  cognitive activities, 85
  culture, 80
  definition of, 77
  dopamine, 87
  economic depression, 82
  endorphins, 83
  experiential purchases, 82
  extroverts, 85
  formula, 79
  hierarchy of needs, 78
  hormones, 83
  humour, 87
  introverts, 85
  Frederickson, Barbara, 78, 86-87
  Geelong Grammar School, 78
  life expectancy, 80
  marriage, 84
  materialistic purchases, 82
  mental wellness, 77
  normal, 77
  positive psychology, 77
  positivity ratio, 86
  poverty, 82-83
  Maslow, Abraham, 77-78
  retail therapy, 81
  Seligman, Martin, 78-79

set point, 79
volitional activities, 85
voluntary activities, 85
wealth, 80-83
Hare, Robert, 106-107
health, 83
heartbreak, 103
help, 44-45, 57-58
hemispheres, 23, 25
hemispheric specialisation, 25
heroin, 56
hierarchy of needs, 78
hippocampus, 4, 23, 49
Hobson, McCarley, 74
homunculus, 95
hormones, 83
human relationships, ch 7 *passim*
    agoraphobia, 94
    autonomic nervous system, 94
    culture, 96-97
    delineation, 91
    fight-or-flight, 94
    flirting, 100-101
    friendship, 98-99
    gestures, 95-97
    Hall, Edward, 92
    heartbreak, 103
    homunculus, 95
    kissing, 101-102
    marriage, 102
    Mehrabian, Albert, 90
    Middlemist, Dennis, 94
    mirror neurons, 98-99
    personal space, 91-95
    personal space zones, 92
    proxemics, 91
    romance, 100
    socio-biological psychology, 92
    socio-cognitive psychology, 92
    territory, 91-92
humour, 87
Hussein, Saddam, 109-110
hypothalamus, 23
hypothesis, 3, 74

informed consent, 125
inpatient, 129
insomnia, 41
interpersonal, 106-107
introverts, 85
involuntary patient, *see* inpatient
involuntary treatment order, 129
Iraq, *see* Baghdad
Karpinski, Brigadier General, 112-115
kissing, 101-102
latent content, 73
laxatives, 41
leucotomy, *see* lobotomy
limbic system, 23
life expectancy, 80
lifestyle, 106-107
lobotomy, 121-122
Lucifer Effect, 109-117
LSD, 56
manifest content, 73
marijuana,
    effect on brain and behaviour, 53-54
    mental illness, 42
    schizophrenia, 9
marriage, 84, 102
Maslow, Abraham, 77-78
materialistic purchases, 82
medication, 43
Mehrabian, Albert, 90
membranes, *see* meninges
memory, 23
meninges, 21
Mental Health Research Institute, 12-13
mental health problem, 33
mental illness, ch 3 *passim*
    adolescence, 31-32
    advice, 44
    anxiety, 35-36
    causes, 42
    cognitive behaviour therapy, 43
    conduct disorder, 33-34
    definition of, 33

    depression, 36-37
    eating disorders, 38-42
    Headspace, 45
    help, 44-45
    medication, 43
    most common, 32
    myths of, 8
    substance dependence disorders, 37-38
    treatments, 43
mental wellness, 77
meth/amphetamines, 55
microsleeps, 70
Middlemist, Dennis, 94
mirror neurons, 98-99
motor neuron disease, 12
multiple personality disorder, 9
multiple relationships, 126
myelin sheath, 48
myths, *see* psychomythology
MHRI, *see* Mental Health Research Institute
MND, *see* motor neuron disease
narcotics, 121
neuroblasts, 16
neurogenesis, 4, 49
neuroimpulses, 18
neurons, 3-4, 16-20, 48
neuroscience, 12
neurotransmitters, 18, 50-51
nicotine, 54-55
normal, 77, 105
obedience, 116
occipital lobe, 22
olfactory bulb, 23
onset, 36
parietal lobe, 22
Parkinson's disease, 27
Patel, Jayent, 127
peripheral nervous system, 17
personal space, 91-95
personal space zones, 92
pineal gland, 61
polysomnography, *see* sleep
positive psychology, 77
positivity ratio, 86

index

poverty, 82-83
prosocial, 108
proxemics, *see* personal space
psychiatry, 5
psychic-driving, 127
psychoanalytic, *see* Freud
psychology
    as a science, 2
    Board of Australia, 14
    definition, 2
    ethics, 120, ch 9 *passim*
    evolutionary, 62
    not psychiatry, 6-7
    registration, 13-14
    socio-biological, 92
    socio-cognitive, 92
psychomythology, 1, ch 1 *passim*
psychopathy, 9, ch 8 *passim*
    affective, 106-107
    antisocial, 106-107
    definition of, 105
    dysfunctional, 105
    executives, 107
    Hare, Robert, 106-107
    interpersonal, 106-107
    lifestyle, 106-107
    normal, 105
    prosocial, 108
    psychopathy checklist revised, 106-107
    psychopathy personality inventory, 106-107
    psychotic, 106
Psychopathy Checklist Revised (PCL-R), 106-107
Psychopathic Personality Inventory (PPI), 106
psychosis, 9, 55, 106
psychosurgery, 121, 128
PCL-R, *see* psychopathy checklist revised
old wives tales, *see* psychomythology
organisational psychology, 13
rapid eye movement, 63-64
replication, 2-3

restraint, 130
retail therapy, 81
rights, 128-130
Roberts, Blaine, 12
romantic relationships, 100
Roth, Sir Henry, 123
Royal Australian and New Zealand College of Psychiatrists, 199-120
Royal Commission, 121-127
RANZCP, *see* Royal Australian and New Zealand College of Psychiatrists
REM, *see* rapid eye movement
Sargent, Wiliam, 121, 123
schizophrenia, 6, 27
    myths of, 9
scientific method, 2-4
Scientology, 122-124
sea squirt, 22
seclusion, 130
Seligman, Martin, 78-79
sensory deprivation, 127
set point, happiness, 79
sleep, ch 5 *passim*
    alpha waves, 65
    apnoea, 67
    beta waves, 65
    circadian rhythm, 61
    delta waves, 65
    deprivation, 62, 68-69
    dreams, 72-74
    eating, 66
    Freud, 72-73
    K-complexes, 63, 64
    microsleeps, 70
    nREM, 63
    parasomnias, 66
    phenomena, 66
    psychoanalytic, 72
    REM, 63-64
    REM behaviour disorder, 67
    REM rebound, 72
    snoring, 67
    spindles, 63, 64
    stages of, 65

    talking, 67
    theta waves, 65
    walking, 66
sleep eating, 66
sleep talking, 67
smell, *see* olfactory bulb
smoking, *see* nicotine
snoring, 67
soma, 18
spatial neglect, 25
Sperry, Roger, 23
spinal cord, 17
split-brain surgery, *see* Sperry
Stanford Prison Experiment, 113-114
Stanford University, 114
stress, 31, 42, ch 4 *passim*
stimulants, 55
substance, 37
substance dependence disorders, 37-38
    alcohol dependence, 38
    symptoms, 37
Sundram, Suresh, 5-6
swearing, 49
synapse, 18, 50-51
Taguba, Major General, 110-115
Tatton, Julian, 13
taste, 23
temporal lobe, 22, 49
territory, 91-92
theory, construction of, 3
tolerance, 37
treatments, 43
Tripp, Peter, 69
THC, *see* marijuana
urban legends, *see* psychomythology
variables, 4
volitional activities, 85
voluntary activities, 85
white matter, 48
withdrawal, 37
Zimbardo, Phillip, 109-117
zygote, 16

For EU product safety concerns, contact us at Calle de José Abascal, 56–1°, 28003 Madrid, Spain or eugpsr@cambridge.org.

www.ingramcontent.com/pod-product-compliance
Ingram Content Group UK Ltd.
Pitfield, Milton Keynes, MK11 3LW, UK
UKHW051239180426
11947UKWH00013B/866